C000185974

The Grail Kingdom

by Alec Kinch

Merry Christmas,

With love,

~~scribbled out~~ x

~~scribbled out~~ x

First published 2020
by Rowanvale Books Ltd
The Gate
Keppoch Street
Roath
Cardiff
CF24 3JW
www.rowanvalebooks.com

A CIP catalogue record for this book is available from the British Library.
ISBN: 978-1-912655-75-5

Contents

Dedication

To Max, who saw in me a spark and fanned it into a flame; for that I am eternally grateful.

And to my twin-soul Pamela in highest Heaven, I shall forever remember our journey together.

To Kathryn, who pulled me down to earth with loving kindness to fulfil the task of writing this book.

To my brother, Norman, for his encouragement and moral support.

And not to forget my good friend, the irrepressible Richard Davies.

Prologue

Where do we go in our dreams? What paths do we tread into the future and the past? There are no maps to guide us, no signposted way, but the knowing of the swallow that flies from Africa to the place of its birth, the knowing of someone who sleeps and dreams of another time and place, familiar as if it were yesterday.

The reality we know is only one of many, some close enough to touch, others elusive as the distant glow at the edge of the Universe.

1

Initiation

The sun felt hot on his face as Dylan walked along the seashore at Llanilltud Fawr, unaware he was in an alternate reality. Sensing he was being followed, he detoured through a copse of trees and into an open space where stood a white castle on whose wall seven maidens danced to and fro like a Greek frieze come to life. Their gowns of white samite flowed with their movements as they chanted over and over their lament through the spiral of time: "The Rose is the symbol of the Lion, and of the Rose not one trace remains."

Dylan turned to see a monk in grey standing there. His face hidden beneath a cowl, he beckoned Dylan to follow him to where two rivers joined on their journey to the sea.

Standing at their apex, he pointed downward and told Dylan of a treasure buried there, before speaking disparagingly of the modern age. He removed his cowl and stared into his soul, silently conveying the power of truth.

Dylan awoke from the vision and wrote down all he'd seen and heard, a point of light visible on the tip of his pen. Bathed in the sublime, otherworldly balm of peace, he closed the notebook to contemplate the meaning of the Rose and

*the Lion, unaware that this was to be the beginning of a
quest that would continue for several decades, one that was
to change his view of reality to one that existed on many
levels, where the binding forces of love and truth would
unravel the mysterious spiral of time that encapsulates the
forces at work within us all.*

He stood waiting under an oak tree for what seemed
a long time. It was a cold May Day morning of misty
sunshine that filled the valley and swam through the
trees like the essence of lost souls. His naked back
rubbed against the rough bark as a rustling in the
undergrowth warned of something approaching. He
felt the touch of a hand on his shoulder, accompanied
by kind words, and was led blindfolded through the
woods into a clearing where a spring bubbled from
the ground. Two men and a woman came forward.
They stood him there, naked, and poured spring
water over his head and body, baptising Dylan into
their Druidic brotherhood.

Birds sang in this temple open to the sky —
beneath the Eye of Light, as the old Celts would
say — and the bubbling water's musical harmonics
spoke to the little things that lived there. The
watercress swayed in the sweet water from deep
underground.

They covered him with a woollen cloak, bade him
to crouch on all fours and placed heavy stones on
his back. They spoke to him of many things — of who
he was, his spirit, his many lives — to lift the burden
of his old self, to lift off the stones and to rise up
reborn. Dylan rose slowly as the stones tumbled to
the ground. They hugged and congratulated him and
held hands to recite the Druidic oath:

"We swear by truth and love to stand,
Heart to heart and hand in hand.
Mark, O spirit, and hear us now,
Confirming this our sacred vow."

He was told to keep three of the stones with him always as a reminder of the past and of his rebirth into a new life.

Yurts, tents and teepees sprawled along the winding river valley. Smoke drifted upward from the fire in the centre of the sacred enclosure with its willow-arched doorways aligned to the four cardinal points. Already, people were about. Kettles hissed and steamed on the fire, and the melodious sound of a flute drifted over the field as Bear gently roused the sleeping incumbents of the Druid encampment.

Bear was the gatekeeper, who greeted new arrivals at camp with the words: "Welcome to the real world; time to leave the apparent world behind."

Wrapped in the woollen cloak, Dylan crouched by the fire, cradling the stones from his initiation. Magpie suggested he let go of them, that he didn't have to carry them everywhere. Others teased and kidded him until he saw the funny side and dropped the stones, laughing. His acute shyness had always inhibited him from opening up to strangers, but here he felt at ease, peaceful and as loved as a ten year old.

A shout went out: "Dance of Life in five minutes!"

He looked at the people around the fire. Eight, who had a natural tendency to laugh and play, an actor-dancer who nodded his approval at the new initiate. Magpie, large and imposing as an earth mother, poked a stick in the fire.

"This fire is sacred. Who put that cigarette in there?" she said in a strong Dutch accent. "I know that the Native American regard that as an offering, but we are not them great people, so we should not do that here, but smoke it with the breath of the One Great Spirit."

Afrique played her guitar and sang an Irish folk song, her dark curly hair falling about her bare shoulders, her loving spirit vibrating the strings. Dylan smiled at the sense of kinship that held them together, a quickening, imaginative and spontaneous interaction.

"Dance of Life nowww!" went out the call once more.

Dylan joined the circle dancing and chanting around the fire, drawing energy from the air and the earth, from the ether and the sun, hands moving and twisting with the intricacy of weaving a loom, stepping forward then back, moving clockwise, chanting light-beams of energy, which they dispersed by throwing it into the ether with a joyful shout.

All the men and women stood in a circle inside the big yurt, holding hands and chanting the Awen, whose harmonic vibration created an aura of peace and calm, fading into what the old Celts called the great circle of life. These people were picking up from where they'd left off aeons ago — the Celtic spirit dormant, like old bears and squirrels waiting for the thaw — as the bells of freedom rang in the long-awaited age of love and compassion. No inquisitional church, no more burnings or fear of reprisal for just being naturally human.

The morning meeting got under way amid laughter and chatting, sitting on blankets and sleeping bags, children huddled together. A mongrel lurcher sniffed for its owner, who sat by the big log-burner called God, though it was hotter than hell.

"Who's on shit-pit duty today?" shouted Ruth, the chairwoman.

A hand shot up from a jumble of clothes. "Me!" yelled Esther. "I'm the shit-pit fairy."

"Of course you are, Esther, and your shit-pit fairy song is brilliant."

"Thank you." Esther bowed.

Ruth clapped her hands rapidly until the laughter and chatter ceased. "We shall initiate the banns after this morning's meeting, which means that the camp will be closed at three o'clock for three days, and no one is allowed in or out except for emergencies. All mobiles off and no exceptions, except for emergencies. Remember that this time is sacred. Men and women go into their separate yurts—no contact, talking or touching, until we've chosen the May King and Queen. We really must be respectful of this as it is a very sacred thing, so we ask that everyone honour that."

"What instruments do we use for the banns?" asked a voice behind the burner.

"Whatever's to hand: tins, rocks, sticks, drums. Just remember that the ceremony is as old as time, connecting us to the ancestors who are our protectors, so do it with remembrance and respect for them that came before, who gave us life on this land of Mother Earth."

One hundred people poured into the open, banging drums and whistles, Irish pipes and bells, driving away unwanted energies in the age-old ceremony to protect a sacred enclosure, as children danced, dynamic and joyful. Dogs barked, and adults abandoned all pretence of so-called normal behaviour on their journey around the camp perimeter.

Pausing at the four nodal points, paying homage to the east where life begins, to the south for the life-giving sun, to the west for its nourishing rain, and lastly to the north, where nature sleeps until the rebirth of spring. They gave thanks to the infinite life and love from the Creator of the Universe, whose warm embrace kisses the vitality of love's purpose into our waking consciousness.

"The gateway to the north is closed," yelled Ruth. "I declare this camp closed. This circle is now under the protection of the ancestral spirits who guard this place."

Later that day, the men and women separated into different yurts like sheep into pens. Yet these were no sheep, but warriors of men and goddesses of women, all proven in their various walks of life, initiated into the fullness of themselves. To the ancient Celts, there was no difference between going to war or becoming a hermit, opting to live alone in a cave or a beehive hut. Merlin was one such hermit. The gift of prophecy is given only to those who have mastered their fears and desires, for this is the highest trust bestowed upon a human being.

They were not how Dylan imagined Druids to be, so unlike the solemn old men in white robes, but full of vitality and humour, as if they'd happened upon some mysterious elixir of life.

What these camp Druids are about is community, Dylan observed as men and women wove around each other, going about daily tasks, cutting wood for the fires, preparing food or tending to each other's needs, as effortlessly as birds in synchronised flight.

Many an impromptu eisteddfod took place around the central fire: music and song, poetry and storytelling, an abundance of talent freely expressed. Dylan loved them all, even oddball Bran, who chopped wood and dug the shit-pits, singing songs of his own devising, who'd once encamped three months up an oak tree marked for destruction. Eco-warriors, lovers of the land—and who's to say who's crazy but the ones in grey?

There was little emphasis on gender, as all were Druids by virtue of their individual accomplishments. To become a Druid in the old days required twenty years of study, memorising hundreds of stories, tribal history, plantlore and philosophy—much of which has survived the pillage of time and the cultural ethnic cleansing of the Church of Rome.

Adrian—the Shining One, as Dylan liked to call him—was a softly spoken gentle giant, always with the whisper of a smile as he walked the field in a battered top-hat and colourful sarong with his soulmate Lani, who ran the healing dome—a kind of camp hospital for children with cuts and adults with everything else, especially loneliness. Formalised comfort and a soothing touch, a spiritual sanctuary amid the tribal mish-mash of daily activity, for here you are naked under the sun, and the heart, for so long hidden away, needs often to hide for a little while.

Adrian was a married man who loved his wife, but camp life was a soul-need, being here with these people. Lani plaited his long fair hair and painted his body, murmuring sweet words into his ear as he sat on his throne, smiling like a noble lord in a happy kingdom.

Elder Druid Jay wore clothes bright as a parrot, his strong yet gentle presence emanating the energy of a man fully alive. "I like you," he said to Dylan, "you speak from the heart," and hugged the life out of him until his black beard made Dylan sneeze.

Dylan felt honoured and accepted. He was uncertain of his role, as this was all new to him, yet he felt very much alive in the 'now' of the present moment. The moment of 'now', he realised, is what truly touches our soul, when each moment seems eternal, immediate and expansive. The courage to live this way is what the life-spirit requires, to reach out to one another in the natural way of a child.

Surrounded by such accomplished individuals, he wondered what he was doing amongst them; was he experimenting with an alternative lifestyle or searching for a doorway to the distant past? Whatever the reason, he felt at home amongst this tribal family, lawless yet obeying the true law, for there is no other law but this law: that we love one another as through the eyes of a child.

Rural communities are now rare, as authentic village life has virtually vanished with the arrival of the new rich who transformed rude dwellings into mini palaces, converting cowsheds into homes for their BMWs and Mercedes. Country living without country-folk, no longer able to afford to dwell in the homes of their ancestors, now occupied by the four-wheel drive brigade having arrived at Shangri-La, whose inn is now an eatery where the wellied farmer and his dog are no longer welcome. Many of the camp Druids lived on smallholdings and grew their own food, imbuing their children with a love of nature, because going forward meant going backwards to retrieve lost values.

Dylan stumbled over his thoughts and shuffled along with his misconceptions without a map or compass. *These people are my friends, whose kinship is strong despite differences, who are willing to dive into the dark waters of unknowing, where the truth of how to live lies buried in the silt of the ages.* Dylan had always followed his intuition and insights, searching for the elusive phantom called 'peace of mind'.

Many years had gone by since his vision of the maidens on the castle wall; years spent investigating the history of the Grail, clues to where or what the Grail was: the chalice of the Last Supper, or a dish or platter termed *graal* on which food was served? Was it the Holy Bloodline of Jesus and Mary, whose living descendants are with us today? What is it that would touch the heart of all mankind? What would alter people's perception of divinity, other than wisdom of the Divine?

Dylan concluded that it had more to do with lost knowledge, the step-by-step stages towards enlightenment. Why else would the monk have pointed to the meeting place of the two rivers to tell him of treasure buried there, if it were not of a spiritual nature? The Grail was a metaphor of the Divine within, hidden and elusive, the last great mystery. Would he find it among these people, in this land of many shadows, a play-board whose centre is the labyrinth where all are free to venture?

2
The Ritual

Twenty-five men sat in a circle to decide who would be the May King. In the centre lay a star-shaped cloth on which was placed crystals and talismans, ogham pendants and eagle feathers. The women had long since immersed themselves in the ritualised process of choosing their May Queen, whilst the men told jokes and swigged non-alcoholic beverages. Keith, the elected overseer of the camp, was a wise man who danced light-heartedly between disputes like a smiling Buddha. Garth, a Quaker farmer with the appearance of a white-haired saint, suggested they each confess their wounded-warrior experiences. Men can relive personal traumas in trusted company, and each confessed deep hurts: of love denied, betrayal, even revenge.

Darkness had fallen by the time each man had surrendered their soul pain. Several wept, though most toughed it out as men do, holding onto an imaginary masculinity.

"I'm for the pillow," yawned Adrian.

"No doubt the women have already chosen their Queen," commented Derwyn. "They're so efficient it's scary."

"Born with a multi-tasking gene," quipped Keiron. "We've no chance keeping up with them."

"They may be quick, but we are thorough," asserted Bear, breaking wind and shifting his huge backside back and forth.

"You mean like shuffling the oracle cards to choose our May King?" said Derwyn. "Roll over and go to sleep."

"Women follow their intuition," cut in Adrian. "Whichever way, it's the powers that be who choose."

Keiron laughed. "Which is why they always choose me."

"How many times you been May King?" asked Adrian.

"Three. This will be the fourth."

"Not even the President of the United States is allowed a third term, never mind the fourth."

"Hands up all those who want Keiron to be May King?" groaned Adrian, as all eyes were on Keiron.

"Unanimous vote of no confidence, I'd say," concluded Adrian.

"You said yourselves that the oracle cards choose," responded Keiron.

"God forbid you're the chosen one," said Keith. "The women will say: 'Oh, it's Keiron again. Hey-ho ladies, let's chuck him in the river.'"

"But they like me," asserted Keiron.

"That why you haven't got one?" commented Adrian.

"I have," retorted Keiron. "Well, sort of."

"You mean crazy Annie who'd jump on a dog if it gave her the eye?"

Chuckles and laughter followed Keith's comment as Keiron hung his head, dejected.

"Hey guys, time for shuteye," yawned Adrian. "Love being with you—keeps me sane."

"In the morning then," suggested Eight. "Whoever the cards choose."

"So be it," agreed Derwyn.

"I'm new to this," Dylan piped up. "So I'll go with whatever you say and let the cards decide."

One by one they slumped onto pillows and bedding, apart from Keiron, who chucked logs into the burner, huffing and puffing like a child denied chocolate. Bear snored so loudly that Adrian suggested smothering him. Garth said it wasn't quite the Druid thing to do.

"You are a Quaker, Garth, a man of peace, whereas I'm a lapsed Christian who just wants to sleep." Adrian stood over Bear lying flat on his back, his abdomen rising and falling like a balloon, "Look at his big fat belly. Maybe we should put him out of his misery."

"He plays the flute well," said Garth. "Wakes us up in the morning after he's kept us up all night with his snoring. Maybe we should let him live—after all, he *is* the gatekeeper."

"Point taken," concurred Adrian, "let the bugger live. As for me being May King, count me out; let the honour go to whoever needs it most, which is usually the way it works anyway."

Eight winced and rubbed his thigh, sore from an arrow that had struck him the day before, for it was the custom that the old May King should die. Covered in a red deerskin with antlers fixed to his head, he had moved on all fours across the field. Onlookers laughed and jeered, Dylan wondering why he scrambled about in an animal costume, when out of a yurt, a tall raven-haired woman appeared, garbed head to toe in tight black leather, with a bow and a quiver full of arrows. She looked serious, for

Marianne had become Diana the Huntress, a fearful sight that made Eight scarper, a dot in the distance. The first arrow flew and struck his thigh, and he tumbled over and lay still.

She moved forward, her gaze fixed on the prey as Eight staggered to his feet and limped on. She loosed another arrow, which arched high as a rainbow to strike him between the shoulder blades. He rolled over and lay still. No one moved or breathed, for the meaning was clear, their reverence deep: the old was gone and the new was about to be born. Everyone clapped and cheered as Eight struggled to his feet and removed his antler crown, which would be worn by the new king about to be forged in the fires of Beltane.

Eight sat by the central fire at the midnight hour to muse on his time as May King. A thoughtful man despite his playful persona, a dancer and actor who encouraged camp-people in role-playing such as activating the jester — qualities that had perhaps been needed for that year, especially as his May Queen had complemented his own gifts. Strange how compatible the king and queen were, a mystical element ever-present amid the ordinary.

Dylan likened Druid Camp to a cauldron in which the process of transformation took place with alarming frequency, as they fluctuated from extreme loneliness to wholehearted joyful belonging, human alchemy exploding into a new way of being, an echo from the dawn of tribal man, a distant drumbeat, a song of resonance rekindling old fires of the soul.

Much had happened that day to tear away Dylan's layers of self-protection, leaving him naked and vulnerable as a child on his first day at school.

≈≈≈

An early morning mist played across the valley as a buzzard's sharp cry caused Eight to look up and smile at such a good omen on his first day as a free man, free from the responsibility of being May King. Dylan joined him by the fire. Bran read a poem of his own devising, imbued with the juices of procreation, nature's gift of ever renewing life, reminding Dylan of Omar Khayyam's poem: 'And in fires of spring, the winter garment of repentance fling.' The phenomenon called life never ceased to amaze Dylan, the extent to which a part of us is the sensual expression of a higher nature. How the heavy cloak of materialism prevents the soul from dancing! Arcadia is everywhere; blackbirds sing loudest in the rain and a robin sings through dark winter nights, reminding us of the beauty of nature's song.

Dylan thought of Pamela, his soulmate. They were as children together, possessing an understanding that swept away all trivia, revealing their true essence. So similar in their thinking, a perfect yin-yang, yet many questions confounded his inner peace, searching for the relevance of his life, and all lives. His knowledge of history and philosophy was quite extensive, veering toward the esoteric—humanity's spiritual evolution rather than events, delving instead into the stream of consciousness that forms the way we think and feel; the real history, the timeless ephemeral reality, whose form encases the invisible soul of humanity.

To Dylan, the Grail was not an object but a current of knowledge which, when applied to oneself, reveals our true nature, where fear and illusion dissolve into the oneness of knowing, where love and compassion predominate and the material world is merely a means to an end. What that knowledge was, he'd yet to discover, but that was his quest: to search for the key to the door to an unknown land.

Dylan sensed something stirring. His intuition held him in stillness and quietude, holding onto an image of communion with the Divine: men and women sharing their roles, complementing one another, each containing the mysterious shadow of the other. And in the weaving of time, an image emerges, the illusive phantom of our primordial self, born before material life ever was. Uniting spirit and nature, intuition and intellect, is the key to mankind's survival, for man's future myth is man's megalith.

Dylan was a blind man in a fog with nothing to guide him but fine words and thoughts that evaporated when raw instinct took the rein. He would fall and he knew it, but he didn't care.

3
The May King

"Who will be our May King?" challenged Keith. "The wheel of the sun has turned full circle, and the women are waiting with their Queen."

"That's women for you," joked Adrian, "getting down to the nitty-gritty while we faff about."

"How do the women choose their May Queen?" said Keith. "Maybe we ought to sneak a spy-cam in there."

"Don't think so," interjected Eight. "Acteon spied on his wife performing her sacred rituals in the forest, so she turned him into a stag and his hounds tore him to pieces."

Keith laughed. "Nowadays they'll just hire a lawyer who'll tear you to pieces instead."

"How do they choose their May Queen?" mumbled Derwyn. "Guess we'll never know."

"For good reason," said Adrian. "They take life seriously."

Eight placed the cards on the altar for a final blessing. "Whoever chooses the eagle, the owl, the stag or the wolf shall be the four candidates, and whoever of the four discovers the hidden antlers shall be our May King."

"So much for the debate on who will qualify to be May King out of us twenty-five," said Garth, "sat here as we are waiting for a finger from above to point him out."

Adrian smiled in his knowing way. "May the cards be their instrument. So shuffle them, Eight, and get this over with."

"The women wouldn't approve the way we do it," said Derwyn. "May be better if we meditated on it first."

"Bollocks!" interjected Keiron. "Got to trust the cards—always works. For me, anyway."

"Shut up, Keiron," said Keith. "You haven't got a clue about the mysterious workings of women when they collude head to head; they've got us beat because they know much more than we'll ever know, which is how they've survived a male-dominated hierarchy for thousands of years by going deep into nature's magic. Ceridwen and all the others, you just don't mess with them."

"Bloody right there, Keith," concurred Eight. "They're stronger than us when it comes to harnessing the intelligence of the cosmos."

"That what it is?" challenged Bear. "Don't know much about women, but what I do know is that I wouldn't want to bring a baby into this world that tears your insides out, no way."

"Hooray for some perspective," cheered Adrian. "So shuffle the cards and let's be done."

The cards were dealt around the circle of eager men up for the honour of being the May King. Bear received the owl, Keiron got the stag and Derwyn held up the eagle card. Dylan drew the wolf, placing it on the altar, thinking maybe he would be the one, though he was only a recent member of the Druidic order. He looked at the others sat cross-legged around the altar, men rich in knowledge and experience, gentle but tough as oaks. Garth poured tea into mugs, and Dylan passed around chocolate to boost their energy for the hunt.

Moments of contemplation followed as Dylan visualised the outside terrain: the river, the trees on the other side, an upturned coracle... Curious, he flipped over his card. The wolf loped along a riverbank opposite three trees and a shrub, which by chance reflected the outside terrain, except there was a coracle in place of the shrub. In an instant, he knew that was where the antlers would be hidden.

"Candidates outside," commanded Keith, "and may the best man be May King, unless it's Keiron, in which case drown him in the river and we'll choose another."

Adrian patted Keiron on the shoulder. "Just joking, you know how much we all love you."

"Off you go, guys," urged Keith. "And who knows? You might find what you need instead of what you desire."

The four waited in the rain for the signal to go. Dylan glanced at his card once again to make sure he wasn't seeing things, looking at the river below and the three trees, the coracle. A shiver ran through him. It was his if he wanted it, but did he? This was all new to him: the May King, and what it entailed—that the gods or higher energies chose whoever was most suited to be of service to the whole. Did he want the honour and the obligation? He glanced at Derwyn. Water ran down the man's cheeks, but it wasn't rain.

"Oh man, I've got to have this," pleaded Derwyn, holding onto Dylan's shoulders. "I've just got to have it. I've never won anything in my life, but please God, let this be mine, just this one thing."

During the intimate revelations of the night before, Derwyn had confessed a life of hardship and cruelty, of soul-destroying put-downs and poverty on a council estate. Now he sensed a new beginning that could redeem much of the sorrow and pain.

"Go!" yelled Adrian. "And may the gods choose the right man."

Derwyn ran down the sloping meadow towards the river, scouring brambles, nettles and tall grass and ramming his arm into badger-holes in a frantic search for his future, which was hidden close by. Dylan strolled nonchalantly towards the coracle, still questioning whether he wished to be the May King. Derwyn was up to his waist in the river searching amongst the weeds. Keiron had gone way off into another field. Bear moved sloth-like along the riverbank, disturbing a family of newly-hatched ducklings bouncing on the water like balls of fluff.

Dylan was torn between achieving glory and abiding by the quiet voice within that asked, *Why do you want this?* Derwyn was now out of the water and looking his way, and for a moment their eyes locked. Dylan smiled and walked slowly towards the coracle, and in the instant it took to draw breath, Derwyn flew past him, swooping like an eagle onto its prey as he flipped over the coracle to seize the antlers.

"I've got it! It's mine!" he yelled, tears running down his face as he knelt on the wet earth, holding the antlers aloft. "Thank you, God, or Great Spirit, or whoever you are, for giving this to me."

His long hair hid the light in the eyes of a man reborn. Dylan smiled and hugged the rugged, scarred warrior who'd reclaimed his own sword of truth, who'd prevailed against all odds to sustain his spirit and now, for the first time in his life, felt possessed of something of value: himself.

Derwyn's victory caused Dylan to reflect upon his own life-changing moments. He reminisced of the time in his early twenties when, drifting from job to job, disillusioned and lost, someone he'd known only as a nodding acquaintance said to him out of the blue: "You are a writer; I can see it in your eyes. Come with me and I will help you."

Max, a highly intuitive teacher and writer of Russian/Jewish descent, knew how to encourage the imagination out of the sleep of ignorance by applying discipline and a love for words in equal measure. Jewish people have that gift, as do the Celtic race, who know how to help a person find that gift buried deep inside.

He spent years reading and writing, several days a week landscape gardening, thinking of his friends enjoying their youth womanising and drinking and all those activities that devour the vitality of the young. Seven years on, he began to sense a subtle change; his voice mellowed, the words flowed sweetly off the typewriter, and his dreams became more vivid, revealing a gateway to another realm. It was the Mother Country, the home of the soul.

Poems flowed swiftly in praise of nature and the veracity of the human spirit, but his dreams revealed a strange conundrum: glimpses of the future and inklings of past lives, of who he was—the people in his dreams, Celtic warriors and Druids, faces he seemed to know. What did they want? What was it they were trying to tell him?

Max had a way about him that could conjure up the past. He told stories to the local children gathered on the lawn, who listened spellbound to tales of Mr Pipperpepperpot, the Toy Gun and Pickwick Papers. Dickens was his favourite novelist, whose characters he knew so well. Smiling cheekily like a little boy, his eyes sparkled with delight recounting stories to the young, a schoolmaster when a penny bought a chocolate bar and two gobstoppers.

"You are a writer," he'd say, "and a writer is only worth his salt when he writes."

It was a constant reminder for Dylan whenever he skipped facing the blank page to run off into the countryside. He'd turned out plays for radio and television until the rejection slips formed a small heap on his desk but a megalithic mountain in his mind.

"Write," goaded Max. "Do what you know you can do. Discipline, round and round, till you get it right."

The seasons marked time as the years rolled on, through country walks with his brother, Norman, who introduced him to the myriad workings of nature, the birds and insects of innumerable form. His mentor in so many ways. *"You must teach others what you know. You have a natural way with you when you talk of nature. I see you in dreams surrounded by birds and butterflies. Teach the children what you know."*

University, and several degrees later, he became a teacher at Epping Forest Field Centre, fulfilling his natural ability to pass on his love for Nature, whose intricate web of life and delicate balance is in jeopardy with GM crops, floods and drought to order in the name of global warming, under whose umbrella the new holocaust emerges in the guise of saviour.

As time rolled on, his dreams became as vivid as a movie show, of Native Americans chanting and drumming, Celtic warriors and Druids of great dignity resolving disputes. The past lurked close by, though he knew not why, only that his journey was about to begin. His dreams told him that something from the past was nearing completion, that his vision of the seven maidens was a wake-up call.

An alternate reality impinged upon his thoughts, behind the veil past which he could not see, until one sunny afternoon walking along a country lane, his perception of the world changed in an instant. The landscape of greens and blues became more vivid, more intense. In the blink of an eye, a camera snapshot of rainbow hues filled his panoramic view of verdant fields and distant hills shimmering beneath a vibrant summer sun.

Dylan walked on, perplexed as to the cause of the perceptual change. We see what we see, but do we truly see the reality we are in? Or is it that nothing changes, static as the stars, yet moving away at the speed of light? Contemplating the cause, he sat in the porch of the church of St. George, whose ancient yews were young in the days of the Druids, who worshipped in circles open to the sky, beneath the eye of God. He wondered if his altered perception was due to the Awen, the three rays of light from the Creator, the manifestation of all life, the inspiration of song and poetry, the soul's creative urge.

Several weeks later, Dylan dreamt he was walking along the country road toward St. George's village in the Vale of Glamorgan when the face of a Chinese woman hovered in front of him, her spirit radiant with peace and love as she spoke these words:

"Now is a very important time for mankind. It is crucial we speak our minds; if we do not, we will all perish. It is up to every individual to play his part. There are things to say and work to do. You must get into a spirit of conviction, otherwise it weakens the whole fabric of the endeavours of all. You have much to say, and your contribution will be most worthwhile." Her name was Min Sun Sang of the temple of Kiang Ti.

Something was about to occur worldwide, and her message was clear: to express our truth fully because indifference would have no effect whatsoever as humanity was in danger of losing its soul to technology and AI, which should be our servant and not our master.

An increasing discontent followed in the wake of such profound awakenings. Max was showing signs of early dementia, his behaviour was becoming more erratic, his mind befuddled as his health deteriorated rapidly. Change was coming. Dylan took to walking alone through the countryside, unwilling to come to terms with his own revelations.

We are such stuff as dreams are made of, because they display the inner workings of the psyche. His depression informed him that he'd compromised his aspirations by his failure to shatter the peace of his self-created plateau. He had few friends apart from Brian the artist, a skinny cat called Loppylugs, and Gypsy Joe, aka The Godfather, the respected go-between in neighbourly disputes.

He began dreaming of a beautiful woman whose Nordic blonde hair winged out slightly, whose azure blue eyes conveyed a deep passion and a love beyond human understanding. The self-assured serenity of her smile intrigued him. She reappeared several weeks later walking along a woodland path wearing a yellow raincoat, while he was a knight in shining armour. There were two rivers of saltbrine of unknown depth, the two rivers that would one day figure prominently in his life.

She soon appeared again standing in the middle of a roofless building, just the bare outline of a Romano-British monastery close to St. Brides in the Vale of Glamorgan. They communicated telepathically on archaeology and religion. Dylan challenged a tall man who stood close by, who replied with his motto: "When Caesar came I stood alone until his defeat."

She simply said, "Close but apart, that is the way she wants us to be."

Synchronicity was moving fast; many events occurred in quick succession as an inner prompting guided Dylan to join a spiritual development group, and he found himself the next day knocking on the door of a house to be welcomed into a meditation room where four women and a man were seated. Among them was the woman he'd spoken with the night before; her name was Pamela. Nine months later she became his lifelong partner, the twin-soul so many speak of, though few know the love that is love for its own sake, free to be oneself without judgement or coercion, to follow one's inner law, for life is a non-negotiable contract between ourselves and the Creator.

He'd met his May Queen, regal as purple, whose spirit shone with an inner light. Unconditional love outweighs its opposite by its very simplicity. Yet life was strange. His dreams and insights often made no sense. Romantic poets composed odes on clouds of laudanum, questing knights strangled dragons with a shoelace, and Orphic rites enticed the seeking soul into the oblivion of their domain. He was content with an occasional glimpse into the fairyland of his imagination, reflecting a yearning for a lost golden-age — not one of marble-pillared pantheons, nor an idyllic Arcadia, but the golden age of the human spirit, of love and compassion for all living things.

4

Beltane

Derwyn stood in the centre of a circle of men, his arms and face painted in swirls of blue. A mantle of green covered his shoulders, a tribute to the victor who'd defeated the obstacles of his past, smiling in triumph, at peace with himself as the men grunted and beat their drums.

"The women are coming!" yelled Keith.

The sound of singing and melodious pipes collided with the rough sounds of the men like two rivers of water and fire as the door opened to a beautiful array of female forms in flower-garlanded white tunics, and children with colourful posies, singing: "The Queen's a-coming, beautiful as may-blossom and longs to see her King."

The instinctual animal sounds from the men in this primitive contest of the rite of spring, the drumming and chanting, faded to a lull of expectation when one of the women stepped forward.

"Do you have your King?" she demanded. "Where is your King? Show him to us."

Derwyn crouched behind the men in a game of hide-and-seek as the women searched the faces of the men.

"Who is your Queen?" responded Adrian. "Present her to us."

"No!" she insisted. "It is our right to see your King first."

Keith put his hand on Derwyn's head to push him down. "Not yet, let them wait. They like to play the waiting game."

"Don't they just?" whispered Derwyn.

"Give him to us," she demanded. "We know you are hiding him."

"Very well," relented Keith, holding up the antler crown. "Will the King step forward and be crowned?"

Derwyn stepped into the centre of the circle, and all the women shrieked and yelled, for they all loved him for his quiet strength and pleasant ways.

Derwyn took up the crown and placed it upon his head. "Where is your Queen?" he demanded.

Four women wove a dance around one another until one of them broke free to stand alone: Rowena, in purple and gold, wearing a mayflower crown. She held out her hand to Derwyn, and in the moment of their first touch, the men and women came together, hugging and kissing, rejoicing in the desire to reunite. Dylan sensed the tangible oneness of a fairy-tale myth of tribal life, where meaningful rituals celebrated the natural rhythms of life as the world outside thundered by without purpose or recollection.

Twenty-five axe-wielding men trampled through the forest searching for a maypole, scaring blackbirds and annoying the cawing crows. All 'expert foresters', they were deciding which tree to cut down. Eco-warrior Bran insisted they chose a dead tree rather than a live one. The dispute continued as they hacked through the undergrowth, until eventually they decided on a sycamore whose bursting buds embraced the life-giving rays of the sun. They hugged, blessed, and Awened the tree to its destruction. Bran walked off, angry, his integrity insulted, the tree's demise mocking his efforts to help save the planet.

"Timber!" yelled Keiron as the sycamore swayed precariously, and everyone ran off in different directions, not knowing which way it would fall. Some said this way, others that, but the tree confounded them all by going nowhere, merely resting in the branches of its neighbour. Serious discussions followed, fingers on chins pondered the dilemma, until a gust of wind brought it crashing down, scattering the men every which way. Bran yelled from the track below that they should never have cut a living tree.

The ancient ceremony of cutting the maypole contains a hidden meaning that only foresters know in the springtime rising of the sap, nature's reproductive juices offered as sacrifice. The men hauled the tree up the wooded hillside and onto the open field of the escarpment. Their din and guttural chants startled roebucks who, in the old days, would have been their Beltane feast. Below in the valley, three mud-covered naked women were digging a hole for the maypole. They gave an orgasmic shriek on seeing the men carry the sycamore over the ridge of the White Horse. The men responded, as men do, with deep-throated guttural testosterone. Dylan loved the primitive feel of their basic instincts given an airing. Primitive man lives just beneath the skin.

With renewed passion, the women dug the hole big enough to receive the great phallus of the sycamore, the sacred tree of Isis, in celebration of the cosmic circle that embodies the male and female dynamic of all creation. The men put the tree down on a ridge to trim it into shape, carving symbols into its bark: Oghams, spirals, hearts and crosses — even Hebrew, for no religion was excluded in this universal celebration of spring. Jay covered himself with may-blossom and green leaves, his brightly coloured clothes reflecting the vitality of the natural world.

They were joined by the Professor, who'd arrived in his working clothes of tweeds, a waistcoat, a flamboyant necktie and polished brogues. An Oxford don to his socks, he spoke melodiously and respectfully to the men, saying it was a delight and a privilege to be amongst them on this day. His extensive knowledge melded easily into the instinctual pagan fire of such rituals as this, joining full on with the drumming and yelling like banshees to the screech of Irish pipes as the call came from below that they were ready to receive the maypole.

The descent into the valley began with the Professor leading the way. He was a shy man — though Dylan suspected more respectful than shy, such was his love for these people that he'd give a talk at every camp on Druidic and Celtic lore, illustrating humanity's striving for eternal truths, which give meaning to man's existence. So eloquently did he weave tales of gods and goddesses and panegyrics on myth and cultural evolution. How the universality of the human condition emerged out of time's dry bones in the search for meaning, and how the power of symbolic ritual awakens a joy that shakes the earth beneath our feet.

"Deep into the earth I go, deep into the earth I know," chanted the men carrying the maypole down the hillside towards the eagerly waiting women.

"Deep in the earth I go," bellowed the men as the women pushed a hoop of streaming ribbons over the Maypole's rounded end, sliding it all the way along its length. The men yelled in orgasm and the women squealed with delight as the pole was pushed down hard into the hole in the ground, the men pushing it ever deeper, sweating muscles trembling to appease the Goddess of Love, until at last the maypole stood upright. Rainbow ribbons dangled to the ground to be taken up by the men, women and children, dancing clockwise and anti-clockwise around the maypole to weave the May King and Queen together.

Winding and binding the chosen ones to the pole of love, exchanging kisses in alternate circles, amongst smiles and laughter, limbs moved to the sound of Irish pipes, flutes and drums. Kisses lingered fondly, shyly obliging as children danced freely and filled the air with glee, joyful as the coloured ribbons binding the May King and Queen to the maypole with each turn of the circle, holding them ever more tightly to the tree of life in the ritual of the rite of spring.

Dylan collapsed exhausted onto the cool grass, feeling privileged to be part of this timeless ritual, until his euphoria fell away and a sadness descended upon him like a shroud, compelling him to go to the hill of the White Horse, where he slumped onto the green grass, sobbing over the recent deaths of his father and brother. The father he'd loved more as he grew older, and the brother who'd been too young to leave this world.

He said to his mother in a dream, "Look, there they are," and touched his father, who sat up, saying, "Hello, son."

Dylan said to his mother, "They're not dead, but alive in spirit."

Then he touched his brother, who opened his eyes and said, "What happened? Did I fall asleep?"

Dylan sobbed as the grief welled up uncontrollably until it evaporated into the stillness of peace, knowing it had served its purpose because there is no death. Madeleine came by and touched him on the shoulder, inviting him to sit with her on the White Horse. They sat in the chalk-white eye, chanting the Aum. She raised her aeolian harp to the wind as a rainbow arched across the sky to touch the ground in the valley below, a celestial maypole of colour, and he thanked Spirit for restoring his peace, for reminding him that the world is of one mind.

Madeleine gave him the Aeolian harp, which he held to the wind, content to not be the May King but king of himself instead.

Sensing his sadness on their way down the hill, she kissed him lightly on the lips. Dylan admired her soft and gentle femininity, her elegant dress flowing in the breeze, the maypole totem to spring standing in the valley below, a Druid's temple open to the sky, beneath the Creator's eye.

They believe that the Spirit of God is everywhere and in everything: the birds, the animals, the plants, even the rocks.

"All life is sacred," declared Madeleine. "Honour the earth and the sky, honour the air that we breathe and the smile upon a child's lips. Kiss the ground we walk on, sing your spirit into life and dance with the unicorn who leads us to our journey's end."

5

Celebration

The May King and Queen sat enthroned in a bower of blue and gold, he in green with a crown of oak leaves and an antler staff, she in purple and pink, a garland of may-blossom upon her head, the crown of the Queen of Heaven. Madeleine sang and stroked her harp strings gently. Scented incense hung in the air, its smoke curling in the candlelight inside the big yurt full of happy people celebrating Beltane, the Fire of Spring.

Outside the yurt three men whispered conspiratorially, conjuring up mischief to inflict on the unwary—among them, Dylan, garbed in black.

"Go on in there," urged Adrian, placing a Green Man mask over Dylan's face. "Challenge the May King with three questions. Say to him that he must answer two out of three correctly to be entitled to be May King. Though not too serious—wind him up with a bit of humour."

"What, three questions?" muttered Dylan. "What kind of questions should I ask?"

"Serious, but funny," said Adrian.

"Yeah," added Jay with a grin. "Make him sweat."

Adrian patted him on the back. "Traditional to challenge the May King to see if he's worthy. So off you go, but remember to be funny."

He backed off with a wicked grin as Dylan gathered his thoughts. He'd almost become the May King himself, so it was with a certain empathy that he formulated the questions before hammering on the yurt door with his staff.

"Who's there?" demanded a woman's voice from inside.

"The Guardian of the White Horse," responded Dylan.

The door opened into a candlelit interior where many a glowing eye followed him in the flickering light.

Empowered beneath his mask, he approached the May King with an air of regal authority. "I am the Guardian of the Hill of the White Horse, and this is my land. You call yourself King? Anyone can call themselves King. We shall see if you are worthy. If you answer two out of three questions correctly, I shall leave you with my blessing. If not, you shall be banished into the wilderness of forlorn hope. You get my drift."

"You're some serious dude," responded Derwyn with an uneasy chuckle. "Okay, go for it. Fire away."

"What makes gold so precious?"

"Because gold is the purest thing on earth, the sun's teardrops and the source of life."

"Well answered, my friend," grunted Dylan, thumping his staff on the ground. "Question number two: Can you recite the Tain backwards in Urdu whilst standing on one leg?"

"You got to be kidding me," he replied grimly. "Couldn't do it in English standing on one leg, never mind Urdu."

"Just as well it's not the full moon then, because if it was you would be sacrificed... so I'll let you off that one." Dylan took a deep breath. "Final question!"

"Fire away," mumbled a dejected Derwyn.

"Can you sing a three-verse song in Welsh?"

Derwyn glanced apprehensively at the candlelit faces all around, before standing upright to sing *Myfanwy* like a songbird, his tenor voice vibrating through the silence. The quiet passion of his voice welled up from the depths of his being, for the spirit of inspiration was upon him, initiating him into rebirth and a new life.

The song ended with a deafening silence, as none had suspected that this rough-edged person with unruly hair and tufty moustache could sing like an angel. When the yurt erupted with loud applause and cheers and whistles, Derwyn beamed and bowed, resuming his position on a throne fit for a May King who'd truly won their respect.

Dylan nodded deferentially to Derwyn and exited the yurt. He'd witnessed many such life-transforming moments in this playground of possibilities where the imagination is allowed to run free. There were rules, to be sure. Drinking alcohol was allowed, albeit with discretion as several amongst them were recovering alcoholics. Drugs were forbidden, though the occasional spliff occurred. There were rotas for cooking duty, wood-chopping and cleaning the shit-pits — though Esther, who called herself the Shit-Pit Fairy, regarded it an honour, singing a song celebrating her role as maiden of the cesspit.

Within the cauldron of Druidic gatherings, magic occurs, though the initial alienation, the stripping away our so-called normality, leaves a sense of isolation. Some hide away until the shell of their protective persona dissolves or they are cajoled out of it with respectful humour. Initiation into the inner child produces a painful vulnerability, adjusting to a new way of being, as when new arrivals are 'gated' they are asked to leave the 'apparent world' behind.

Children possess the natural ability to live in the moment, unlike our conditioned adult selves, hooked into the money world to survive, constantly on the move, living for a debt-free future. We forget that the 'now moment' is all there is in which to be truly at one with the miracle of life.

Dylan observed how the elusive phantom of peace weaved within the joyful activity of kindred spirits, joining one to another with divine love, dancing around the fire in an elemental celebration of the miracle of life. There were often meditations, music, dance, poetry and storytelling, talents expanded by appreciation. The cauldron holds it all, gives to each a place of honour, where love sings many a song to those who sit in the circle of their home, beneath the stars, on Mother Earth.

What is our true history? Where do we come from? Why are we all so different? A professor of history formulates conclusions from events, but what of the constellation of our own history, the missing element of past lives, the mysterious equation that holds the key to aspects of personality and attributes, natural talents and modes of behaviour? Certain elements of Dylan's own life only made sense in light of glimpses into his previous incarnations, and why he had been born into a particular family and location, why he'd been drawn to certain people or group souls, reuniting for a specific purpose.

Dylan concluded life to be a culmination of our past and a preparation for our future. Anana, Chief Scribe to Seti I, declared: 'We do not live only once and depart hence forever, but we live many times in many places, although not always on this world.

6
Eco-Warrior

The primitive moan of a conch shell announced the morning meeting. The central fire steamed with kettles, smoke and conversation. Many sat talking or playing musical instruments, singing songs or telling stories. Men and women came and went with bowls of porridge. Dance of Life participants threw their arms in the air, yelling 'ho-ha!', dispersing their group energy into the ether. No frail gesture, but a powerful affirmation of their belief in the power of people to change the world, passing energy and thoughts from one person to another. This was how it worked, how it has always been from the beginning, from Buddha, to Krishna, to Christ, and all the saints and love-filled waters are as ripples on a pond, celebrating the life of the Cosmos.

Keith took the chair and cracked a joke about the Shit-Pit Fairy. Sky, the wolfhound, licked its way through a group of giggling children. Josie suggested that everyone give special thanks to Bran for all his hard work constructing the camp and maintaining the firewood for the sauna and log burners.

Bran, who never attended morning meeting, stood in the doorway, waiting for the applause to wane. Josie hugged him with genuine affection, and Bran grinned a stammered response. He walked purposefully toward the May King and, kneeling with solemn ceremony, presented him with a wooden dagger he'd carved from a branch of the maypole tree.

He turned to face the circle, imposing his height of six foot four in a manner of proud defiance to address the gathering.

"I only came to present my little offering to the May King as a token of my respect. I wasn't going to talk at all, but I will now, so listen to what I have to say. You said yesterday before you cut the maypole that you wouldn't cut a living tree. I said I'd walk out of camp if you did. I said, why cut a living tree when there are dead ones to choose from? But you cut a living tree. You shouldn't have done that. I have campaigned to save trees. I lived three months up an oak tree to stop them cutting it down at the Newbury bypass. I don't just talk about saving trees. You know me and the other eco-warriors—that's what we do. What I say is true: the birds have one less tree to nest in. You get what I'm saying to you? I've said what I wanted to say, so now I shall go."

Bran exited the hobbit door, leaving a reproachful silence hovering over the gathering. Dylan liked him—he kept things together, the silent one working away unselfishly for all. He was upset, that was obvious. Dylan had helped cut the tree despite Bran's objection, thinking that a living tree had the energy needed for the ceremony.

Everyone was asked to comment in turn as the talking stick was passed around, allowing one person at a time to speak without interruption. Some spoke of the beauty of the day before, of the love that was there and what a precious ritual the making of the

May King and May Queen was. Now a sadness cast a shadow over the joy.

To help resolve the issue, Josie mimed a dance in front of the May King, gently weaving her thoughts around him with the elegance of a ballet, breathless and silent. Her hands moved with gestures mimicking her thoughts of disapproval, even though he was innocent, merely the representative of all the people there. The beauty of the dance and her feminine grace conveyed a sublime emotion more powerful than words.

She returned to her family as a calm descended like the wings of a butterfly: ethereal, delicate, though destined not to last. Shaman Darew seized the wooden dagger from the May King, weaving it like a pinnacle of power, up, down, and across, like a warrior defending his king. With a final sacrificial gesture, he slashed the dagger across his chest to pledge allegiance to his sovereign, then kissed its hilt and returned the dagger to the King.

Dylan was overawed by such a spectacle of unspoken passion, from the depths where words have no dominion, where imagining conjures up archetypes of meaning in the profound silence of simple gesture, born before language came into being, before words were carved into stone, a language prevalent in the natural world of birds and animals, no longer utilised by people, yet still alive in our psyche.

He sensed this missing link contained in the symbols of dreams, whose encoded emotions contained elements of our primitive past, whose meanings lay submerged in language and sigils. The cauldron of human intelligence is a vessel in which all disparity dissolves into love and compassion for all living things. Only when this is found and tasted, whether through dance or poetry, music or play, does the thread of a truth weave its way into our souls to realign our spirit-selves with all other forms of life.

When all was done, the celebrations over, the Awens sounded and the loud snores of those sleeping cut through the silence of the night, but for the stars hissing like wet logs on a fire, Dylan slipped out of the yurt to sit by glowing embers and ghost-like images inviting him into their world of fire, the doorway to their domain.

"Hello, Dylan," greeted a voice from the dark.

Dylan turned to see Jay standing there with a big smile.

"Don't wish to intrude," he said, sitting on a log next to Dylan. "You are a very private person; you keep your thoughts to yourself."

"Do I?" replied Dylan in mild surprise. "Guess I'm just a bit shy."

"Perhaps, but when you do speak, you speak from the heart." Jay threw a stick on the fire. "Often see you lost in your own world."

"I do wander off a lot."

"You are a dreamer, you know things."

Dylan stirred the fire with a stick, causing sparks to dance about like imaginary beings. "What's to say, Jay? I like you and the way your spirit shows through, the way you show your love for everyone. I feel at home here, one of you, brothers on a quest searching for a new way of living."

"We are," replied Jay. "We want a better life, one of honour and respect, one where men and women are equal, caring for one another. We look to the past to resurrect what was lost, what we once had: our common humanity."

Dylan glanced at the tall man in multi-coloured clothes, vibrant as a child's laughter. "That's why I love being with you all, feeling that connection again, sat here talking to you by the sacred fire."

"Sacred, very much so, though few understand the concept." Jay paused to look up at the night sky. "We're in great danger of losing our connection to nature and ourselves, but we can still turn things around if we continue to do what we're doing here, through our rituals, expressing our gratitude, beyond personal issues force-fed us by the corrupt otherworld."

"That's what I love about being with you all: the loving respect that's natural as spring water. Was it you led me blindfolded through the woods?"

Jay smiled and placed his hand on Dylan's shoulder. "You are a good man. It is an honour to know you."

"Likewise, Jay," responded Dylan. "My true family, living from the heart that binds us together regardless of personal beliefs."

"Well put, my friend," replied Jay. "An experiment in alternative living, with a smattering of ancient ritual connecting us to the ancestors and nature spirits: fairies, elves, call them what you will, though some refer to them as elementals."

"Children see them often, that I know."

"Who knows what relevance that has in our sophisticated technological age, when we've yet to solve the mysterious workings of the natural world, human consciousness and the alchemical magic that occurs between people? The May King feels the tribal energy, takes it onto himself, the responsibility. That's the key, taking on the welfare of the tribe for a year."

"Almost had that honour bestowed upon me," replied Dylan, "but I said no."

"Yours only if you truly need it. Discovered that conundrum a long time ago, surrendering to the powers that be, and by letting go of desire I found what I really needed." Jay paused to stare into the fire. "You are a dreamer, Dylan. You dream your future."

"Perhaps the future dreams us all."

"What sustains us is living and loving in tribal fashion. We come to camp to fortify us for the struggle of living out there. What is the first thing that happens when you come to camp? You are gated and asked to leave the apparent world behind, which means stepping into a different mode of being, surrendering to what is inside you, going back millennia to our instinctual mode of being. Our true nature wants to express itself, wants to move with the rhythms of Nature, our guide and teacher. Sometimes it takes days for that to happen, but sure as the sun rises in the morning, She is there waiting for you, once you learn to let go. Millions out there don't know what to do or where to turn for relevant guidance on how to find the elusive fulfilment they crave." Jay turned to Dylan directly. "How did you find yours?"

"Mine?"

"Your peace and sense of fulfilment."

"I became a hermit for fourteen years. Reading, writing, meditating… Best thing I'd ever done."

"No mean achievement," affirmed Jay. "Letting go of the world, finding yourself. For that, you have my respect."

"I was fortunate, most are not."

"But you can help show the way by your own experience."

"I know what I know, which isn't much if truth be known."

"Yet you found the courage to do it, which is enough in itself to live by example." Jay paused. "We are all here on a quest to find the grail of meaning in our lives, to find the golden meaning hidden within this illusory reality of phantasmagorical symbols rarely seen, touched or tasted, like a half-awake dream of Shangri-La. We go deep because we're not the only ones searching for what's lost." Jay grasped Dylan's arm and pulled him upright. "One day we shall build our lives on what we do here, because here is sanity and out there is madness."

Dylan knew this small gathering of people looking for a new way was but a drop in the ocean. All over the world were others of like-mind—tribal peoples, Druid and pagan gatherings—rekindling the embers of an ancient culture long-forgotten but not gone. Beneath the ground on which they stood was a way of life waiting to be reborn into the hearts and minds of twenty-first century humankind.

Jay stood, touching Dylan gently on the shoulder. "Remember that here we are free, here we can dream of a better world. Remember that we are never alone in the world of our ancestors who watch over us from beyond."

Dylan watched him go as the firelight danced into spirit companions for the man who shone like a beacon of loving strength. Sparks flew like thoughts into the ether, images of children in the garden of the unseen, running through a bluebell wood, swimming in a river of rainbow trout skittering amongst golden weed before the river died, before thatched cottages were replaced by modern flats and dream days trampled on by progress into the new world of efficient science. A battle-line was drawn between the opposing forces of nature and man. Nature our friend, and our enemy, the distorted reflection of our true being untainted by greed and the laws that govern a people trapped in never-ending servitude.

When will the clouds part to reveal the truth? What are we if we do not know who we are? A child knows the secret of the 'now': that there is no other now but *this* now, that this is the now in which we all live, in which we love.

Dylan had become the Now Lover. Peace descended upon him like morning mist. He would no longer extend himself into the future or belong to the past. Why do birds sing in the rain when we bemoan our lot? What do they know that we have forgotten? What did the ancients know of continuity that they played out their parts in such heroic fashion? That was what he was searching for, that something, that lost part of ourselves, longing for the peace that once was.

7

Lucy

Dylan had ventured into the world of Druid Camp like a dreaming child, a holiday away from the humdrum of everyday existence. He observed the activities that united them, the shared experience of ritualised ceremony elevating mind, body and spirit with a sense of oneness. He wished his soul-partner were with him so they could share the experience together, but Pamela abhorred the thought of camping in a muddy field.

"You go and enjoy yourself," she would say, though he often wondered what she meant by that.

Single women came to the camp, where nudity was optional and naked dancers performed bodily movements to ritualise inner feeling. Dylan was not of a mind to consider anything other than enjoying involvement within the bounds of friendship and sociability, even though his inner daemon would challenge the moral perception he had of himself, awakening an aspect that would nail his hands and feet to an unspoken agreement between mind and body, between dreams and reality.

Her name was Lucy. She sat in the lotus position, transcribing thoughts into a notebook when all

45

around was mayhem. He stood in the yurt doorway observing her disciplined focus, her pen moving quickly across the page. She glanced up; her blue eyes sparkled with a sharp intelligence.

"Hiya," she said, her greeting punctuated by a beguiling smile.

"I see you're busy, so I won't disturb you."

"That's alright," she replied. "I'm done for now, writing up descriptive text for the tarot pack I've just created. Deadline to fulfil, got till the end of next week."

They stared at one another. She put away her notebook. He sensed an attraction, a warmth.

"Good luck with that. You will do it—you have that discipline. I'm parked just here by the door."

"So you can escape quickly?" she jested with a deep-throated giggle.

"I'll leave you to it," he said, turning away.

"I'm not doing anything now, so why don't you come and sit by me? Talk to me, tell me about yourself and why you came to camp."

"Why are any of us here?" He sat close to her but not too close.

"Why so evasive? What's the big secret? What are you searching for?"

"Wish I knew," he lied, almost confessing his obsession with the Grail.

She gave him a piercing look and held him there. "I don't think that you are the sort of person not to know. I mean, you didn't just wander into camp willy-nilly. Don't have to tell me if you don't want to."

"A friend suggested that I come, and I had no idea what to expect."

"I saw you arrive, you and your friend."

"He had to go back, family emergency of some kind."

"It was dark when you joined us by the fire."

"I remember you."

"So?"

"What?"

"Camp life, do you like it?"

"Like being chucked into a cauldron."

She laughed. "Bloody good way of putting it."

"The rituals and ceremonies kind of go deep, like touching on something that's been long out of use, like a muscle that's been inactive for a long time, and the feeling you have when you yawn and stretch and say, ah, that's better."

"Oh boy, you can spill it out. Not so shy and retiring as I first thought. You are a deep one. You a writer, too?"

"Scribbled a little prose in the small hours of my life. Pretentious gobbledygook fit only for deranged cop-outs on mescal."

"Oh, one of those." She frowned. "Do you always put yourself down?"

Dylan winced. "Not always."

"You will like my tarot. It's called intuitive, as that is how I operate, seeing beyond the bullshit, such as you've just delivered to me. So what's on with you? Are you fey also? I think so, by the look in your eyes."

She rummaged through her bag to show him a painting of a man standing beneath a thunderstorm, dark and blue. A light glowed in the distance, far away and out of reach. "That is you looking for that something. You are a seeker, the Holy Fool who dares tread on pathways without guidance or a map, except for your inner sat-nav. Am I getting close? I read people better than I read the cards. Watkins bookshop in London is where I practice."

"Watkins?" Dylan was surprised and impressed. She'd read him right: his questing nature, bordering on foolhardy, living in a dream world where angelic visions were as Pinocchio to a woodcarver.

"We've just met," she said, eyeing him with curious interest, "and already we're contesting a difference of opinion. Shadow stuff is my game. Love and light birds had better not perch on my shoulder or I'll bite their heads off." Her light laughter suited her impish way. She bit with her tongue, but her eyes were full of fun. What mattered to her was sincerity.

A warm glow wrapped itself around them until she shivered and stood up. "Time for food. I bring my own. I don't like camp food. No bacon. I like my bacon and my coffee. Join me if you like."

He smiled at her invitation, though it wasn't only the food that she wanted to share. They left the yurt and walked across the field to where she'd parked her car. The food tent was full, and the smoke from the fire drifted into his nostrils with the smell of hot chocolate boiling in a pot on the fire.

"I am searching for something."

"What?"

"The Grail."

"Hah! I knew it," she replied jubilantly. "You're the Holy Fool."

Dylan hadn't a clue what she was talking about, but he enjoyed her coffee.

"What are you searching for?" she asked him several days later. "What do you want from me?" She wanted to know he wasn't just using her.

"Nothing."

"Everyone wants something."

"Not everyone," he answered defensively. "I enjoy being with you, but if you ask me why, it's just that you seem to be a very interesting person, a strong-minded woman who knows where she is going."

"Oh," she replied, surprised. "Suppose that I do know who I am—I mean, if I don't know then nobody knows. You say you are searching for a way of life that's got lost somewhere in the mists of time. Well, what about this one now? Is it to your liking? I think it's just about all I can stand of country living, if that's what you mean. Do you think all the people here are bloody angels?"

"Of course not, but at least they're real, expressing themselves more fully than out there in the streets of suburbia where it's all about what you got, mumbling hello to the neighbour and shutting the door."

"Point taken," she replied, "but not too seriously. City life separates, here is different. Camp life is a cauldron of emotion, though you may choose to be alone to preserve your own space, as I have to if I'm to finish the tarot in time. But I do like my own company." She observed his downcast expression. "Maybe you need to wake up to what's going on and get involved instead of sitting on the sidelines."

"But I do get involved," he protested.

"Then why are you always with me? Not that I mind, but you need to mix more, talk to the other Druids. Besides, there's many a woman out there who'd love to have you for company. They're jealous you're with me and not them. A man many women would die for, and who gets him? Lucy. Elaine thought you were her ex-boyfriend when she saw you lying naked on the grass. She'd have you in a shot."

Dylan felt flattered. He rarely thought of himself as desirable. "Elaine?"

"Garth and Elaine, Garth the Quaker."

"Garth who looks like a white-haired saint? Peaceful man, I like him a lot. He exudes peace, and strength."

"But he's now with us, the Druid weirdos, and he loves it."

"Craziest bunch I've ever been with." Dylan smiled. "Can only describe it as disciplined freedom."

"They have an arrangement; she has her boyfriends, yet they love one another. How's that for true acceptance? One that transcends normal relationships, because at the core of it all is love — call it unconditional or whatever, but for them it is right."

"I can imagine."

"Camp relationships can be fluid as a river, or rocky and thorny if they've got unresolved issues. So don't be naïve, see them as they are and not as you'd like them to be."

"I do see people as they are," he protested. "I sense their energy, their sensitivity — "

"Yes, but do you know them?" she interjected. "You don't know me, not properly anyway. Not saying I'm a total freak, but we've all got unresolved issues. Perhaps you need to wipe the romantic dew from your eyes that's blurring your vision."

She'd exposed his Achilles' heel. Was everything that he believed nothing but fairy-tale imaginings? Had he created in his mind a construct that had little to do with reality?

"You're a good, kind, attractive man," she said softly, "and very bright, except when it comes to women, but then most men haven't a clue what women want. Men are romantics, women are realists.

Men see their mothers, and women see babies that need feeding."

She liked Dylan a lot. His innocent openness was to her a reflection of a long-ago love taken from her by a mother she truly disliked, whose shadow had forced her into the dynamics of self-exploration.

"You're right. I must get out there and join in more," he said with sudden conviction, though his real reason was to get away from her probing questions that rattled the cage of his illusions.

"Why have you come here, Dylan? What do you want?" she called out.

"Nothing!" he snapped, turning to face her. "Love, understanding, a new way of living, uncomplicated and true to the spirit of our ancestors."

She laughed, amused by his annoyance and fiery spirit. "I know what I need from being here."

"Easy for you to say, being so sure of yourself. You know who you are, but I don't."

"Then it's about time you found out," she retorted. "The answer's right in front of you. Just look, and you will find it."

"No. I can never belong—not here, not anywhere. I'm a little boat adrift on an ocean current taking me where it will."

"Poetic waffle," she replied. "We all feel like that, bobbing up and down through one storm after another; it's called life. Come and sit with me, I promise not to wind you up any more."

"No! I'll watch the ceremony about to take place, Draig's initiation into manhood."

"Maybe you should join him," she laughed, knowing that deep down he enjoyed their banter.

Dylan joined the group of twelve men who'd formed a circle around the fire. Shaman Wolf stood

by his teenage son, Simon, and Simon's friend
Draig, a youth of seventeen, both apprehensive
of the ritual that lay ahead. Draig's bare arms
revealed tribal tattoos of swirling spirals. Around
his neck hung hag-stones and a bear's claw he'd
found in river gravel. Two women stood in the
sacred enclosure, preparing to lead the initiates
into manhood as a mother surrenders her child to
the world of men.

"My own recollection of initiation into manhood,"
declared Adrian, leaning on his staff, "was me and
nine others belting ninety miles an hour along a
motorway in a borrowed minivan, yelling like wolves
with hashish coming out of our ears. Though truth be
told, I would've preferred to go through an initiation
with you Druids instead."

Garth smiled. "One should never underestimate
the power of love when it comes to respect for oneself
and others. This is the gift that we give to each other
freely, not just within this sacred enclosure, but also
out there in the world we choose to forget during our
time here. We return to it fortified with the knowledge
that we are all one."

Adrian placed a hand on Draig's shoulder. "Just
as Simon and Draig will soon know what it means
to be a true compatriot of the Druid brotherhood
when they return."

Marianne escorted Draig to the river. Immersing
him in the cold water, she whispered tenets of
wisdom into his ears, secrets of the song of life that
echoed somewhere deep inside his soul. Then she
left him in the water and the rain.

Simon, son of Wolf, climbed the hill of the White
Horse, stretching his sinews to breaking point by
the time he got to the eye where Dylan had sat

with Madeleine and her aeolian harp. Simon's father was a powerful figure in the Druid world, a global phenomenon of groups searching for a more natural way of life, for nature we are, in the world of the Great Mother.

Simon was joined by the May Queen, Rowena, who put her arms around him and told him not to heed the voice of his ego and the shadow of his father's disapproval. She told him it was illusory, that he had not yet walked the plank into his own darkness, that no one could do it for him, not even his father, and that no one was exempt from the journey into the shadow. Holding back his tears, he curled into a foetal ball on the rain-soaked ground and wished that this was not happening to him, that he was the son of a man who knew all the answers, that he did not need to find them for himself.

"Wake up!" she shouted, and left him there as the cry of a buzzard tore through his cold isolation like fire through ice.

The voice of Nature spoke to him that day and that night, until the time came when he was ready to return to the safety of the camp and to the world of men, who waited in the yurt for his return.

It was half-past midnight. The camp slept in the glow of the sacred fire and the stars in the sky that wound up the circle of the day. The men swapped stories, told jokes and anecdotes, but secretly wondered how the trials of initiation had been for Simon and Draig, how it was done in the old days when living was so much harder than now, in a warrior society where only the strong survive. Today's young men are warriors of light and regeneration, and elder warriors contemplate their own strengths against trials testing their belief to live with dignity in honouring the Creator Spirit of all life.

Many lifetimes ago, they fought to survive. Now the fight was against ego, in a society seemingly bereft of compassion, the feminine quality many men embraced, knowing surrender of self brings love to the fore in all their actions. Adrian had dedicated his life to helping those addicted to drugs, encouraging them to live a more meaningful life, the kind of life he'd discovered for himself fighting through his own lost-soul phase. Jay had recently returned from a voyage to Patagonia in a three-masted schooner crewed by disaffected youths. Once a chemist in a government establishment, he'd chosen the Druidic life in total, as had Garth, a Quaker, who with his partner Elaine practised woodcraft and the shamanic arts at their hill-farm in North Wales. All in their own way were strong, loving, compassionate human beings.

Draig burst into the yurt grinning from ear to ear, a great thing achieved; he was also very wet.

"Been fishing, have you?" joked Jay, throwing a blanket over his shoulders.

"Yeah, and I caught the big one... myself."

He quickly responded to the warmth of their loving embrace as each presented him with a gift and told him of their love and respect, that they were bound heart to heart in true Druidic fashion. Dylan gave him an Ogham stick Adrian had given to him at his own bardic initiation. It was precious to him, but its purpose fulfilled, he passed it on to Draig in the hope that it would mean as much to him.

Simon followed a little later, no longer the boy who had left the gathering of the circle to climb the hill of the White Horse. He was calm and his poise more sure. His wayward energy had hit the ground hard, but he'd awoken to his own individuality. He would hate his father for a while, until the dethroned god became once more human in his eyes; only then could he give his love.

In the candlelight flickered the faces of the few who'd dared embrace a new way of being. Beneath the stars of night glowed a million lights with worlds of their own, in whose care the Great Spirit entrusted the unity of all things that live and grow, as Draig and Simon realised their own value as equal to all and the gift of self-value and love, as nature intends for all living things.

8
The Shadow

They would lie together without making love. He felt good about that, safe from the inner persecution that would follow if they had sex.

She told him, "I am your animus, which you give life to by being with me, the reason why you were attracted to me in the first place. You must learn to embrace your masculine side more fully, because you are actually an alpha male who's afraid to stand in the limelight."

"That isn't how I feel at all," replied Dylan.

"Of course it isn't, which is why it is hidden from you. You really do need to become more involved."

Her words bit deep, disturbing the inner sanctuary he'd created through years of isolation.

"I'm searching for a way of life that's been lost. Most are starved of the connection to Spirit, or God, or whatever we call the Creator, drugged by the soporific world of mass media where, for two cents, you can create your very own virtual reality."

She listened to his idealistic talk with amused interest but was quick to tease him out of introspection by goading him into camp activities such as re-enacting *Lord of the Rings*. As orcs with blackened faces, they'd battled like warriors from another time. A sense of the otherness of a long-ago connection pervaded the dance of love that raged between them.

He told her of his dreams, that he could sometimes foresee the future.

"Go on," she prompted. "Tell me more."

"All I can say is that my dreams tell me things, point the way. Not a map exactly, but an inner indication, an occasional peek into the past. Being here at this Druid Camp, I sense something long forgotten, but it's coming back to life like a seed that's been dormant and needs only a drop of water for it to start to grow again."

"You're such a romantic," she said teasingly.

"Wouldn't have it any other way," he replied.

"Not the way of things though, is it?"

"But it could be," he answered brightly. "We have the power within us to create our own reality."

Ducklings bobbed on the water near the coracle where Derwyn's desperate desire to be May King had been fulfilled. Good things occur when droplets of transformation splash out of the cauldron to touch the tongue with otherworldly inspiration.

"You put great store in your experiences of an alternate reality," she said, aware of his sensitivity about the subject, "but what relevance does it have for us in today's world?"

"I don't know, but if I relate to you a vision I experienced years ago, perhaps you will understand me more."

"Tell it to me."

"I am frolicking through a forest with three children, gliding and flying will-o'-the-wisp-like through the trees, happily disobeying the law, obeying our own Law, running through the forest brightly lit, happy birds singing, brooks tinkling down the valley, everything vibrant with light and life.

"On the other side of a bridge is where the people are, where we must go, for we are on a mission to restore the Law and to change their law in accordance with our Law; a boy of seven, a girl of eleven and a boy of thirteen cross the bridge to confront the people in a little hamlet somewhere in Wales.

"I watch from my safe spot amongst the trees. I see them pleading to let the protestors go, but all three are arrested. I don't want to go there, but I know I must, for something other than myself impels me to.

"The woods are bright, the trees are green, the rivers flow sweetly, the sun shines through the leaves. I am the leaves and trees and springs and sunshine, I am all, and the Spirit of Life is inside me, illuminating my consciousness.

"I cross the bridge to confront the policeman who stands between me and the friends I must protect. I demand he returns them to me, but he just smiles in a sure, almost patronising way, his young, bland face acquiescent.

"'Go back,' he says. 'If you trespass here, I shall arrest you.'

"'That's right,' I say, 'By your law you will arrest me. By my Law I will fight, and your law will be no more.'

"He just smiles, though I sense something move beneath his conditioned exterior, but he has his job to do and repeats as before, 'If you attempt to intervene, you will leave me no alternative but to arrest you.'

"I stand up to him and say, 'By the law of man you will put down that which has made man. I say that the Law which made man will come again, and you will be subservient to that Law once more, and your work will be to uphold that Law, and all others will abide by it, for that Law was the first Law, and will be so for evermore. Let me pass through! Your law forbids, but my Law commands. Pass by, you and all you people watching; those you have arrested are my friends and you must let them go.'"

"That it?" asked Lucy.

"I was arrested and thrown into the paddy wagon with the others, but the message was clear: I must enter the fray in order to win, from the inside, as that is the only way."

Lucy considered his vision, realising that it had been no ordinary insight into the world of nature. "You said that you were the leaves and trees and everything. In what way do you mean?"

"That I was all, simultaneously."

"Were you on ayahuasca?"

Dylan laughed. "No, Lucy. If you live like a hermit for fifteen years, strange things happen."

"A superconscious experience; fascinating."

"In a way. But what it did do was force me to change, to get out and into life once more."

"I can imagine you living like a monk; you've that ethereal otherworldly quality about you. So tell me more about this Grail thing?"

"What about it?"

"Bugger me!" she exclaimed. "Elusive as a butterfly."

"Have to," he replied.

"What?"

"Obfuscate what scares the hell out of me."

"What does that mean?" she demanded.

"It means that my dreams and visions lead me where I do not wish to go."

"What kind of conundrum is that?" she replied. "Enlighten me, Dylan."

Sat on the riverbank, he told her of the vision of the Rose and the Lion, and the maidens' lament.

"So that's what got you started on the Grail."

"Plus other things, such as past-life recollections."

"Right pickle then?"

"I believe so."

"So?"

"So why me, who just wants to live a quiet life?"

"Seems you made the choice long before you were dumped on this planet." She chuckled, amused at his dilemma. "Trouble with you, Dylan, is that you are afraid of your own masculinity, afraid to be forceful, afraid to be who you really are, who you're supposed to be. If I were you, I'd get on with looking instead of waiting for someone to lead you there, which won't happen."

They walked in silence towards Eight, who stood alone and forlorn on the escarpment overlooking the river and smiled on seeing them approach.

"Hi, Eight." Lucy greeted him and put her arms around him. "You must know how much it means to us all for you to hold the tribal energy for a whole year, the invisible glue that binds us all together."

"An honour and an obligation I was happy to uphold," he replied. "The new King is a gentle soul, as is the May Queen."

He shook himself like a dog shucking off rainwater and danced like a dervish around the sacred fire. No one paid heed, no matter what one did on the spur of the moment—children do it all the time.

That night as the camp slept and the stars shone in the clear night sky, Dylan crouched by the fire, preoccupied with his vision of the riddle of the seven maidens, whose lament of the Rose had grown like a tree reaching ever upward, for the Rose symbolised spiritual perfection like the lotus flower of the Buddhists, the feminine heart of loving creation. The Rose also represents Sophia, the Goddess of Wisdom and the Logos of the creative mind.

The maidens' dance on the wall in the garden of the ancient monastery spoke of lost wisdom concealed within the feminine psyche, as the three houses on the shoreline he'd seen in the vision represented the trinity of Heaven, Earth and Man.

The Grail conundrum had dominated Dylan's mind for several decades. Research had produced conflicting definitions: the cup of the Last Supper, the cauldron of the Celts — the possibilities were endless. Waleran's *Le Seynt Graal*, 717 AD, describes a vision of Jesus and the Grail: *'Here is the book of thy descent, here begins the book of the Sangreal.'* Chretien De Troyes describes the Castle of the Fisher King, whose Grail is his sustenance. Robert de Boron's Fisher King is kinsman to Joseph of Arimathea by marriage to his sister, Enygeus.

Dylan threw a log on the fire, creating sparks that flew into the silence of his thoughts. A million times a million have asked the question: "What is the Grail?"

What was so important to the people of those days, beyond the conflict, beyond the wars? The spiritual salvation of Jesus Christ? Jesus the Prophet, not the son of God, but the son of the Holy Spirit, the feminine emanation of the Creator.

The world changes as the Great Awakening pours energy over the Earth to fill the void in people's hearts. Twenty-six thousand years, and the great wheel turns towards the centre.

The heart knows many things concerning love. Wandering through times long gone, something lingers, unfulfilled, a taste of love that went away; death came quickly and often. Souls talk when they sleep. Lucy talked of shadows, images on the walls of our minds that sleep or wake when the resonant soul makes contact with its kin. Mysteries are just that, a taste on the tip of the tongue. Longings are best when they lead to the goal.

Lucy held a lantern to his reflection. Laughter would come, and sorrow. Fates are worse when unheeded. Open the eyes; it is there, shining for all to see. Perhaps not all. Not the profane, for life is careful not to divulge its secrets to those who despise the love that made us.

Druid Camp was a quest of sorts. The alchemy of the psyche works its magic in the most unlikely of places, such as a field of yurts and teepees, beneath the open sky and the light of the sun. Human nature doesn't change in its longing to belong to the greater whole, to Mother Earth.

9

Journey to Camelot

Seven days after the Beltane Druid Camp, Dylan found himself wandering through the ruins of the ancient city of Caerwent, whose Roman walls towered above lush pasture beneath Wentwood, where megaliths stood like sentinels to a forgotten time, just like the foundations of the Roman forum and basilica, whose cyclopean remains remind us of a once mighty empire, whose broken columns and capitals lay as if an earthquake had struck the day before.

A Roman inscription stood in the porch of St Stephen's Church, declaring the city to be a *Civitas*, governed by the tribe of the Silures. This was their city, set away from the troubled mountains where warfare stuck like mud to the invaders of this free land. Here they ran their own show, skilled craftsmen in metal and leather, a free-trade zone, much to the satisfaction of the Romans who gained the best of both worlds: conquest and trade.

Dylan wandered among the remains of villas whose mosaic floors adorned a local museum, where a Chi Rho insignia scratched on a pewter vessel told of early Christianity long before Augustine came to pronounce everlasting judgement on all those who stood in the way of the Church of Rome.

St Stephen's Church bell rang three times, and Dylan considered the legend of Arthur and Gwenhyver marrying in the Church of St Stephen in Winchester, that Winchester translated into Welsh is Caerwent. Leyland, the sixteenth-century historian, declared Caerwent to be Camelot, as Winchester had been under Saxon control during Arthur's time.

Hidden amongst the trees to the north lay the hillfort of Llanmelyn, which some say is Camelot, though Dylan knew that dream city to mean many things to the Cymric Celts, who aspired towards true equality between men and women, between their way of life and the land, between knowledge of the past and hope for the future, between self-sufficiency and avarice. There are many Camelots, and each age has its own.

Dylan walked along the high wall stretching the length of the city. Its four towers, three times the height of a man, stood unbreached to this day. Dylan held onto his hat as a wild wind blew from the north-west like Celts descending upon the killing machine of Roman usurpers. He touched the stones whose story lay hidden beneath mounds of rubble frequented only by grazing sheep. What tales of the past could they unfold to our inquiring minds? What did they think and feel, those who for a generation defied the might of the Roman Empire?

Who was Merlin? Who was the Arthur who stood against the Saxons? What was it in the spirit of the Cymric Silurians that they allowed none to destroy their heritage and their land?

A shiver ran through Dylan, standing where they had stood fifteen centuries before. He recalled a dream where a white-robed Druid stood in the centre of a circle of stones, holding a sword by its tip to testify that the Bards of Britain were men of peace and heavenly tranquillity, attested to by the three-rayed sigil of the Awen of the flowing spirit, the creative force of the Universe—the source of spiritual strength, inspiration and prophetic insight.

Events of those long-ago days had told of a configuration of circumstance that would fire the imagination with its living truth. This was the road he was on, to discover that truth, yet every insight was a test to his integrity, as his greatest enemy was himself, his egoistic desire luring him away in order to discover the true from the false of his own nature and natural instincts. It is the same in love and war, for whoever enters either unprepared perishes. Relationships are like that, in the search for love, for who we are, but also who we *were*, as he knew that we are all a culmination of our past lives moving in a spiral of knowledge and understanding.

He walked on, perplexed as to why he should relive such events as the Saxon wars, warriors fighting single combat, a ship burial of a young prince, or how the vision of the Rose and the Lion should fall onto a canvas of disparate images. Shaking his head in bewilderment, he slipped on a molehill and cut his hand on a piece of metal, a fragment of a bronze brooch worn by a Silurian tamed by Roman ways.

"This is Camelot," he said aloud, venting annoyance at the injury. Yet he could not undo his sense of injustice at how little the Welsh knew of their own history, that the city of Caerwent was the Camelot of a thousand tales.

He scanned the alluvial plain with its fertile soil stretching towards the Wentwood Hills, green with beech and oak, and craggy Gray Hill, whose megaliths lay amongst sweet grass and fern beneath the gaze of birds of prey. Archaeologists came and went with their finds of Roman hairpins and gladiatorial memorabilia, paying respects to a lost empire that scarred the land with the blood of human dignity.

Sheep grazed on hillocks between the walls where the forum slept, stripped down to the ground, forlorn pillars and pilasters languishing in a hawthorn copse. The basilica once imposed the power of Rome upon a people of mud huts who lived in a land free of tyranny. The earth holds tight to its past, as now they lay, mute witnesses to those days in a land whose people sang their songs of liberty, defiant as ever, yet a sense of loss haunts the hills whose valleys are the people, and the people are the valleys, at one with the spirit of the land.

Dylan walked away from the city unaware of his dreaming and sense of frailty, the precarious value of his thoughts disturbed by the rushing traffic that cut through tranquillity like a knife. Was Leland right: was Caerwent Camelot? Did anyone know? Did anyone care?

He followed the ancient Roman road of the Via Julia towards the City of the Legions. Windshield eyes glared at the wanderer on a pilgrimage as traffic sped by on a journey to a future of bits and bytes, to quote a local poet. The rope to the moorings of the past had been cut, and the boat drifted over the ocean of hopes and dreams towards the Promised Land of Arthur's return.

10
City of the Legions

The City of the Legions glowed red in the evening sun alongside the River Usk becalmed at high tide, a majestic moment as the swans glided on the water below the quay of the Hanbury Arms where Dylan sat, and where Alfred Lord Tennyson wrote: *'I sit here like King Arthur as the mighty Usk murmurs by'*, whose commemorative plaque hangs in the inn opposite a photograph of Arthur Machen, whose *Hill of Dreams* conjures up Caerleon's enchanted past.

Dylan sat with his legs dangling over the quay and wrote on his notepad: *A poet was I in the small hours of my life. Contemplation rules my hours with a rod of straw woven from dreams of what once was. Who is he, say they? Who is they? The Shadow calls through the noise of the living. The river flows by majestic and serene as Orpheus on the silver stream, rafting memories constant as the tide. A sparrow hawk hovers above balsam, mallow drifts in the breeze and the sun shelters daylight, wafting gentle rays into the sky of conscience as a man, bitter as ale, spits on the quayside where Orpheus plays a flute to charm these devils of our time; and there is the killing of love where Arthur stood to call up the Lady of the Waters to bring peace once more to this land.*

Dylan wended his way around the Roman walls of this once proud city, walls still strong after two thousand years, dominating the land where green grass grew stunted and shivering. Its power carved into the chiselled stone features of Roman senators, enshrined forever in a frieze of cruelly misnamed civilisation.

Dylan touched the sandstone pillars of the amphitheatre, where games are played out to this day: gladiators from Italy re-enacted sword thrusts into their opponents gills with muscle-taut efficiency; a Roman cavalry officer sat astride a stallion, looking down in disdain on woad-daubed Silurians, who laughed at his arrogance and won the game by bashing shields in contempt at such vain superiority.

School children marched up and down, repeating a mantra in perfect Latin: "We who are about to die salute you!" A Jack Russell wagged its tail and pissed in the centre of the arena, a just offering to the Roman gods. Ten thousand sat here in those days—and in Arthur's day, who knows but the stones that murmur beneath the hissing stars of all-seeing photons of light? We in our dark corner recall our time, but the neighbouring trees hold the stones fast by their roots.

"They say if you stand there long enough, you will see Arthur and his knights go by."

Dylan looked up to see a man standing on the ramparts next to a feisty Jack Russell. "That another of those old legends?"

"Knock on any door and you'll hear stories that'll make your hair stand on end."

The Jack Russell wagged its tail, shivered and yapped.

"A woman who lives on Lodge Hill told me that when her mother went into her bedroom, she asked her daughter if she wouldn't mind telling the Roman soldier to leave so she could get some sleep. She described a six-foot centurion in full regalia. Can't get rid of the buggers. Must be stuck in a time-warp or something."

"Aren't we all?" replied Dylan, who was beginning to like the way this man thought. "Do you believe this amphitheatre to be the Round Table?"

"Does the Pope wear a mitre? No one's top dog in a circle. Celts love circles for the obvious reason that no one's above another, even if one of them's a chieftain." He descended the ramparts and approached Dylan. "Where you from then?"

"Wales."

"Fellow Cymbrogi," he replied, offering a hand of friendship.

Dylan shook his hand and sensed his magnetic energy, ebullient, upbeat, his ready smile revealing a missing front tooth.

"Do you believe that King Arthur was here?"

"Do you think this great walled city stood empty throughout the Dark Ages? Do me a favour — course he was."

"So why do tourists go looking for him at Tintagel and Glastonbury?"

"The *Saesneg*, the English, stole him from us. Arthur was Welsh. Only got to read the old stories to know that."

"So why don't the tourists come here then?"

"Because we have a Welsh Assembly who don't give a damn about our history being usurped by the *Saesneg*, our heritage buried in the undergrowth of poverty and disillusion."

Dylan admired his passionate verve and his Jack Russell that shook like it was plugged into the national grid.

"Between fifty and a hundred Roman buildings lie under those fields," said Dylan, pointing to the flood-plain along the river. "I was a volunteer on a dig here, unearthing a forum, basilica, and mosaics, hypocausts and a quay. Caerleon was a bustling port, as you probably know."

"Yep, but where's the evidence of the dig now? Covered up like the rest of our history?"

"Perfect analogy of the Welsh dilemma: history deleted to suit the English agenda of superiority," replied Dylan. "Archaeologists are generally unbiased, except when it comes to Arthur. 'We don't want to find King Arthur do we?' said the head honcho, holding up the front page of the local newspaper with the headline: *Will they discover King Arthur?* 'No!' said all with scathing laughter, afraid their version of Welsh history might be shattered."

"Do you think," the man continued, "that they'd ever allow a dig on Welsh soil that might throw up evidence of the Once and Future King? Most don't care because they believe the lies they've been told of our history. Excuse my language, but it pisses me off the way the Welsh are regarded by the *Saesneg* as good-for-nothings, relying on handouts like beggars from a rich man's bowl."

"Rape of the Fair Country, say no more," responded Dylan.

"Could say a lot, but I won't, except that this is the lost city of legend where Arthur entertained kings, and Taliesin spoke his verse, where the quest was championed by Arthur and his warrior knights."

"The quest for the Holy Grail. What is the Holy Grail?" asked Dylan. "What were they searching for?"

"Join me in the Hanbury for a pint and I'll tell you."

"Okay, I'm in."

"I'm Richard."

"I am Dylan, whose bardic namesake still haunts the world of prose."

"Good to meet you, Dylan."

The Hanbury Arms stood on the quayside with its Roman tower, whose battlements could readily hurl hell onto intrepid pirates or invading Saxons. The pub's antiquated interior was sodomised by a megascreen showing Welsh rugby highlights, as bums on seats and food in bellies had become the modus operandi to ethnically cleanse fishing nets, trout in glass cages and the chalked wit of generations on blackened oak-beams, whitewashed into oblivion.

Richard pointed to an old framed photograph of Alfred, Lord Tennyson. "Tennyson sat here to write his *Idylls of the King* after Lady Charlotte Guest suggested he come to Caerleon—she being the first to translate the *Mabinogion* into English. She knew the truth of the legends of Arthur, that Caerleon was his stronghold."

"So, what's your profession, Richard? What do you do for a living?"

"Apart from breathing and being Welsh, I'm an artist who runs the Ancient Cwmbran Society," he said, raising his glass. "*Iechyd da!*"

"Cheers!" responded Dylan, curious as to what Richard might know of the Grail.

"You are Welsh then?"

"Welsh and Irish."

Richard laughed. "Twice as mad then."

"And a Gemini to boot."

"Me likewise, which makes four of us."

"Rollercoaster ride, you and me, dreamers on the Grail trail."

"No, not me," laughed Richard. "Just your everyday Valleys boy who walks the hills talking to nature spirits up there on Twm Barlwm along with my Druid."

"Your Druid?"

"Yeah, my Druid," asserted Richard. "The Saxons called the Welsh *Wallach*, which means foreigner. How can you be a foreigner in your own land? That's mad! Cymru is Wales. *Cymbrogi* means comrade or fellow countryman."

Richard laughed readily; his generous nature and strong voice radiated a certain integrity. "I'm an artist with a passion for history," he said, quaffing half a pint in one gulp, "which is why I'm running a project about the Cistercians at Llantarnam Abbey. Truth is, it's more to do with St Derfel, one of three survivors of the Battle of Camlann, whose ruined chapel is up on Mynydd Maen. We've also discovered a sixth-century llan, a sacred enclosure, and hundreds of massive quartz boulders, Neolithic megaliths. No one knows who put them there or why."

"Twenty-nine bronze axes were discovered amongst those trees," said Dylan, pointing to the wooded hillside opposite, "each wrapped separately as votive offerings from different tribes, brought to what was a Druidic Cor, where they would chant and pronounce prophecy."

"You think Caerleon was a Druid stronghold?"

"Why'd you suppose the Romans built their city here, if not to impose their gods on top of the Celtic ones, even though the Druids believed in one god."

Richard's Jack Russell leapt onto Dylan's lap, frantically licking his face.

"Gerroff, Rocky!" yelled Richard. "He's just trying to dominate you. It's their nature being so small, it's how they survive; it's called friendly aggression."

"Like some of the kids I grew up with," said Dylan, wiping saliva off his face. "Okay, let's get a handle on this Grail thing. The old stories describe such a vessel in allegorical terms to ward off pagan-hunting Catholics. The *Mabinogion* story of Culwch and Olwen describes a magic cauldron; Taliesin received his inspiration from the cauldron of Ceridwen after stirring it for a year and a day, when three drops touched his tongue."

"Whatever that means," interjected Richard.

"The Awen, the spirit of inspiration."

"Of course, idiot that I am."

"Not the Christian Grail but the pagan equivalent, the treasure of knowledge which heals the sick and brings the dead back to life. So where is it now, the Grail, the font of wisdom? Or more to the point: is it an object, or lost knowledge, a magic formula to attain the Divine?"

"Local legends claim that Derfel and Frechfa ran off with it, that Illtud was its guardian, or Arthur's son, Morgan, took it westward out of reach of the invading Saxons. No one knows, except that they lost something very important to them, that without it, bad things happen."

Dylan was quick to realise that Richard was quite knowledgeable on the subject. "What about the theory that a comet struck Britain in the mid-sixth century, causing famine and plague that wiped out half the population, creating the Arthurian Wasteland? Chroniclers describe seven months of darkness. Gildas, the historian, said it was God's punishment due to the corrupt rulers."

"Gildas would find fault with Gandhi." Richard grinned. "Blackett and Wilson claim the devastation allowed the Saxons to conquer England. The Druids and warlords were tame compared to the Saxon's rule of blood-law and Woden, whereas the Celts venerated natural phenomena such as rivers and lakes, forests and mountains. They called their God, Duw, the Supreme Being who pervades the Universe, Creator of all Life."

Dylan paused, sipped his drink and spoke in a low voice. "An object is a beacon only if light shines out from its centre. All trees point to the sun, all eyes look upward to the stars, all hearts look inward to its source. We are all one at the end of the day."

"Don't go Biblical on me now," rebuked Richard. "I'm more pagan than Christian, a spiritual healer who believes in a universal energy field taught to me by a Druid on Twm Barlwm."

"A real Druid?" asked Dylan.

"Yeah, kind of," he answered evasively. "Just he's been dead a long time — though very much alive, if you get my drift."

Dylan was beginning to realise Richard functioned on many levels. "That I do. So this Druid...?"

"True story, got me to change my wild ways and walk the spiritual path. Twm Barlwm's a sacred mountain overlooking Cwmbran. Used to be quiet before kids on scrambler bikes began churning up the old tracks and creating havoc and desecrating the land."

"Can well understand why you were angry."

"Not so much angry," replied Richard, sipping his lager to gather his thoughts. "Just knew I had to do something, so I waited for them up a tree with a lump of wood, saying to myself, 'Right, you buggers, you don't give a damn about this sacred mountain, so now it's comeuppance time.' I could hear them coming and they were almost beneath me when all of a sudden a voice yelled at me to get off the tree. I shit myself. It was a Druid with a shaggy beard, clad in one of those monkish cloak things. Fierce, I tell you."

"You actually saw him?"

"Oh yeah, he's my spirit guide, or whatever, who taught me to practise spiritual healing, and to set up the Ancient Cwmbran Society."

Dylan wasn't sure if he was half-crazy or just spinning a yarn, though he inclined toward the former. "So, you had an encounter with a discarnate Druid. Does this Druid have a name?"

"Wouldn't tell me. Names are not important anyway. I only know he's with me whenever I go up there. Scary though, won't take any messing, tells me off for drinking too much or showing off. Heal people, he says, and you will find your reason for being."

"Something about the Druids," Dylan chimed in. "They had their finger on the pulse of life, living in harmony with nature and a deep respect for one another and all life, as best they could, that is, considering the adverse conditions back then."

"You a Druid then? You sound like one."

"I belong to a Druidic organisation, OBOD, the Order of Bards, Ovates and Druids."

"Why am I not surprised?" interjected Richard. "You've that look about you, not just your long hair either."

"They put a lot of love into whatever they do, whether it be rituals or activities that free up our conditioned ways. Feel like a child and lose sight of who I think I am when I'm with them, a weirdly revealing way to our true nature, free of judgement and expectation. Days roll one into another in a constellated adventure into the self we know only in dreams, but it's more real than any stimulus our sick society can offer."

"I grasp what you're saying, out of your comfort zone with strange people." Richard was beginning to realise Dylan's multi-faceted personality was as eccentric as his own. "We are here to help one another in whatever way we can. I heal, that's what I do, that and the Ancient Cwmbran Society. History's important because the land is important. Who are we if we forget? Nothing. That's what we shall become if we fail to respect our ancestors by honouring their lives by revering one another."

"Question," cut in Dylan. "Why has the Church hidden the truth of who we are? They've abused their power for so long, but we are now free to decide for ourselves what to believe, allowing our hearts and intuition to guide us, knowing what we know now, that the Universe was created out of love."

Richard leaned back in his chair as though he'd discovered the secret of life, comfortable with himself and his world. "The Druids are the guardians of the land. My Druid tells me that we must protect the land, and he's very concerned at the lack of spirituality, that if we lose our connection to the past, we lose everything."

Dylan realised Richard's thinking was similar to his own, a kindred spirit. "My quest is to discover the truth of our history. The valleys of South Wales are like a dried-up spring where people go to drink to quench their thirst, but the rains no longer come and the land is dry. I tell you, my friend, a deep mystery is waiting to be revealed."

"Are you that person?"

"What person?"

"You're a Grail seeker, aren't you?"

"Yes," answered Dylan, reluctantly.

"And if the old ways are to be reinstated at all, then it has to be where the land meets the sea, where matter touches spirit. You have your quest, and I have mine, which is the Ancient Cwmbran Society. We conduct archaeological investigations to piece the past together, gluing one sequence of events to another. Number one project is to investigate the ancient chapel and shrine of St Derfel, but will we be given permission by Cadw to dig there? Not on your nelly."

"Why not?"

Richard laughed mockingly. "They don't want people to know about Welsh history. The Treachery of the Blue Books was a long time ago, but little has changed."

"To change the subject," said Dylan, pointing to the field adjoining the river. "You see that field? The grandfather of someone I know —"

"Who?" interjected Richard.

"Pete Davies."

"I know Pete... Go on."

"Told me that his grandfather sees three angels standing there every night, looking towards Caerleon."

"What do they look like, these angels?"

"Well over six foot tall with long white robes, but no wings, because angels don't have wings as such. What you see is their aura, which can look like wings."

"Why are they facing the city wall? "

"A question to which I have no answer," replied Dylan, "unless they're guarding something, such as the Mynd, the pre-Roman mound almost as big as Silbury Hill, hidden behind the trees and the wall and flanked by Roman pillars leading to a spiral path circling the Mynd to the top and the remains of a ruined temple."

"The Mynd is just outside the Roman wall. It's ancient."

"Me, Pam and Emma, who'd left her roundhouse existence in the Preselis to sort out the Romans, as she put it, went up there to meditate. A Roman soldier with shield and spear stood in front of us. I can see his face now — clean shaven, mid-thirties, good-looking features. Further away, a gathering of white-robed men were conversing with the Emperor Claudius. Figured that they were discussing terms of peace, a truce, which actually happened when Caractacus and Arviragus were invited to Rome, because the war here was going badly for the Romans and Claudius needed to save face."

"What I know of the Silurian Wars is that it took thirty years of fighting before they could build Caerleon."

"That's the truth of it," replied Dylan. "On leaving the Mynd, the old gardener asked if we saw the Roman soldier. I said that I had, and he nodded with a knowing smile."

"Roman ghosts are everywhere in Caerleon," responded Richard.

"Tell me about it. We have a wee shop in the Ffwrwm Courtyard where I sculpt and sell things Celtic."

"Ah, I knew I'd seen you before, you and the blonde-haired lady."

"Pamela."

"Beautiful lady," responded Richard with an approving smile. "Had an artist's studio there once, before your time."

Dylan raises his glass. "Here's to the Grail and the spirits who haunt this ancient city."

"*Iechyd da!*"

Dylan raised his glass to Lord Tennyson for reviving the old legends of King Arthur, and to Arthur Machen for rekindling the essence of the Celtic spirit, conjuring up the magic and mysticism of an unconquerable race.

Dylan stood on the bridge over the Usk to take in the beauty of the early morning mist enveloping the river like a sacred kiss. There were secrets buried in the tidal mud, stories of long-forgotten truths. He saw Roman galleys unloading cargoes of oil and wine at the quayside, and auxiliary troops marching along the Via Julia towards Caerwent. With ships came strangers from Gaul and Spain and Rome, from Alexandria and Smyrna, bringing with them stories from the eastern empire, of a new religion called Christianity.

Dylan glanced at the wooded hill of Bulmore, where several years prior an ancient underground tomb had been found containing two stone sarcophagi of a man and a woman. Alongside the man's skeleton was a jewelled sword. The well-known historian who'd told him this said that the sword ended up in the boot of the boss's car, the billionaire who owns the Celtic Manor. A rumour perhaps, or as real as the Celtic offerings to the River Goddess Sabrina dredged from the muddy Usk.

Black cormorants skimmed the calm water, and a sea of silver dew glistened on the meadows as traffic grumbled over the bridge to disturb the early morning peace. A helicopter whirred over the hill towards the temple to the god of golf on its summit, a citadel of futility, the temple of the New Rome, where senators of politics and kings of big business gathered to drink from the empty cup of the Grail in a land barren of meaning, bereft of hope without the glory.

God save and bless this land, thought Dylan, *for there is no tomorrow without yesterday, and the yesterday of our fathers is no longer apparent to the eye of power and wealth, whose mocking laughter echoes along the valley to disturb the spirits sleeping there, and the spirits stir from their slumber to call out what is lost: 'Those who have ears hear, and those who have eyes follow the trail to the broken pot and sing it back together again.'*

11
Derfel

Richard walked upright and proud, breathing the air of freedom, leading the way up the ancient track flanked by quartz boulders protruding out of the undergrowth alongside a fast-running brook. Sheep took shelter under an old oak, and Dylan held onto his hat in the wind on the mountain of Mynydd Maen.

Richard placed his hands on a boulder. "This is just one of hundreds strewn all over this mountain. Got to ask yourself who put them here and why. In the woods below us are walls constructed of huge quartz boulders. Were they built by the Cistercians, or are they from the Neolithic period? I think both, that the Cistercians realised their healing potential, as did the Beaker people. Stonehenge was built for the same purpose."

Dylan pulled his hat on tight as low cloud and drizzle smothered the mountain.

"This ancient track is the pilgrim route to Derfel's shrine," continued Richard. "These white-quartz boulders reflect the moonlight."

"Must have been quite a sight during days of candle and sword, glistening on the ridge in the light of the full moon." Dylan squelched his way up the deep-cut track, where rivulets of rainwater cut channels through unyielding granite.

"Only a people who believed in the 'Other'," said Richard, "who struggled with everyday existence in a land that was harsh and unforgiving, could devote the time and energy to put all those megaliths in place."

"What do the archaeologists say about them?" asked Dylan, still holding onto his hat.

"An unexplained anomaly is the general consensus, except for one archaeologist who said to me, 'Well, it's bloody obvious, isn't it? They were put here to ward off negativity.'"

"Good to know that at least one archaeologist thinks outside the box, aware of the spiritual element of the past," yelled Dylan above the whistling wind.

"The Druids believed in the power of the stones to heal," said Richard. "Pieces of quartz have been found in many Celtic Christian burials, a tradition inherited from the Druids."

The ruins of St Derfel's Chapel lay desolate and forlorn beneath a grey sky, its crumbling walls painted by nature's hand with green lichen, marking time since long-ago pilgrims payed homage to the warrior monk who survived the ill-fated Battle of Camlann, where Arthur was mortally wounded and taken to Avalon by Morgan le Fey.

"Welcome to the Lourdes of South Wales," said Richard, standing on a heap of rubble with a staff of blackthorn. "Down below is the Valley of Bran— Welsh for raven. Or maybe it's named after the historical Bran who led Welsh warriors to Ireland to bring back the cauldron of immortality, which many say is the original Grail."

"So we create a history out of imagination."

"Derfel was a warrior monk who fought bloody battles against the Saxons before retiring to live a life of solitude. Going to war or into a monastery was very much the same to the Celts, as both required courage."

"Going into oneself is tough," expounded Dylan. "I've done it, as have you."

"Yeah, been there, done that, got the sackcloth tee-shirt," replied Richard, glancing at the rough terrain. "This is wild; Derfel must've been mad to live up here."

"The price of peace never changes," Dylan agreed with a wry grin, zipping up his jacket against the wind.

Richard paraded on the ruins he hoped to one day excavate. "Once there was a statue here of St Derfel riding a stag and holding a spear and shield. An ancient prophecy foretold that it would one day burn a forest. Come the dissolution of the monasteries, it was used in the pyre that burned John Forrest, who'd refused to acknowledge Henry the Eighth's marriage to Anne Boleyn."

They continued along the old pilgrim route towards Twm Barlwm, a Neolithic fairy mound assaulted by wind and rain, and rounded like an egg of the Great Mother.

"Tradition says it's the burial mound of King Baram, who burned Caerleon to the ground, a reminder to the Romans to respect those warriors of the hills."

"Tradition says that the Druids were taught by Enoch in the Vale of Hebron, and the Greeks called the Cymry the Cimmeroi, and the Hittites called them the Cymru."

"Never!" exclaimed Richard.

"Taliesin wrote of their origins in the sixth century when he said: 'I was in Africa before the birth of Rome, I came here to the remnant of Troy.'"

"So the Cymru were the Trojans?" queried Richard.

"Chariots were used against the Romans."

"This track we're walking on was built for chariots — told this by an archaeologist."

"Which by itself isn't proof that the Silurians were the Trojans, but there are certain women in Wales and Cornwall who possess palm-sized stones on which is carved a labyrinth, which are used for healing and seeing into the future. They call them the Stones of Troy."

"Never!" exclaimed Richard.

"So you never know."

"Welsh women know a thing or two, especially the Valleys women. I know because I'm married to one."

Richard gazed towards the sea and the far-off shore of England, then turned towards the Brecon Beacons and the Land of Song as sunshine burst through the clouds, creating a kaleidoscope of colour as the ridgeway wind rustled through gorse and heather growing between rocks worn smooth by centuries of horse and cart, and even chariots.

Twm Barlwm, Arthur Machen's 'Hill of Dreams', was alive with stick people out of a Lowry painting. Others clambered up the steep slopes of Mynydd Maen, hair blowing wildly and holding onto hats in a terrain fit only for sheep and buzzards, yet once home to hardy hunter-gatherers inured to the elements.

Dylan gazed at the land sloping towards the Usk and the Severn Estuary, visualising the Roman legions coming ashore to subdue the Silurian Celts.

Thirty years of warfare ensued, allowing Christianity to gain a foothold in South Wales. He thought of the blood and slaughter of those days and shuddered. Today's slaughter is bloodless but just as deadly; it is the destruction of the history of a people called the Cymric Celts.

"Why are all these people here?" asked Dylan, as they joined a stream of people heading towards the tumulus.

"Whitsun," replied Richard. "Tradition going back hundreds of years. Easter's the same — hundreds celebrating Oestre, the Goddess of Spring."

Dylan sensed this was more than just a gathering huddled together against the wind, children clinging to mothers wrapped in woollies, celebrating Whitsun on a mountain top in preference to attending church.

"You can't walk these hills without walking on the trail of the Cymru," shouted Richard, dancing wildly to the beat of a drum.

Dylan sensed a quickening of the spirit as dance and music played out on the summit of an earthen mound, paying homage to the ancestors, the people of the land who had kept alive their connection to heaven and earth.

"Listen, my friend," said Dylan on their way down the mountain. "Wales has been air-brushed out of history, not by circumstance but by design. If only the Cymry knew the truth of their history, they would walk tall, knowing they belong to a brave race of people who could've ruled the world but chose not to, knowing that to conquer oneself is the highest good and the greatest challenge any human being can undertake."

"You may be right," said Richard, "but the poverty of imposed ignorance is something else. The

Welsh are a stubborn race who've never surrendered to the dictates of a foreign power."

"Only to the Normans."

"They conquered by stealth and clever infiltration through marriage, or setting one faction against another."

"The method used to create the British Empire," Dylan cut in.

Richard stopped walking. "Dylan, what else can we do except resurrect something of our history? I'm all out keeping the Society going. So many ongoing projects… It's overwhelming our resources, and I have to go cap in hand to the council for more funds."

"You're doing a great thing, Richard. The people of Cwmbran know more of their history now than they ever did."

"That's the idea—give people a sense of belonging, living on a council estate. They can feel it for themselves, that they are part of something beyond going to work to pay the rent. Slave labour is what most do in short-term jobs, or they don't have a job at all and their self-respect hits the floor and they start on drugs or alcohol, and end up with nothing to keep body and soul together. So, maybe me doing what I do will help in some way. It is a community project, and we've so many volunteers who join in, who love being part of something."

They'd reached the bottom of the mountain when the rain returned, sufficient to extinguish the fires of hell, and they ran into a little inn on the edge of Cwmbran. They sat wet but content with beer and crisps beneath a veranda.

"Who knows the origins of the Neolithic people?" wondered Richard. "The people who built Stonehenge and all the other megalithic stone circles."

Dylan shook his wet hat. "What if I told you that I once dreamt of them arriving on our shores? I've experienced many dreams and visions, as you know. Not that I ask for them; they just happen, like being in a never-ending movie."

"Figured that soon as we met, got that faraway look about you," replied Richard, puffing on his e-cigarette. "Tell me, then?"

"I saw a fleet of fifteen to twenty single-masted ships moored off the coast of Cardigan Bay. I watched as they left the ships and came ashore. The men, who were short and stocky, led the way along the headland. I was close enough to see gold rings attached to their curly black hair. The women and children followed the men cautiously leading the way, though it seemed to me that they knew where to land, that it was where they wanted to be."

"Gold hair rings were found in the grave of the archer at Stonehenge," Richard cut in.

"Yes, I know."

"So where were these people from?"

"The Middle East, perhaps Sumerians, but what's interesting is that they landed where the Preselis meet the sea, close to the Blue Stones and Carn Ingli, the Mountain of the Angels. A voice in my head told me that these were the Proto-Celts."

"That's not a past-life recall," blurted Richard. "That's time travel." He was convinced that Dylan spoke the truth, as he knew from his own experiences that such things were possible. Dylan was familiar to him in more ways than one, though he dared not say yet what he knew of Dylan's distant past, deciding to leave that for another time.

"So they came ashore at the seaward end of the Preselis," suggested Richard. "Years later they hauled the Bluestones to Stonehenge. The original Druids perhaps?"

"Wasn't it Taliesin who said: 'By the wisest of Druids was I made before the world began, and I know the star law from the beginning of time?' Meaning that he knew the movements of the planetary orbits around the sun, the cycles of the moon and stars and the transit of Venus. Such initiates were well versed in astrology and astronomy and the transmigration of the soul."

"How did the Druids know these things?"

"Beyond comprehension to our present-day thinking, but they knew that past, present and future unfold over time, in which the Seer sees the probability of events occurring on the spiritual realms before manifesting on earth. They came here with a profound understanding that the cycles of life move in spirals, that one dimension overlaps another. They knew that with proper training it was possible to access the otherworldly dimensions, as do shamans from other cultures. It's just that no one believes the Celts were also adepts in the mysteries."

"I'm sure they could, from what little I know of the Druids."

"That vision told me that the Bluestones are actually healing crystals."

"You're right, it's called dolerite," added Richard. "I've a huge chunk in my garden."

"So you know the latest theory about Stonehenge, that apart from being a celestial calendar, it was a place of healing."

"Just like the quartz megaliths strewn over these hills. I sometimes sense them when we're excavating a cairn or cyst burial."

Dylan admired his sensitivity and soulfulness, a true brother-in-arms seeking the truth of the past. "You and me are heretics ripe for burning, wandering about searching for the light of a thousand suns that appears to saints but not to sinners."

"Leaves me out then," laughed Richard. "Religion? We are our religion. I'm a spiritualist who heals with the laying on of hands. Spiritualism just is. Has no name, no founder, but has always been. Body and mind tuned to a higher vibration to allow spirit helpers to come through via the universal energy of love."

"But isn't the Grail also higher vibrational energy?" queried Dylan as the sun's rays burst through the clouds.

"Would you look at that!" exclaimed Richard pointing to the sky above Mynydd Maen. "The three rays of the Awen."

"No wonder they worshipped the sun, the Druids, who were the shamans of their day."

"Something special about South Wales," mused Richard. "Feel it in my bones."

"Me too, tumbling over ruins and heathered hills, wondering if I'm a fool or a wiseman, searching for the origins of the myth of Joseph of Arimathea."

"You mean Glastonbury?"

"No, I mean here," responded Dylan.

"Knew when we first met that you were weird, and no one's weirder than me. Ask anyone and they'll tell you: 'Oh, Richard? He's mad as a bag of gerbils, talking past-life stuff, Derfel and all that.'"

"Something's going on; the past is coming to fruition and completion. Racial memory, call it what you will, but the wheel has turned full circle."

Richard stared knowingly into Dylan's eyes. "We've met before, you and me, a long time ago."

Dylan quickly changed the subject. "Why were all those people there today?"

"Paying homage to nature," replied Richard. "We're free to believe whatever we like. Jews, Christians, Muslims, Hindus—it's all the same. Spiritualism is simple; you meditate on the healing power of love and you give out that love. Where's the religion in that? None, except love is at the heart of all religions."

Dylan looked hard at this battle-scarred man bursting with enthusiasm, who didn't give a damn what others thought, concealing an acute sensitivity and integrity of purpose.

"Come back to my house and meet Anne," suggested Richard. "She's a follower of Krishna, and her food is exquisite."

Dylan agreed and they walked on through a housing estate of roundabouts and trees.

"Spiritual evolution," said Dylan. "Christ planted a seed, the disciples watered the seed, which became a tree, which was uprooted and transplanted into Caesar's garden and pruned of its branches. A few cuttings survived during those early days, which rooted in the Coptic Church of Egypt and the Celtic tribes-people of Britannia. Nurtured by the Druids, it became Celtic Christianity, allowing the Gnostic teachings of Jesus to survive for a thousand years."

Anne greeted Dylan with a warm smile. She was a quiet, thoughtful person, a perfect foil for Richard's garrulous personality. She loved him, that was obvious, and he cared for her as she cared for him. Food was served in bowls: dahl, rice and steamed vegetables lightly spiced, finished off with blueberries and cream.

Richard's garden studio overlooked the valley of Bran. Quartz boulders were strewn about or piled in heaps; Richard lived his past in the present. Dylan's past was all around in the ever-changing landscape of hills and valleys, rocks and springs, where oak and yew umbrella the graves of Druid and Christian.

12
Lughnasadh

Dylan returned to Druid Camp in early August to celebrate the festival of Lughnasadh. He'd barely been 'gated' when he saw Lucy Firebird walk across the field towards him. He called her that because of her fiery nature, the faery queen who initiated warriors into their own shadow, the battle between Mars and Venus, the male and female warring in each of us until reconciled into the whole.

"I dreamt about us last night," said Dylan, guiding her towards the central fire. But she rejected being controlled and shrugged him off.

"So?" she said, facing him with a look that would freeze hell. "Tell me, what profound insight have you come up with this time?"

"Regaining a lost soul connection because of how much love there is between us. Perhaps the dream was unreal, a compensation of sorts, but to me it was real."

"Would be, wouldn't it?" She laughed. "Within your fertile imagination, all things become possible, including your imagined love for me."

"I'll tell you anyway," said Dylan. "I was walking down a dark lane away from you. I came back and you were sitting in the top row of an auditorium with a woman friend. I went to meet you, and you came down halfway and we hugged and cried."

"You know what that is, don't you?" she said, unfazed by his emotional outpouring. "As I've told you before, I am your animus, which is why we met halfway as a balancing compromise."

"Why must love be reduced to an archetype?"

"Because love relates either to the anima or the animus. I don't wish to become a figment of your imagined love for me because of that undeveloped aspect of yourself. Archetypes must be grounded to have substance."

"Quite so," he retaliated. "Because at the heart of all myth and legend exists an actual truth. From heaven to earth falls a seed: Jesus, Buddha, Mohammed, to name a few. Myths take many forms and are mutable enough to accommodate the spirit of the time. Twenty-first-century psychology would like to chuck all legends and archetypes into a wok and stir-fry the lot."

"What are you babbling on about?" interjected Lucy. "I'm talking about us, and you're off on some metaphysical discourse about avatars."

"And you want to put me into a window box of your off-the-wall psychology."

"I'd like to put you into a window box and keep you there until you wake up from your romanticised imaginings," she said, tickling his ribs. "If only to stop you running off into your dream world."

Dylan enjoyed their banter; they had no hang-ups about male and female sexuality, a taboo subject for many, but not Lucy, for her sexual polarity was about exploration, touch and joyful fun.

"Alchemy's what we create," she said. "The magic formula of sexual fulfilment. The joy of sex has been promulgated for a long time now, and still people choose to spoil it with outmoded religious morality that separates men from women."

"Sexuality is the key to understanding who we are, because sexual love creates a union with the divine force of the Universe."

She pondered upon his words, looking deep into his blue eyes. "You mean when we fuck?"

"We don't fuck," responded Dylan. "We lie together and exchange energies."

"That what you call it?" she said, laughing. "Come to think of it, that is what we do... Feels like sex though, the intimacy."

"The ancients were well aware of the exchange of energies between man and woman, what Hindus call tantra, knowledge of the finer elements of sexual energy, both subtle and transforming, the delicate balance between the anima and animus."

"You talking alchemy?"

"Kundalini," replied Dylan. "When man becomes woman the joy celestial descends."

"Who said that?"

"Me, though Jesus expressed it differently: 'When the two become one, and the outside is as the inside, you shall find the Kingdom within.'"

"Meaning to be balanced and whole to feel the joy?"

"Yes, and what you said about the shadow makes sense. Many reject it because they're afraid to own it, such as those men who don't do compassion or express their feelings in case they're judged to be too soft."

"Women no longer want to be with a man who has that kind of attitude—not anymore they don't. Not now they're free from persecution." She looked deep into Dylan's blue eyes. "Why are you here?"

"Here?" he responded. "You mean, here with you?"

"No," she said. "Here with us Druids."

"Because they're the kind of people I choose to be with."

"But what's the real reason?"

"Our past—yours, mine, the others. Reconnecting to the way things were."

"Nope, don't think so," she replied in softer tones. "You've a dream that's not of this world, looking for that elusive thing that will connect this world to the spiritual."

"Otherwise no one will ever be truly at peace with themselves and one another."

"Just take care to protect yourself, Dylan, because there are those who don't want that and will do anything to stop it."

"I know what's going on, how wars are engineered and famines created, why so many become ill and die before their time."

"Be careful they don't gobble you up and kick you in the goolies just for fun." Giggling like a gurgling spring, she pulled his hat tight on his head. "The order of the hat to Dylan, the Galileo of the world within, the lone wolf who talks to angels and dreams of a past that never was."

"But it was," he challenged. "Our past, and the people we know—we are all connected."

"Shit! No wonder I don't like them."

"You say that about children, but you love them really."

"As long as they're somebody else's and not mine."

"How can you say you don't like people and laugh at the same time?"

"Am I laughing now?" she said with a straight face. "Truth is, I'd rather go back to Africa to live in the Kalahari Desert with the dik dik."

He never knew if she was winding him up or just being playful. Fiercely independent and strong minded, she belonged to no one but herself.

"You taunt and cajole, tease and ridicule and prize me open like a can of sardines."

Lucy chuckled. "You love the games we play."

"What you do to me is magical alchemy, which is why I'm determined to see it through to the end, dead or alive."

"Preferably dead," she retorted, whipping the hat off his head. "Martyrdom's much overrated, doesn't gel with the Dylan I know, whose cool presence women would die for. Fortunately, I know the difference between the dream and the reality; though to be fair, you do possess several admirable qualities, though what they are slips my mind right now."

Dylan laughed, realising that she was winding him up. Or was she? "Are you okay with me then? I know that I sometimes disappoint you, not always being able to come to camp because of circumstance..."

"You come when you can, that's what matters," she lied, turning away so he wouldn't see her hurt.

"Am I a fool?"

"Yes, albeit a wise one. It's your destiny to go where angels fear to tread."

"Guess I do stick my neck out, especially on moral issues, and I don't even know why I do that."

"Because you like being with me?"

He looked at her, afraid of his own insincerity, loving two women at once, though not in the same way. "Whatever's between us is so intense it's likely to burn itself out like a meteor, though I still want to be with you."

"So long as it's not just my animus you want to be with."

"Why would I roll around in the mud of my animus complex when I'd rather roll around in the mud with you?"

She grinned. "I like mud. There, I have confessed. And sex, preferably not in the mud, unless it's warm mud. l don't go for cow-shit or cold water to shower. Don't like being in the yurt with everyone either, prefer my own space."

"We all need that," he replied light-heartedly. "I love the way you laugh, the way you fool around and make light of serious issues, the way you perform rituals with all your heart. You love some more than others, and you don't like the fluffy bunnies who hide from their own shadows."

"I'm a psychologist who sees through the crap, even yours."

Dylan ignored her remark. "I agree with what you say that the camps should be more about confronting the shadow, that that's what its purpose should be."

"Have mentioned that to Keith several times, but he thinks the rituals do that anyway, though not far enough in my opinion."

"Can't force them to if they don't want to."

"Wouldn't dream of it, their shadow stuff is their own affair."

"I remember my first experience confronting the shadow with you and Anna, and Roland with the sword he had made on the first full moon of spring, wearing a silvery-blue Merlin cloak. You wore a black robe and a mask of silver and gold. I thought I was in some otherworld surrounded by your goddess persona. I shall never forget the effect of that ritual."

"Good, that's the intention, to bring out the shadow stuff, to know that we are darkness as well as light. God forbid we neglect the responsibility we have to own our psyche, with guidance from people who know what they're doing. Professionals who know how far to take you, people of honour, knowledge and wisdom, guardians of the threshold beyond which we tread with steps of great humility. You know that. You have gone beyond the threshold many times."

"Yes, I have," replied Dylan. "'Steps in humility before the great unknown', to quote Jung."

"I'm studying psychology, but I haven't heard that one."

"He spoke to me in a dream, said that my admiration for him was getting in the way, that I had become mentally lazy. 'What's the use of carrying apples to the needy if you haven't the wherewithal to hold them together and you drop them?' is how he put it."

"He's right about that."

"Then he drew a three-sided monad, depicting reason as guide, truth the light, and structure of form. All three are interchangeable, a representation of the three norms of visual and intuitive understanding that conveys a Universal Law that is insurmountable via the human mind."

"Did you really dream of him, or was it your imagination?"

"It seemed real. I was at his house in Bollingen. To get there I had to cross a dilapidated bridge. I'm not afraid to do that because of the way I am."

Lucy laughed. "Got that right. The Holy Fool, that's you. Brave but often dumb. You know the risks but ignore them; crossing the threshold into danger, you come back with the offering and give it out."

"If you don't give out that which you have, then that which you have will destroy you."

"Who said that?"

"Jesus."

"No idea you were that religious."

"I'm not."

"Then what are you?"

"A Gnostic. Which means knowing through inner experience."

"I know what it means."

"Inner harmony is as inherent in us as it is in nature."

"Is it?" she challenged. "I don't think so. Psychology may not be the gateway to the soul, but it teaches you an awful lot about human nature. That we are conditioned to act in certain ways. That our dark side, our shadow, inclines toward evil if neglected or ignored."

"The duality we see in nature is the governing principle, but not in us — we are outside that..."

Lucy cut him off with derisive laughter. "Just trying to ingest a little realty into your world, risking life and sanity delving into realms most would run away from. Yet you have the quality of the fool who tip-toes into the water of the subconscious to find the you who is truly you. I don't do that."

"But you do, with the tarot, conjuring up archetypal images of the tarot you create, or when giving a reading."

"Yes I do," she said smiling. "But I'm much more grounded."

"I came to camp to find that happy medium, to interact more, do camp things, chop wood and join in with rituals. Hey, have you heard this one? Before enlightenment, carry water up the hill; after enlightenment, carry water up the hill."

"I love it," she said with a laugh that was deep and gentle. "Sorry I misjudged you. Only trying to prick out your shortfalls, your overly romantic views."

"But don't you get it?" he implored. "We create our world by our thoughts."

"Hogwash! You're just afraid to stand up to reality."

"But it is my reality, not yours."

"Go away with you! Get out of my tent. You think you can come here when you like, when you deem you want to see me for a few days of camp, and that's all right? Well, it isn't. The last time you said you were coming, but you couldn't make it because of difficulties on the home front—either you were ill or you had back problems. Excuses, all of it. If you truly wanted to be with me then you would come, hell or whatever. So bugger off!"

Despite her words, Lucy liked this long-haired truth-seeker for whom she held a grudging respect, who drank her coffee, though drank her words with less enthusiasm. She felt that he was truly 'gated', that this otherworld had kicked him into being painfully human, that transformation meant being gutsy and raw to get to the truth laid bare.

Dylan sat on the grass outside the yurt, deeply troubled by her stinging words. Activities in the field moved in a silent and surreal ballet of fluidic ease, of people at peace in a place they called home.

Lucy dragged an airbed and dumped it next to him. "Could you do this for me? Pump some air into the bloody thing—it's leaking."

Dylan pumped furiously to relieve his tension. "You and me, we war. Sexual tension. It is electric.

You shock me through. You wake me up to what I have to do, which is to write and search for the truth, my truth and the truth of others. The past, what was lost, what is called the Holy Grail of the soul of Man, to know who we truly are. Through you to me exists an energy that will either burn me through, or I'll come out the other end stronger and wiser."

"Let's hope it's the latter then," she replied. "You know this can't last forever. Perhaps I am the catalyst meant to shake you out of yourself for you to be your true self. You have told me certain things about your home life, of the difficulties in dealing with that person — not Pamela, but the other, whose jealousy has almost destroyed you. I think that's the reason you became a Druid: to escape and find yourself."

"Perhaps, but I've been a hedge Druid all my life, so what you say isn't the only reason why I'm here. I am searching for something. Being here is like being reborn and gives me strength to deal with my home life. I know it is hard for you to accept my love for Pamela, but I would be lying to you if I told you that I didn't love her."

"I know how difficult it is for you, and I respect your honesty. Most men would play it both ways and say that they love the one but not the other."

"I can't do that, hide behind a lie."

She could see the pain of his dilemma but also his bravery in putting his heart on the line for the sake of his personal journey. She loved him despite his quirky nature, how he was elusive and impossible to pin down, often away with the fairies.

"I know it's difficult for you to take me on with all my baggage," he said with a bold look. "So believe me when I say that if you want to back off, I understand why."

"Come on," she cajoled, smiling. "Let's go to the Eisteddfod. Enough talking, time to play. Think of who you want to be tonight, what you'd like to wear or not wear."

"You make a suggestion," he replied.

She led him into the big yurt where a flurry of activity was taking place. Jay smeared paint on Adrian's face and body, black and red, a tribal way of dividing night from day. Draig squeezed into a Green Man costume, and the Shit-Pit Fairy pranced about in a gossamer gown waving a magic wand whilst sitting astride a broomstick shouting, "This must be the only place on the planet where you can try out a new broomstick and nobody takes a blind bit of notice."

Dylan pulled Lucy aside. "All a bit surreal for me. Think I'll go and chop logs for the fires and have a sauna. Meet up later, if that's ok?"

Dylan strode over to the woodpile, picked up an axe and split logs till the sweat soaked his clothes. It wasn't her fault he felt this way. The frustration he felt was as much due to his home circumstances as her justified demands. Lucy's fiery nature and need to be loved in the short time they were together frustrated her, whilst his dilemma of how much of himself he could give bothered him to distraction. Their emotive maelstrom had quickly become camp entertainment; would they stay together, or would it end in a furore of anger and frustration?

She found him in the sauna as evening descended on the village of tents. She wore a black dress decked with leaves, her face covered by a Green Lady mask. She stood him naked on the grass and painted his body red and placed the mask of Cernunnos over his head. They entered the yurt where dancers cavorted in the candlelight to loud drumming as poets recited prose with passion and humour. Others sang, choral and solo, as a living buzz of creativity filled the air. Stories, original or known, regaled the audience, as had been witnessed in the halls of mighty kings long gone but alive in these people who lived and loved with an exuberant fullness.

Jay and Rowena hugged one another and rolled about the floor laughing. Angie and Rick massaged one another's feet, and Steiner sang of his first experience of love, watching a girl from a tree, a boy dreaming under the moon. The song was about her belonging to the moon and how the moon came down to claim her, until he was left with nothing but a memory of perfect love. Owl sang of a soldier going to war. Chris played the Irish pipes and sang an old English folksong. Behind them sat Donal, a big Irishman with wide, staring eyes who liked to be the centre of attention. A follower of Odin who acted accordingly, working with drug addicts with forceful inspiration until they were branded with good qualities and the power of self-belief.

Louise, a poet-performer, whose long hair swirled like hay on a windy day, confessed her take on yurt folk:

"Does it seem stupid to you that we do what we do?

Us boundary-less beautiful souls exposing our nipples and shyest of holes.

More like tigers of courage than shuffling moles.

We are eagles and foxes of human endeavour.

So give your life new direction, your body new form.

Paint over fine lines, bypass the norm.

So come join us—the painted, the magically acquainted.

More like werewolves of wonder than spiritually sainted.

We are the lions and wasps of creative invention,

Enjoying our animal potential by defying convention.

Does it seem crazy to you — that we do what we do — us boundary-less beautiful souls?"

Louise called Dylan a deep man of the fire. He was too over-burdened with care to think that she might see in him a spark of life. Druid Camp was replete with imperfections and idiosyncrasies, all equally certifiable, but Dylan wouldn't miss it for the world.

The Brigida ceremony began with Angie and Sarah placing a candle at each of the four cardinal points, along with a piece of tree root to symbolise new growth. Steiner banged hammer and tongs together to call in the spirits of place to bless the ceremony in the half-light of the moon.

The circle formed around the central fire. Some wore their ceremonial cloaks, others threw on blankets to keep out the cold. Lucy walked the circle with a flaming torch, marking each forehead with earth. Jay sprinkled water over everyone with a warm smile, though performing the ceremony with serious intent.

Lucy laughed a lot that night, as they lay together in the quiet of the early hours, happy to be with Dylan during this interlude of their lives, wishing it could be forever. But she was used to holding on and letting go of love and pain in equal proportion; fuel to fire her art. She knew it could not be otherwise and that winter would soon arrive.

13

Duma

"There you go," said Richard, placing a glass of cider in front of Dylan. "*Iechyd da!* To the oldest pub in Gwent, and to Llantarnam Abbey, also known as Duma, whose origins remain a mystery."

"Duma?"

"Duma is an old Celtic word which means Mother of God," replied Richard. "Llantarnam Abbey was Cistercian, now it's St Anne's Hospice, run by two crazy Irish nuns who shut up shop for two weeks to watch the World Cup."

Dylan laughed. "That's the Irish for you."

"The Irish and Welsh are wild as guinea pigs in a barn of straw. They laugh at anything—worse things get, the more they laugh. The Celtic temperament that doesn't give a damn for kings or authority, a kind of inborn legacy of the Round Table, where no man's above another."

"Love the Welsh, though I'm only half Welsh myself—the other half being Irish."

"Mad bastard then,"

"Only on Sundays," chuckled Dylan, glancing at families sat at tables, laden with drinks and crisps, and children running about, laughing and chasing one another around the trees and shrubs, playing hide-and-seek.

"Love it here," enthused Richard. "I was just talking to a guy who knows more about the history of this place than I do. Lots of people want to know about the past. It's what we are, who we are."

"Sure is," concurred Dylan. "The trail of our ancestors winds through the valleys and the rivers and the stone circle. There's also the theory that memories of our previous lives are locked into our DNA, which links to the fourth dimension, where past, present and future are one."

"That's the theory," replied Richard. "But how do we prove it?"

"No idea, except that we are each torsion fields of energy, a spiralling dynamic of consciousness that knows no bounds except when tied to a physical body."

"So we're really screwed then," interjected Richard with a wild laugh.

"You know how spirit operates. Our consciousness exists outside the body, which is why we can travel to the past and even to the future in our sleep, when the disembodied spirit is free to roam, to explore many levels of existence."

"You mean like a free bus-pass?" interjected Richard.

Dylan laughed. "A mystery road trip might be a better description. Truthfully though, if you could recall exactly where you go when you are asleep, recall with accuracy your travels, the people that you meet, the knowledge they impart, we would know the answers to many of our questions."

"Such as?"

"The timeless question: Whom does the Grail serve?"

"The King and the Land are one."

"The vessel that will heal mankind," said Dylan. "But what is it?"

"The blood of Jesus Christ?"

"Not His blood, but His words, the true meaning of which were censored by the Church of Rome under Constantine and his heirs, who deleted the gospels down from twenty-nine to four."

"The Lost Gospels then?"

"But not lost to the Celtic Church, which, as we know, was as much Druidic as Christian, a marriage of two philosophies, both Gnostic in belief, as were the Essenes, of which Jesus was one."

"Jesus the Essene?"

"Yes, something that they knew, something so profound that if we could access that something, then a great mystery would be revealed to all mankind."

"Your Mona Lisa enigmatic smile supposed to convince me that you know the answer to a great secret?"

"I just know that there's something that was lost: the true meaning of the Grail."

"You mean the lost teachings?"

Dylan pondered momentarily. "Consider what Taliesin was telling us when he wrote of his origins, remembering that he was an initiate into the Druidic Mysteries: 'When the great knowledge of the stars is imparted then will be understood every high thing.'"

"Taliesin talking quantum physics?"

"A shaman's version?" suggested Dylan. "If people only knew that they have more than one shot at life, that life is a circle, that we return over and over until we get it right, no matter how many lifetimes it takes."

"You have a way with words and riddles, Dylan, but you're not telling me what I don't know already."

"Okay then, answer me this: who was Derfel, and what did he stand for? Who was Arthur, and what did he stand for? Ask, and if the Spirit of the Awen answers, then it will be valid."

"*Duw!*" exclaimed Richard. "What a thought, if only we knew."

"Just be aware that there are certain people who'll do anything to obfuscate the truth of who we are as human beings, immortal souls of infinite potential."

"I'll fight for the truth any day," asserted Richard. "That's what spiritual warriors do: fight with the mind and the heart."

Dylan observed Richard's mutable behaviour, which oscillated from humorously wild to enthusiastically energetic to a serious and ferocious warrior whenever his integrity was challenged.

Richard poured the remainder of his ale onto the ground as an offering before placing a hand on Dylan's shoulder. "Follow me, I want to show you something."

He led the way over the wall between the inn and the church, which stood grey and silent as the yews and the graves with their lopsided memorials, until they stood facing the east wall of the church, the sandstone blocks of shape and size common to Roman buildings.

"Look there," said Richard, pointing to a relief carved high up on the wall.

Dylan followed his line of sight to see four spirals, each enclosed by a square, one spiral clearly the shape of a bearded head. "Looks like zoomorphic art typical of the Celts, though the bearded face in the centre might be Christ if the other spirals represent arms and legs."

"But why the squares?" Richard pointed to another carving some ten feet to the left. "What about that one, then?"

Dylan stared at a clearly defined depiction of an elongated animal with patches similar to a Friesian cow, suckling a calf. "That is the Milch Cow of the Gallicanae."

"The who?"

"The Gallicanae, an Helio Arkite goddess cult from the Near East. The Milch Cow is their symbol, and Duma may have been their place of worship. Their sacred enclosure, the triangle of the sacred feminine, was the land between two rivers."

"The Avon Llwydd and the Dowlais?"

"The Ynys Avalonia."

"But isn't Ynys an island?"

"Ynys also means the land between two rivers, and if those stones originated from Caerleon, then were used to construct the sanctuary of the Mother Goddess?"

"That's wild!" interjected Richard. "You're saying that the Milch Cow is the Goddess?"

"Which would make the Abbey of Duma the sanctuary of the Great Mother, the Arkite Goddess, the Ceridwen of the Britons and the Nine Maidens of the cauldron, where Morgan le Fey practised her arts, where magic worked through into this world."

"Jumping way ahead of me there, Dylan."

"Nothing like a bit of imaginative conjecture to spice up proceedings. Archaeologists do it often."

"That's true, we're often biased one way or another."

"Why do crystals resonate healing energy?" challenged Dylan. "Why were white stones so important? Why did Celtic warriors assemble in the 'Circle of White Stones' called the Round Table, where holy Druids pronounced prophecy and bards sang praises to the brave. And who are we to unearth these things?"

"Two Cymbrogi in search of the truth?" proposed Richard.

"I'll drink to that. Cheers!"

"*Iechyd da!*" concurred Richard. "Archaeologists I've spoken to are dumbfounded by the carvings. A committee member discovered them; he also traced a mason's mark from the old abbey to an identical one at Rosslyn. Llantarnams was a Cistercian monastery, the religious arm of the Templars."

"Who were prominent in South Wales," interjected Dylan. "Robert Fitzhammon and his twelve knights ruled South Wales, Arthur's kingdom of Siluria. Fitzhammon's ancestors had fled to Brittany to escape the pestilence that ravaged Britain during the mid-sixth century. Fitzhammon's family were related to the Sinclairs of Rosslyn. His daughter, Elizabeth St Claire, married Hugh de Payens, founder of the Knights Templar. It was Payens and nine Templars who excavated Solomon's temple in Jerusalem. Fitzhammon's ancestor was Maelgwn Gwynedd, who succeeded Arthur after Camlann."

"What did Fitzhammon know of Arthur that we don't?"

"Three books written by Maelgwn: *Antiquitantibus Brittannicis*, *De Gestis Britannorum*, and *De Regis Arthurii Mensa Rotunda*."

"I presume 'Mensa Rotunda' means the Round Table?"

"Of course," replied Dylan. "Fitzhammon knew of Arthur's association with South Wales, particularly the monastery of Illtud at Llanilltud Fawr, which he chose for his residence. He also knew of the Prophecy of Melkin, aka Maelgwn, describing the burial place of Joseph of Arimathea."

"Do you mind if I ask you a personal question?"

"Not at all," replied Dylan. "Fire away."

"What is the ultimate goal of your quest?"

"To restore what has been lost."

"Which is what?"

"Knowledge."

"What knowledge?"

"What I just told you: the true meaning of the Grail."

"The blood of Christ? The cup of the Last Supper?"

"Neither," said Dylan.

"What then?"

"*Graal* refers to a platter on which food is served, a grail is a cup or chalice, whereas *Gradalis* refers to steps toward enlightenment."

"You mean like the Consolamentum of the Cathars?"

"Or something similar," replied Dylan. "Talking of the Cathars, Hugh de Payens' ancestors were Muslims from Cordoba, before settling in Toulouse amongst the Albigensians, the so-called Gnostic heretics, who were the Cathars of course. Much of Templar wealth and power was focussed in that region."

"De Payens was a Muslim?"

"Which was why he was given permission to dig one of the holiest sites of Islam, second only to Mecca. Why else would the Caliph of Cairo loan them a fleet of ships, and why would the Muslims refer to them as the Knights Templar of Islam?"

"So how do Arthur and the Holy Grail come into this?"

"Maelgwn, is mentioned in the ancient Triads as the Knight of a Hundred Horses, also as Chief Elder..." Dylan broke off from revealing what he knew of Maelgwn.

"Maelgwn's Prophecy?" inquired Richard, unnerved by Dylan's sudden silence.

"Maelgwn, who was Arthur's contemporary, wrote a prophecy in which he describes the burial place of Joseph of Arimathea."

"The Joseph who took Jesus off the cross and buried him?" replied Richard. "Who kept two small vessels filled with blood and sweat?"

"The very same," concurred Dylan.

"So you know where it is then, the Holy Grail?"

"The cruets aren't the Holy Grail. That's just make-believe to hide the truth of what the Grail is."

"Alright, so you know where he's buried then?"

"Not sure yet, but South Wales for certain," replied Dylan. "Need time to work it out, or to put it another way: impetuosity killed the cat."

Richard relaxed and smiled. "I get where you're coming from, so I won't push."

"It's complicated, trust me, but one thing's for sure: it isn't Glastonbury." Dylan was more relaxed and changed the subject. "Suss this one out, something Taliesin said: 'John the Divine called me Merlin, all future kings shall call me Taliesin.'"

"Taliesin was Merlin?"

"Both were gifted in the art of prophecy, both were great poets and councillors to kings, and both lived in the days of Arthur."

"Taliesin translates as 'Bright Brow', or 'Enlightened', and Merlin means 'Teacher'."

"So who was who? Was Taliesin Merlin, or Merlin Taliesin? Confusing, huh? Well that's the pickle I'm in right now, an identity crisis spanning several lifetimes."

"Sounds like a tough one, Dylan. Be careful, overlaying identities can lead you into deep water."

Dylan gave an uneasy laugh, drank some more cider and stared at Richard.

"Okay, Butty," said Richard in a nonchalant manner, "we may walk the tightrope between the two worlds from time to time. Just make sure there's a safety net to fall into."

"Pelagius," mumbled Dylan abstractly, "Welsh for Morgan, fourth century, educated at Llanilltud Fawr, refuted the doctrine of original sin by declaring that we are born pure, that it is our born duty to live a good life. In other words, personal responsibility."

"A fire-breathing Welshman?"

"Who said that life is a never-ending circle governed solely by our actions, as God had given free will to all, that the thousand-headed serpent of original sin was intended to enslave people to the tyranny of the Rome." Dylan downed the remainder of his drink and slammed the glass on the table. "Sorry to sound like a mad preacher on Benzedrine, so I'll shut up now."

Richard laughed. "Relax, Dylan, the Church has hammered people on their anvil for two thousand years, forcing truth-seekers to comply or die. Now we're free to think for ourselves with regards to religion."

"But the riddle of Jesus remains. Who was He? Was He truly resurrected? Will the Vatican ever tell us the truth?"

"Doubt they'll ever do that," said Richard, smiling, happy to know that another was treading the same path as himself. "My round, but think on this while I'm gone. Your knowledge of the Grail, who or what gave it to you?"

Dylan pondered his question amid the laughter of a family at a nearby table. Thoughts on the origin of dreams crumbled like the churchyard wall, its masonry swallowed by the leaves and grass and the soft brown earth.

Why do you make a riddle of our story? he wondered. *Why do you muffle the sounds of our footsteps? Why does our past disappear into the folding layers of your domain? What survives but the dumb stones buried with memories of a time long ago? A phantom is Arthur, a constellation in the heavens, a mere archetype of wishful thinking.*

"There you go," said Richard, placing a glass of cider on the table, bemused by the synchronicity of their meeting, how this phenomenon had become a frequent occurrence in his life and in the lives of many on the spiritual path. "So where's it all come from then?"

"Nowhere, everywhere," replied Dylan, distracted by children playing hide-and-seek, darting in and out of the trees and shrubs like will-o'-the-wisps. "I'm a great believer in psychogeography, a concept coined by Arthur Machen, whose novels on Celtic mysticism conjure up the ancient past. Psychogeography suggests that if you live on the land long enough, it speaks to you."

"Through nature spirits, elves and fairy-folk?"

"I think what he meant is that the land contains imprints of the past."

"Often wondered why they used quartz megaliths. Is it possible they knew, as quartz is used in computers to do just that?"

"Yes, but the land communicates in an abstract way," said Dylan, "like a vast library of time that sensitives tune into. Plantlore, healing medicine, evolves over centuries, what plants for what aliment."

"Shamans communicate with nature through dreams to know what plants to use. Carlos Castenada is famous for it."

"Because he practised love and respect for all life, that to give and receive is the first law of Nature."

"Which it is, though few practise it."

"Better bloody well do before we're all buggered." Richard laughed, his long hair thrown back like a horse's mane. "Didn't the Templars believe John the Baptist to be the true Messiah?"

"Yes, they took on the beliefs of the Nabateans of Petra in the Jordan Valley during the Crusades."

"And worship the head of Baphomet, a kind of devil?"

Dylan chuckled. "Baphomet is actually a cryptogram for Sophia, the Gnostic Goddess of Wisdom."

"Gnosis — inner knowledge leading to individual salvation?"

"Yes, to know deep down that you are a divine being, that the foundation of life is love."

"Goes without saying for the likes of you and me, but most are too busy just trying to survive to even think about who they are, never mind what life means on a spiritual level."

"Tragic," uttered Dylan, "the impasse humanity has come to, the slave mentality, afraid to rock the boat, afraid to question authority. 'Listen my people, if the clouds part too many times there will be nowhere for mankind to go, and he'll become

numberless, and the stars will shake down their dew
upon him, and only then will he know the truth.'"

"That some kind of prophecy?"

"Could say."

"One of your visions?"

"Yes." Dylan frowned. "And we're truly running
out of time."

Conversation and laughter elevated by alcohol
filled the garden of the inn. Dylan often wished for
such anonymity, free from the sense of responsibility
to fulfil his task, to uncover the age-old mystery of
who we are as human beings on a planet seemingly
groaning and moaning in its death throes. Richard's
field of activity involved the local community, his
passion and enthusiasm for the history of Cwmbran,
whereas Dylan was walking into the jaws of religious
censorship and controversy.

"Think on this, Richard: the Celtic Church was
Gnostic, as were the Cathars, as was Jesus the
Nazarene, a member of the Essene community at
Qumran. Essenes were taught by 'Angels', which
were the High Priests. A peace-loving people whose
teachings were unknown until the discovery of the
Dead Sea Scrolls."

"Which took forty years to decipher," interjected
Richard.

"But there's something else, something so
profound. If we could access the truth of Jesus's
words, then a great mystery would be revealed to
all mankind.

"Myths are invariably founded on fact. Their
underlying imagery conveys a language of forms that
change over time, just as all religions mutate and take
on new meanings. Such universal symbols exist in the
collective unconscious to which we are programmed

to respond. Even crop-circle imagery can awaken dormant energies within our subconscious. All myths contain hidden truths that can teach us new ways of being, flowing through dimensions of time."

"Nice words, Dylan, but what are you saying?"

"Listen to the silence within and you'll know all you need to know. Be as gentle as Gandhi and wise as Confucius. The mirror of recollection conceals itself within dreams emerging from the eternal now of the quantum sourcefield, which is everything and everywhere."

"You mean the Akashic Records?"

"The collective unconscious, call it what you will, contained within the matrix of the Earth's energy field, even our DNA."

"I'll go for that." Richard yawned. "Sorry to have to end our conversation, but I have to go and pick Anne up from work."

Richard stood up to finish his drink and gazed around at the people there. He turned to Dylan in earnest. "Do you think the discovery of the Grail would make one iota of difference to people's lives?"

Dylan glanced at the families sat around tables conversing on everyday matters — their jobs, children and all the things that filled their lives — laughing and chatting in the dappled evening sunlight. Would they even know or care? Would it matter at all? He looked at Richard texting Anne, concluding that it probably wouldn't matter at all if Joseph's tomb was discovered.

"I'm off to Llandaff Cathedral tomorrow to check out Uther Pendragon's tomb," declared Dylan. "Join me if you like."

"Not ever been to Llandaff Cathedral, though I do know of the King Arthur windows."

"And the Pre-Raphaelite art?" queried Dylan. "Burne-Jones, Rossetti?"

"Never!"

"They are there, have been for a long time, Rossetti's triptych being the prize, and Burne-Jones' 'Seven Days of Creation', is a real gem."

"You put it like that, what can I say? Of course I'll be there. What time?"

"Three o'clock?"

"Midday meeting with the Ancient Cwmbran Society should be over by two. Let you know if I can't make it."

"I know how busy you are."

"Busy? You've no idea. Always somebody calling or texting—if it's not the council about the grant it's one member or another. 'Oh, Richard'," he said, mimicking a woman's voice, "'can you help me? I'm stuck on the info you asked for.' 'That's okay, darling, don't worry, I'll see to it.'

"Daphne's nice, she's the treasurer—not that we got any money, not till the grant comes through." He looked quizzically at Dylan adjusting his heavy-duty rucksack. "You know things, but you don't say. Why is that?"

"Protection," murmured Dylan, averting his gaze.

"Relax, buddy, I'm not interrogating you. Curious is all—me being Derfel and you whoever."

"Tell you more tomorrow of what I know, what's been told to me."

"Sure. Layer by layer like an archaeological dig through time, bottom line is you can't cheat time."

Dylan walked the mile to their shop in Caerleon, where Pamela waited for his return.

"How did it go?" she asked. "You and Richard."

"Went okay. You know the Glasshouse Inn—we sat in the garden."

"So what was the something he wanted to show you?"

"Two carvings on the wall of St Michael's Church, possibly from the old abbey. Did you know that its original name was Duma?" Dylan switched on the kettle to make coffee. "So it was very fruitful. We talked on many things, including the Templars and Robert Fitzhammon, who's a key player in Melkin's prophecy."

"Did you tell him about your dream as Maelgwn?"

"Not yet. Don't want him thinking I'm totally crazy."

"You and Richard, both Gemini, can talk the hind legs off a donkey. Worse when you, Richard and your Gemini brother Norman get together and there's six of you. Bad enough just one!"

"Like you say to me in the morning sometimes: 'Which one are you today?'"

Pamela laughed. "Well, it's true. Talk about mood swings."

"Not easy being a Gemini. So how's it been in my absence?"

"Quiet for the most part, a few customers. Almost sold one of your sculptures."

"Which one?"

"The Taliesin. Said they'd be back, young Irish couple."

"Sometimes they do, and sometimes they don't."

"Had a good chat with Rafi next door. Showed me the guitar he'd just finished making—very gifted, and his jewellery designs are exquisite."

"Rafi's the most peaceful man I know."

"Pippa came by with their dog, she left her with Rafi as she had to attend an important meeting with the Green Party."

"She's so upbeat and cheery, I like her," said Dylan, making the coffee in the sparse space behind the counter cluttered with books, jars of pencils and pens, also CDs, as music was essential for ambience in enhancing the vibration of such a small space. "Didn't intend to be so long, but you know how it is with conversation—one thing leads to another."

"No need to apologise. Met a very special six-year-old, a truly beautiful soul who came with her mother. A little angel with curly blonde hair, wide open blue eyes that could see right through you. She stood in front of the crystal fountain staring at the water and said, 'They will never know what water is, the science people. They will never know the magic of water.' She looked directly at me and said that Jesus is coming back. I asked her how did she know, and she said that God told her that Jesus is coming. So I asked her when and she said, 'He's coming soon. God told me.'"

"She sounds like one of them," said Dylan, stirring the coffee.

"She carried on talking, her face changing from a six-year-old to someone much older, then back to the child. All the time a light radiated around her, then she would stop, and she would go into herself, into a silence. An old soul. Her mother said that she talks to people in her bedroom all the time, that they come every night—her friends, as she calls them—and talk to her."

Dylan handed Pamela a cup of coffee. "Wish I was here to have seen her."

"Reminds me of me during the bombing raids on Croydon during the Blitz, when the people who were killed would come to me frightened and shivering, so I would tell them to go towards the light, that that's what they must do. I was only three, and my father thought I was talking to the flowers, which he still believes, even to this day. I've told you all this before."

"You have, but it's a fascinating story," replied Dylan, knowing full well how aware she was, even as a child.

"Dad's friend, Mr Futter, kept pigs, and whenever he came, I'd run off into the woods with my rabbit and chickens so he couldn't have any of them for some bacon. I called the chickens guk-guks. That's how it was in Croydon, being bombed every day and talking to all those dead people."

They lapsed into a peaceful silence, as it so often was between them, the peace and the joy, their natural state together.

"An advanced soul," she said, sipping her coffee. "You know, the children you dreamt about years ago."

"The thousands of blue children marching over the Marlborough Downs, the Children of the Wise who are incarnating to help us and the planet. Others call them the Indigo Children, and they might well have been as I'm colour-blind, though how you could be colour-blind in a dream, I don't know."

They smiled at one another, knowing that the truth of these things was as natural to them as breathing.

"Gone quiet, Dylan. What are you thinking?"

"Nothing," he lied, lighting a stick of incense.

"You don't fool me; I know you too well. What is it?"

"Tomorrow."

"What about tomorrow?" she asked. "What do you have in mind?"

"Llandaff Cathedral."

"Why?"

"Retracing a journey, so to speak."

She frowned, knowing that ferreting out the past had become his overriding obsession.

"I've asked Richard to join me there."

"That's all very well, but you can't always leave me to manage the shop every time you want to go off on your Grail quest, as you call it."

"I know what you're saying, but I'm not on a fool's errand. You know my dreams and what they mean. I've sat on them for years, until now, when something impels me to do something, to follow them through."

"To where, to what?" responded Pamela. "To you they're real, but you must keep a balance between that and the real world."

"What can I say except that I'm getting close, and I wish that you would come with me."

"No, it's your personal thing," she acceded. "But please try not to be late."

Dylan felt torn between guilt and the urgent need to chase the rainbow's pot of gold somewhere between this life and the other of long ago.

14

The First Vatican

Dylan stood facing the iron-studded doors of Llandaff Cathedral. Above the Romanesque doorway, the weathered effigy of St Teilo bespoke the cathedral's ancient origins. Dylan stared up at two figures in the north-west tower set beneath modelled versions of the cathedral. One held a sword and wore a tunic; the other, who was bearded, wore a crown.

Visiting the cathedral invariably rekindled his vision of long ago where he'd seen himself standing facing the doorway in the light of an iridescent red-gold sunrise, gripping a great sword, its point touching the flagstone floor between his leather boots. The heavy object on his head was either a helmet or a crown, and he had the distinct sensation of being several inches taller that his present six foot. A man to his right wore a purple cloak over armour, and another to his left held a shepherd's crook and wore a mitre. Everything vibrated as if he were inside a shimmering desert mirage, a miasma of half seen, half sensed reality of overlapping time. The only thing he knew for certain was that it was sunrise, May the eighteenth, Anno Domini 558.

Was it a past-life experience or simply an overactive imagination? Dylan had opted for the latter, refusing to accept its significance, deducing that the ruin by the river was the site of the original church. It was a full year after the vision that he came across an old map identifying it as the old bishop's palace, and several years after that he came across a reference stating that the Church of Llandaff was erected under the patronage of Uther Pendragon and Maelgwn Gwynedd, dedicated in the year of our Lord, Anno Domini, 558. Maelgwn Hir, Lord of Gwynedd, the tallest man in Britain, succeeded Arthur after the ill-fated Battle of Camlann.

Dylan sat on a wall awaiting Richard's arrival, attempting still to make sense of the riddles of the past. Other recollections had followed over the ensuing years, relating to events during the sixth century. Dylan wished to just bumble about and live a quiet life, but such glimpses through time's window had taken him to levels of perception whose meaning was becoming extremely uncertain, winding from past to present, integrating legend and myth into a reality that encapsulated the Grail as the central goal.

Letting go of any preconceptions he might have had concerning its true meaning, he thought it wise to follow the carrot of his dreams, revealing the relevance of the past to the present, even though the never-ending cycle of incarnation remains an intangible mystery to our formulating mind.

"Hiya, Dylan," greeted Richard, slapping him on the shoulder.

"Richard!" exclaimed Dylan. "You took me by surprise."

"Away with the fairies?" He laughed whilst looking up to the gothic edifice. "Impressive, but not impressed."

"The first Vatican, some say."

"Who says?"

"Historians, though not of the Oxford kind."

"But Llandaff's twelfth century."

"There were two others before this one: the first by Lucius the Great Luminary, built during the second century, and another during the mid-sixth century."

Richard pushed open the heavy oak cathedral door to be confronted by Epstein's Christ, a gaunt image of suffering straddling the nave in the painful agony of puerile humanity. All sounds echoed in a stone mausoleum, heightened by a cavernous interior that dominated their frail biology, safe within nature's care, beneath the eye of God, vulnerable but loved, as it was unthinkable to the Celts to shut out the light.

They gazed upon Pre-Raphaelite stained-glass windows by Burne-Jones, Ford Madox Brown, Lord Leighton and William Morris, depicting St Teilo and Tudval, Elfan and Dyfrig, in all their colourful glory. Others portrayed Biblical prophets and scenes from the Gospels.

. Dylan pointed to three windows above the choir. "Arthur after the battle of Mons Badonicus, the other two are Ambrosius and Cadwaladr."

"So there's our man," enthused Richard. "Impressive Pre-Raphaelite portrayals of the Grail legends, but why here, when the clergy deny all knowledge of the cathedral's history prior to the Normans?"

"Someone knew the truth of Llandaff's past," said Dylan, running his hand over the smooth marble cadaver of Uther Pendragon. "Here lies Uther, removed from Bardsey Island by Bishop Urban, placed here next to the altar as the founder of the sixth-century church."

"You know what," said Richard, gazing up at the roof. "I'm impressed, but also depressed that no healing of the spirit takes place here anymore."

"The mystery has gone," said Dylan matter-of-factly. "Flown away like a little bird, void of love and cold as stone. They killed the Goddess long ago; now nothing remains but an echo chamber of dead doctrine. The Church blinded itself when they buried the truth in favour of power."

Richard gazed up at the statue of Christ. "If Christ were to climb down off that cross right now, He'd climb right back up and hammer in the nails Himself."

"I'm sure He would." Dylan smiled. "This cathedral's a mausoleum to the fallen idols of the age of the Norman lords, whose castles of oppression testify to the resistance of the Cymry who fought for freedom."

"The castles bring tourists to Wales," replied Richard. "Least we get something back from them. So what of Arthur and Uther? How do we know they were here?"

"The Llandaff Charters are a who's who of the Arthurian legends: Arthur and Uther, St Teilo and Dubricius, Illtud and Cadoc; signatories of land grants, such as when Arthur's son Morgan killed Arthur's brother, Frioc, and donated land between the Taff and the Ely rivers as penance. The charters also record thirty-seven monasteries between here and Swansea."

"Thirty-eight, if you include St Derfel's on Mynydd Maen," interjected Richard.

Their footsteps tapped the tiled floor of Teilo's Chapel with its ancient cross. They passed by souvenirs and the muffled whispers of the ladies behind a counter flanked by cards of haloed saints, apologetic in their pose of self-surrender in an age of selling the soul for gain.

Exiting the cathedral along the path towards the Red Lion Inn, they pondered the portrayal of Arthur and Uther, and the Pre-Raphaelites, who had dominated the art world on the subject of Arthurian legends during the Victorian era. Dylan knew something of those far-off days of the sixth century, even though past-life recollections are about as valid as moonrock to orthodox thinkers.

"Cheers, Dylan," said Richard, sipping his lager.

"Here's to our Celtic heritage," replied Dylan.

"Whoever commissioned those windows must have known Arthur was Welsh."

"Of course, but no one with authority in Wales will let on what they know about the real King Arthur." Dylan paused, hesitant and cautious. "Listen. What I'm about to tell you is God's honest truth."

"Go ahead, I'm listening," replied Richard respectfully.

"You know how it is on the spiritual path—you meet all sorts, some strange, some crazy, some real."

"An adventure not for the faint-hearted," commented Richard.

"We met this man, me and Pam. His name is Vivian. He told us about his life in the valleys of South Wales, how one evening, walking through a woods, he saw a bright light amongst the trees come towards him. He stood petrified as it came right up to him and pervaded his thoughts, instructing him to return the next day, that it was important he did so."

"So what did he do?" joked Richard. "Run away yelling he'd never drink another drop in his life?"

Dylan laughed at the absurd truth of it. "He returned to the same spot the next day, and the light, which he said was like an elongated star with blue rays, appeared and told him of his past life as Uther Pendragon, that he had much work to do this lifetime, that it is imperative that he help heal the planet. It told him that he had always been a healer — even as Uther, who was a very spiritual man — that he'd no need of a sword, being a spiritual warrior like so many others who'd fought for their country, for their beliefs, and that he would soon meet Arthur, who had returned to help mankind move towards an age of peace."

Richard listened intently, once a warrior himself, now a man of peace, as was Derfel who'd fought at Camlann.

"The Spirit told him that his purpose now was to help clear the astral of discordant energies, which were preventing the higher vibrational energies from entering the Earth plane." Dylan glanced around to make sure no one was listening. "The Spirit, whom he referred to as She, instructed him to run blindfolded through the woods, guided solely by his own inner light."

"In the dark?" interjected Richard. "That's mad."

"The spirit guide was his mentor, so his faith and belief had to be tested to the limit."

"Bloody glad my Druid didn't ask me to do anything as crazy as that."

"We first met him at a healing exhibition. Pamela is a clairvoyant healer and medium. Opposite our table was a large photograph of Glastonbury Tor. Two men who occupied the table next to ours introduced themselves as Owain and Vivian, spiritual healers. Cheri Lunghi, who played Guinevere in the film

Excalibur, walked into the hall and waited at our table, which we'd left to say hello to an old friend on the other side of the hall. She had gone by the time we returned."

"A real beauty," added Richard. "I remember her as Arthur's Queen."

"The epitome of nobility," concurred Dylan. "Synchronicity? Because two weeks later we received a letter from Owain inviting us to participate in a ceremony on Glastonbury Tor on Saturday, May eighteenth, to cleanse the energy there. This ceremony had been performed only once before in the history of Great Britain, which Owain, as King Arthur the Second, carried out. The Tor had to be cleansed and re-energised, which was a crucial part of the divine plan for this planet and he asked us both to keep this matter private until after the event. The letter was signed with numerous sigils: crosses, circles, Aquarian waves, and letters of the Coelbren alphabet, which is similar to Hebrew."

"King Arthur the Second?"

"Who was the true Arthur of legend. The first Arthur was Victor, son of the Emperor Maximus. It was he who conquered Europe in the late fourth century, hence the confusion with Arthur the Second's exploits. Arthur the Second was battle sovereign of the Silurian Cymry during the sixth century, whose stronghold was Caerleon, and whose Camelot was Caerwent. Just to let you know, Owain isn't his real name, as we gave a solemn oath never to divulge his true identity."

"I respect his need for anonymity, but surely you can tell *me*," replied Richard, offended by Dylan's seeming mistrust.

"Sorry, Richard, can't do that."

Dylan broke the ensuing awkward silence by slapping the table. "Stonehenge! Owain removed an object from a tree trunk outside the perimeter of Stonehenge. He said that the object, which he referred to as a sentinel, was placed there by the powers that be. He became ill soon afterwards, so I'm inclined to believe that he was telling the truth."

"This was after you went to Glastonbury?"

"Yes, we dashed to Stonehenge immediately after the cleansing of the Tor."

"How did that go?"

"Kind of dramatic, or so it seemed at the time. Owain had brought with him twelve rocks collected from the mountains of Wales."

"Which mountains?"

"Dinas Bran, Carn Ingli, Snowden and Twm Barlwm."

"Good man."

"Most of the time," explained Dylan. "Arthur's human like the rest of us, albeit a brilliant tactician who gives not a dot for his own life, except to do the will of the higher forces... So Owain laid out the stones in the form of a Celtic cross, reciting the Great Invocation as he and Uther called up the energy of Excalibur to pierce the darkness and clear the Tor of discordant energies, then we faced the four directions as a sharp wind battered the Tor."

"I know what that's like up there."

"This was different, because it ceased as soon as the ceremony ended by introducing the Purple Ray of Sananda Essu, who you know as Christ."

"That what you saw?"

"Seemed so at the time. Twelve of us, including Chris Kasparis, founder of *Chalice Magazine*, who babbled incoherently due to the disturbing effects of the old energies. April, his partner, was seven months pregnant and felt unwell, so Pamela gave her healing. They say the energies of the Tor affect women more than men."

"Anne would rather cross the Rockies than go up there."

"Also with us was Frank 'the Gatherer' of the Usk Lighthouse, and his wife and son. Owain's wife, Fey, completed the circle, with Stella, a woman of spirit, who sees the soul's journey through many lifetimes."

"That's eleven, you said twelve."

"That's right, I've precluded 'The Challenger', called so by Owain due to his confrontational ways, whose jealous and aggressive nature almost destroyed me."

"Say no more."

"Immediately after the ceremony ended, a boy and girl entered the tower and sat opposite one another, then seven young girls with painted faces arrived and laughed and danced around the Tor."

"Sounds all a bit surreal to me," joked Richard.

"Looking back, you ask yourself: did I see Excalibur pierce the purple ray, or was it wishful thinking? How do we know what occurs in the invisible realm during such rituals?"

"Similar to giving healing," concurred Richard. "You don't know, you just hope."

"Quite an intense time, but you just do it in the hope of changing things for the better. Strangely enough, Owain pointed towards the west and said that when America changes, the whole world will change. That was twenty years ago, and America is changing."

"You're right, something is going on."

"The Great Awakening, Richard. It's happening now."

"Well," said Richard, inhaling deeply, "I can believe that, and everything else that's happening. So, tell me more of you and Arthur?"

"I'll warn you — it gets weirder. Owain and Vivian called in on us several weeks later. We were all stood in the kitchen talking when all of a suddenly I began to feel supercharged and began to shake and felt impelled to withdraw into the living room where I picked up pen and paper and started to write as every atom in my body vibrated."

"What caused the vibration?"

"No idea whilst it was occurring," replied Dylan. "Things happen when he's around."

"What did you write down?"

"Instructions on how to live a more meaningful life, and commands towards achieving what I came to do. The communication ended with the words: *I am Jophial, who has been with you all day.*"

"Who is Jophial?"

"Jophial, I discovered ten years later, is an Ascended Master."

"Can you recall what he said to you?"

"Some of it," replied Dylan. "Along the lines that our position here is of prime importance, like the shell that breaks the love inside into the light of day. We ask that you fulfil your heart's desire, and in so doing release into the temporal the lifeseed contained in the shell. That we are three parts of the whole, which is immense but small without one as the number required is exact, for one atom more would upset the chromosome, and one atom less would serve a different purpose, that the vitality of the whole is of prime importance." Dylan broke off to sip his drink.

"Is there more?" asked Richard.

"Yes, there is, something to do with the stars. He said that if you listen to the stars, they will tell you that nothing exists without the support of its kind, that variance at odds with its number creates discord. Harmony results from fine and exacting measurements of mean through the theatre of life, threading as if it were a semblance of miracles in the becoming of self."

"Some message, Dylan."

"He said to follow the code within, that for two thousand years we are obeying the Second Coming into this life when a stream of light so strong will bond or break the structure. There can be no going back to ponder the choices, that every deed done is a clue smitten from the whole through suffering of God's Law upon a people so vainglorious of their efforts they decry the simple ant and make a butcher's hook for the strivings of your kind. That this is the anger of the gods who know no way but love, and that the song will sing again through the hearts and minds of a people scorning a race of men who become in deed what they become in heart and mind, and the wish-fulfilment of a paradise will be the hearts of all. Then he said, 'The threads weave together.'"

"I'm impressed," said Richard. "So they do actually exist?"

"Albeit on a much higher frequency that ours, which is why they're careful not to come to close in case we blow a fuse."

"Maybe we ought to upgrade ourselves to meet them halfway," suggested Richard, "though I'm no Buddhist monk and neither are you."

"Got to laugh haven't you? Me, you, doing what we do. Guess they must have said: these two are the best we got around here, so might as well make use of them."

Richard laughed so loud the barman looked their way. "Right pair of nutters, drawing the short straw."

"Good thing we don't take ourselves too seriously."

"Go mad if we did."

"Haven't finished yet, so hold on to your reality whilst I conclude the story. I figured Jophial to be associated with Owain, as I could find no other explanation."

"That makes sense."

"That winter I worked as chef on board a container ship going from Goole in Lancashire, across the Zuider Zee and up the Rhine to Duesenburg, where fireballs rolled across the night sky and furnaces belched flames from cathedral-like steelworks, reflecting on the dark river a satanic dance. That night, in a dream-like state when we are free to enter the astral, Owain and I fought Saxons with sword and shield. From the Dark Age to the present, we stood against them, yet they kept coming. What is it about the Saxons? Why have they always been the enemy of the Celts? In the days of Caractacus it was the Romans. Why are the Celts always up against an enemy that wants to destroy what they don't have, which is an understanding of what life is about? Why does it go on, why now, when brotherly love is the answer to world peace?"

"Maybe they just love war," replied Richard. "So tell me about Owain who was King Arthur; is he the powerful, invincible warrior as depicted in the legends?"

"Perhaps if I give you a general description of his human characteristics as opposed to the mythic Arthur of Legend?"

"Yes, the real Arthur."

"Okay, let me think a sec. Average height, broad features with high cheekbones and strong chin, firm lips, short light-brown hair turning grey. Clean shaven, apart from an occasional short beard. Short hair, he used to say, prevents an enemy from grabbing hold of it."

"Me and you wouldn't stand a chance then would we?" said Richard with a laugh.

"Nope, though I think you and I have always had long hair—I don't mean just in this life either."

"Sorry, interrupted you. Carry on."

"They say the eyes are the windows of the soul. Well, his are grey-blue and intense as a forest fire and relatively deep-set. Along with the slightly flattened nose of a boxer, he's very much a physical man who's light on his feet. Overall, tough looking and battle scarred, though easy to laugh, doesn't take himself too seriously, except when focussing on the end game, and swift to act when needs be. Describes himself as an instrument to be used in working towards peace and harmony for all."

"Complex person, sounds like."

"Very," affirmed Dylan. "Tell you this little story: A woman I knew from that time told me that when she first saw Owain and Vivian outside Owain's house, she saw two soldiers conspiring. She'd no idea that they were Arthur and Uther. She's not into this as we are, but that was her impression. We'd had a brief relationship before I'd met Pamela, though we'd retained a kind of loose contact for many years, and I asked her to meet them without telling her anything about them. I could say more about Jacqueline Briton, which is her name, and how she connects with Arthur."

"Tell me then?" pleaded Richard.

"You'll find this far-fetched—"

"Try me," cut in Richard.

"What I didn't tell you about when she met Owain and Vivian is that she was attacked by a dog."

"So?"

"She'd never been attacked by a dog in her life before this."

"She'd been lucky then."

"I'm not explaining this right. The story of Gwenhyver and her liaison with Lancelot—she fled north to Perth to avoid Arthur's retribution. He found out, cornered her there and set the dogs on her. There's even a stone carving depicting that there."

"Come on, Dylan, that's a fairy story, surely?"

"No, it isn't. The night before I first met Jacqueline, I dreamt that I was to meet someone very soon. I was shown a church clock with its hands on three p.m. That day, I went to Coldknap on a whim, caught a bus to there and was walking towards the beach when I happened to pass a church whose tower-clock arms were on three p.m. exactly. It was then I remembered the dream.

"Later on, as I was sat on the beach, I saw this woman with several friends. When she saw me sat on the pebbles, she came over and popped a cherry into my mouth, and that was the beginning of our relationship."

"You saying she was Gwenhyver and you were Lancelot?"

"Yes, I am. Too many coincidences to discount the probability of it being so. She lived in Cwmbran quite close to Owain before going to India to teach at an ashram, where she's lived ever since. Our relationship was short-lived. I was devastated when she broke it off. Threw me headlong into the dark night of the soul, pining for her, writing long letters asking why she ended it so abruptly. I was totally bereft, until one night a Tibetan monk came to me in my sleep, and I knew he was her spirit guide. I said to him; 'I love her', to which he replied, 'Yes, but what do you want from her?' I repeated what I'd just said, so he repeated the same question. Shortly after that dream the penny dropped: Love is all very well, but you cannot expect others to fulfil your expectations for you, as that is down to you alone to fulfil."

"Phew! You've been through the meat-grinder alright, Butt.'

"Yeah, recycled and resuscitated."

"Nice one."

"One year later, I met Pamela, also through my dreams."

"Curious mixture is what you are, Dylan."

"Weird's the correct description." Dylan grimaced, raising his glass of cider to toast life's unfathomable twists and turns. "Bottom line is, we all have our parts to play, actors on a stage, choose your role. Arthur knows his, you know yours, and I know mine. We meet again on the playing field and the stakes are high. We may flounder or fall, but we pick ourselves up. We go against convention, we cry, we laugh, and Abdullah is in his heaven too, where angels chant on our behalf. We live in the dungeon of the Archons, they who are the old enemy of man, whom St Paul referred to as the Principalities of darkness. The resurrected Christ describes how he tricked them on his way to the highest sphere, to bypass their karmic snares that trap those whose belief in God is weak. They prey on us all as the karmic wheel spins, and we are their captive slaves."

"Hell of a tale there, Dylan. Where'd you get that from?"

"The Nag Hammadi Gospels, which lay hidden in the desert sands of Egypt for sixteen centuries. You and I also, lying amongst the hills of Wales till our comeback. So come hell or high water, we press our own olives and drink our own wine matured over a span of time. So where were we since then, coming and going, or far away on another land, or on another planet? Who knows where we go, other than here."

Richard's rugged features creased into a smile as he gazed studiously at Dylan. "Not to worry, Butty. We all die and we all return to pick up where we left off."

"Yeah, sure, except I have difficulty remembering what I did yesterday, never mind fifteen hundred years ago," said Dylan, amused by Richard's easy manner. "So you, Derfel, wish to do what?"

"Heal and be healed, there's no other way for me. That and to be a family man. And an artist, my curse, or my blessing if I get it right. So what exactly did you do on the astral plane, apart from fighting Saxons?"

"We cleared ley-lines of blockages affecting their energy, connecting the matrix of the world energy grid known to the ancients, hence why Stonehenge and thousands of sacred sites are located on nodal points of telluric forces used for healing, gateways to other realms of existence. What has been forgotten will come again; old memories are beginning to stir. War for the soul of man is occurring right now as negative entities create havoc attempting to control the energy grids of the planet."

"As a spiritual healer, I know what you say is true."

"What I'm about to tell you is also true," replied Dylan. "Several months after Stonehenge, Vivian came to me on the astral plane in great distress, ridiculed for his beliefs by his brother, so I said to his brother, 'You are as a flea compared to Vivian who is like the Titanic.' He went away, leaving Vivian shaking uncontrollably and shouting, 'I think I am about to crack up!' Suddenly, his hair turned black, he had a beard and wore a purple cloak emblazoned with a red dragon."

"Uther?"

"Yes, he'd become Uther Pendragon and was about to blow, growling and roaring like a lion, so I held him in a bear hug to calm him down. Then he said to me to stand on a pedestal, and I saw white houses stretching all the way to the distant hills."

"Amazing, but how do you keep on top of it all, the astral and all the past-life stuff?"

"We exist on more than one level, and our past lives often impinge on this one, whether we're aware of it or not."

Richard leaned confidentially towards Dylan. "There's more to this story than what you've told me, isn't there?"

"You know who you were, and I know who I was, so why else are we here if not to restore the lost connection to Spirit? Not just you and me, but millions all over the world who are dedicated to creating a world of peace and love, for we are all God's children, born to live as free souls on this beautiful planet." Dylan rubbed his eyes and ran his fingers through his hair to relieve the tension of confessional truth.

Richard sipped his lager, wondering how much of what Dylan had confessed was the truth, and how much an elaboration of wishful thinking.

"All of what I've told you is true," declared Dylan. "We cleared ley-lines and fought discarnates, often with swords, symbolic except when reliving past-life events fighting the Saxons. The Arthurian wars were as much about religion as seizing the land from the Britons. The Church of Rome had inculcated the pagan Saxons to do their fighting for them by paying them in gold, saying they'd be doing God's work as the Celts were false Christians. Arthur knew that it was a war of genocide. Gregory of Tours attempted to force the Britons to accept the doctrine of predestination and original sin, determined to exterminate the Celtic Church, but the Cymry were battle-ready, and their courage won in the end."

"Tell me more about this Arthur. What do you feel in his presence?"

"Someone who sees a game-plan, a global struggle, in which the fate of all is in jeopardy and time is running out. Those in power know that their time is up, but will do whatever they can to hold on to it."

"You mean the Cabal, the elite who control everything?"

"Including us," added Dylan. "Millions all over the world are fighting for the rights of God's children, dedicating their lives to create a world of peace and love, to live as free souls on this beautiful planet."

"We'll get there in the end, Spirit told me," declared Richard.

"The Great Awakening is happening now, even though most believe technology to be the way of the future, that the past is obsolete. Deluded, they've fallen in love with numbers, but they are in for a rude awakening, because the god of science will devour their spirit, and they'll lose the most precious thing of all, their humanity, and nothing will remain but the sterile husk of what once was."

"Bugger that for a bunch of candles and choir-boys singing in the rain."

"Not over yet. The young are asking questions; they see what's going on around them, the devastation of the planet, the wars, the lack of love and compassion. They know something is seriously wrong."

"Our last hope," said Richard, finishing his drink. "Let's go outside and wander."

They entered the walled garden of the Bishop's Palace, where children played on a daisy lawn, and they sat on a bench watching a boy climb up a fig tree. Down in the hollow nestled the cathedral, its spire almost at eye level.

"You still in touch with Owain?" asked Richard.

Dylan frowned. "During the time of my involvement with Owain and Vivian, I'd adapted a book into a screenplay concerning the author's sexual abuse suffered as a young woman. Owain invited her to join our group. She suffered badly from Crohn's disease, exacerbated by emotional turmoil. Owain gave her healing many times. He suggested that part of the book's royalties be given over to the construction of a healing centre. Her husband was against it, concerned she'd be taken advantage of."

"What about the screenplay?"

"My London agent passed it around film and TV producers. Hollywood was interested and options proposed, but Carol, the author, became ill. We'd been giving talks on the subject matter, a sensitive topic at the time—newspapers were covering the Orkney abuse scandal—and the book publication was purposefully delayed. Carol broke contact and we went our separate ways."

"Sorry it had to end that way."

"Not quite the end," said Dylan, "because soon after, I saw Owain standing on Cefn Onn Ridge, the old hill-fort of Caermelin."

"Cefn On Ridge, overlooking Cardiff, I know it."

"*Melin* is Norman French for yellow, and it was customary in that area to use the sulphur from the hot spring at Taff's Well to paint buildings and walls," explained Dylan. "Hence why I dreamt of him three nights in succession standing on a yellow field at Kibor."

"Kibor?" queried Richard.

"Kibor was once the heart of his kingdom," replied Dylan. "Pamela asked if I was certain that Owain was who he claims to be. I said that I was, or my dreams were moondust, that I'd dreamt of him shortly after Stonehenge. He said to me: 'I am James come to Kibor'. She asked what that meant. I said that in a previous incarnation he was James. She said, which James? I said James the Apostle, the brother of Christ."

"Warriors of the Light, healers of souls," asserted Richard, observing the boy in the fig tree whose ripe fruit he was after but could not reach. "Arthur returns to aid the Cymry during this time of transition."

"Why not?" suggested Dylan with a gesture of self-surrender.

"You've got your finger on the pulse of the world chess-game of salvation to free us from the nightmare of controlling monsters."

"Discernment is knowing that what we see and feel is true, which is why I always wait for three confirmations before deciding if a person is genuine or not."

"That's wise," replied Richard. "I do the same to avoid being duped."

Dylan recounted his visionary experience of the church dedication in AD 558, which Richard accepted as matter-of-factly as the weather forecast.

"So you were Maelgwn?"

"Yes, but am I wanting this to be true. Arthur, Uther and Maelgwn, players in the great game, feeling the fire of inner conviction, pushing us on through the dark days of a spiritual war."

"Armageddon?"

"In which we all have our parts to play, big or small, known and unknown, which is why I felt compelled to seek out others from Arthur's time: Merlin, Taliesin the Bard, Gildas the Wise."

"And?" said Richard, busy texting.

"Several months later, Merlin came to me in a dream to show me three lines of a poem, though I could recall only one, which said: 'Thunderbug, waiting to be used.'"

"Thunderbug?"

"No idea." Dylan gestured, spreading his arms out like a bird. "I only remember him telling me that Taliesin had a neck problem due to his previous incarnation as John the Baptist."

Richard's incredulous expression made Dylan smile. "Taliesin was John the Baptist? No wonder he has a neck problem."

"We often inherit injuries from our past lives."

"So they say," concurred Richard.

"We went to Glastonbury some weeks later, as we were involved with *Chalice Magazine* at the time, and we went there for that reason, also to purchase books you can't find anywhere else, esoteric and otherwise, and enter a shop called Pendragon—not that that means much in Glastonbury."

"I know the shop," Richard chimed in. "Celtic art and ornaments, ornate round Celtic shields, books on Merlin, Arthurian myths and legends."

"That's the one," confirmed Dylan. "A bearded man with long hair stood behind the counter. We looked at each other and our eyes locked as if magnetized, and a strange feeling came over me as if I were suspended in a place of no time. When I returned to myself, I was aware of an object suspended between us that was spinning and reflecting light."

"Hanging crystal?"

"Excalibur."

"Never!" exclaimed Richard, putting his hands on his head. "How weird is that?"

"Just a shop prop," replied Dylan with an easy smile. "Not that coming across an Excalibur sword in Glastonbury would be unusual."

"Like finding chickens in a farmyard."

"Or Muslims in a mosque." Dylan paused, looking directly into Richard's eyes. "I'd found Taliesin."

"How do you know it was him?"

"A sense of kinship and recognition on a soul level, as it was with Arthur." Dylan observed the boy up the fig tree reaching for its ripe fruit. "There was much history between Maelgwn and Taliesin, who often praised or cursed the King of Gwynedd. 'I saw Maelgwn battling, the host acclaimed him. Seven spears, seven rivers of blood from seven chieftains fallen', then cursing him with equal eloquence in another poem."

"Did you speak to him?"

"Just a brief hello when I handed him the book we wished to purchase. I'd given up searching for

Taliesin long before, and it was only later that day I realised who he was. Besides, I couldn't just blurt out, 'Hi, Taliesin, good to see you again.'"

Richard laughed, relieved Dylan wasn't an egoist out for praise.

"We called back weeks later to see him and hopefully discuss certain aspects of his past. He wasn't there, but his father-in-law who owns the shop was. He said what had occurred had never happened to Jon before."

"John?" queried Richard.

"Jon, J-o-n, Kuthumi Jon, who'd named his son Taliesin. That Jon does indeed have a neck problem, and he'd written a novel based on his past life in first-century Israel."

"You couldn't make this up, nobody would believe it."

"Kuthumi's a guru; ashrams had been set up in his name. He is a powerful spiritual healer who operates on many levels." Dylan looked at Richard, knowing he could trust him utterly. "I know this because of a vision—"

"Not another one?" Richard interjected. "Seems you have visions like others have a rash."

"You live like a hermit for fourteen years and weird things happen."

"Isolation can have that effect, but you've often been a monk, even as Maelgwn." Richard smiled knowingly. "I know, I was there."

Dylan brushed his comment aside to continue. "Three hundred miles above the Earth, I saw fields of wheat as far as the eye could see. Each field was ready for harvesting, each one cultivated by a particular religious group, whether it be Quakers or Christians, Muslims or Hindus. I look over to the east to see a pink light rising over the Earth like a new dawn, one that will transform the Earth and every living thing."

"Must've been a beautiful sight, Dylan, seeing a pink dawn."

"Pink is the colour of unconditional love." Dylan sipped his drink before continuing. "So I look down to the Earth to see someone sat in the corner of a room meditating, just a tiny speck, so I go down to have a closer look and see Kuthumi Jon sat in a lotus position. Then I find myself sliding down a helter-skelter to hit the ground with a bump, right in front of the great sarsen at Stonehenge."

"That's mad!" exclaimed Richard with an easy laugh, always able to see the funny side of life.

Dylan lapsed into a thoughtful silence as the boy climbed down from the tree to eat the figs like a monkey. The girls tried to take them from him, but he held on tight to the figs and they ran off.

"Incredible, what you've told me. Uther, Arthur, Taliesin. What do you think it all means?"

"That we've come back to finish what was started then, the struggle for spiritual freedom."

"The Grail?"

"Is just a metaphor for gnosis, the true way to the inner self, blanked off in our materialistic frenzy for all things that divert us from the inner soul-connection."

Richard's mobile played a Stereophonics tune. "Anne's calling me, have to go."

As they walked towards Richard's car, Dylan paused to look down at the cathedral. "The first church was built by Lucius, grandson of Claudia and Rufus Pudens, half-brother to St Paul. Claudia was the grand-daughter of Joseph of Arimathea. How's that for a bloodline and verification of Llandaff's ancient past, whose charters prove South Wales to be the centre of British Christianity."

"So where does that leave Glastonbury?" enquired Richard.

"A great fiction, artfully put together by the Normans. Fitzhammon knew the location of Joseph's tomb, although his soldier's military logic almost destroyed the last relic of early Christianity, buried deep in the bowels of the true Avalon, where the protecting spirits of the Goddess prevail to this day."

"How did he know?"

"Maelgwn wrote several books on Arthur and the Grail, one of which reappeared in the court of Eleanor of Aquitaine, patron to Chretien de Troyes, the first to write of the Grail."

"Why did Fitzhammon keep it a secret?"

"I know but cannot say, as even you would find it hard to believe."

"Surprise me!" replied Richard, hurt by this slight to his spiritual integrity.

Dylan refrained from divulging what he knew, for inner knowing often lies in the wisdom of silence. "Angels always know, Richard. Our invisible mentors, they always know."

"You must do what you have to do, no matter what. We've all been ridiculed for our beliefs, which make us stronger and more determined."

"That's the way of it," replied Dylan, not wishing to hurt his feelings. "We're both healers. We stick our necks out because we must, brothers-in-arms with diverse opinions."

Richard leant against the wall of the Bishop's Palace and stared into the dungeon below. "Wales has been pillaged of its history, its values ridiculed and its land despoiled, but one thing remains: the truth of our ancestors: *'Gwir Erbin Y Bydd'*. 'Truth Against the World' was their motto, their battle cry. Lest we forget our true standing in this mad world."

Richard got into his car and drove off, leaving Dylan in the middle of the road, staring at the effigies of Uther and Maelgwn in the north-west tower of the cathedral.

Would they mock him as he often mocked himself? Saying to those who come searching, *"What was here has flown back to the source from whence it came."*

"What source?" demanded Dylan, imagining that they were laughing at him, and a rebellious surge of energy welled up from the depths of his being. "No!" he protested. "I know who I was, who I am now, why I am here, where I am going."

The silent statues, whose sightless eyes glowed red in the evening sun, conveyed a living presence to Dylan as the cathedral bell rang seven times. The ringing tones revealed a questioning presence. *"Why are you here? What are you searching for? Who sent you?"*

"I was Maelgwn Hir. I have returned to complete what was started in the days of Arthur, to restore the Holy Grail to his people, the Cymry."

During the silence that followed his proclamation to the wind, three white doves flew out of the bell tower to alight upon the ruins of the Bishop's Palace and coo in unison, a chorus of harmonic sound, causing him to cover his eyes with his hands. Peeking through the gaps between his fingers, he saw a tall man looking down at him, a bottle of wine barely contained in the pocket of a rag-tag coat that fell about the body of someone well into middle age.

"Look around and tell me what you see?" he asked, his mischievous blue eyes piercing Dylan's indifference. The riddling question intrigued him. "Everyone's posing, can't you see? Open your eyes, everywhere people are posing. Open your eyes and see."

He took a swig from the bottle and sat next to Dylan, observing a Japanese couple snapshotting the cathedral between selfies. Likewise, three teenage girls, sat on the bonnet of a white Porsche, also took selfies, its owner smiling as if he was onto a sure thing. What this man said was true: they and millions of others were addicted to posing, so much so that an anomaly had become the norm.

Dylan glanced at the man, who had the look of someone who'd resigned himself to life's pitfalls.

"Open your eyes and see," he repeated, though the meaning was other than the obvious.

Dylan observed the body language of the tourists who sought recognition, having forgotten the dignity of the self that desired nothing.

He glanced at the old drunk philosophising on the human race. How degraded were his ragged clothes, as he scratched his scraggy beard with soil-black fingers. His twinkling, mischievous blue eyes awakened a memory that disturbed Dylan. He looked away quickly. Those eyes, where had he seen those eyes before? So familiar, perhaps an old friend from long ago.

"Pleasure to meet you, sir," the man grinned, exposing surprisingly white teeth.

"Good to meet you also," responded Dylan with a handshake. "I am Dylan."

"If you say so," he said, looking Dylan straight in the eye. "Remember this: it has to be lost, because if it isn't lost, it cannot be found, and if it cannot be found, it cannot be written about."

Dylan watched him walk away towards the cathedral, perplexed, with an overwhelming sense of knowing him from long ago. Then he remembered the dream, the loud hammering on the door of the hut where he'd slept and opened his eyes to darkness. The woman with him had stirred as the insistent knocking continued. He'd reached for a tunic before unlatching the door to let in the blinding early morning sunlight, and saw a goliath of a warrior standing in the doorway, with bull-horned helmet, padded leather armour and tied leggings, conjuring up an image of formidable invincibility.

A hundred armed men lined the track leading to the bay below, where two dragon-prowed ships with white sails lay at anchor. He stood in front of the bearded man, their eye contact saying all that was needed, and glanced at the woman, who'd covered her slender body in a dark green cloak, her long auburn hair dancing in the sunlight. He looked again at the line of men as one broke rank to look his way, whom he instantly recognised as an old school-friend in his present life, and was puzzled as to why he should look the same fifteen hundred years ago.

Maelgwn Hir put on his armour and strapped on his sword. He was their warlord, and the man who stood in the doorway, and the man who mocked the posers and the vanity of the day, was Rhuvon Bevre, Arthur's cavalry commander.

Dylan blinked the past-life recollection into the ether in time to catch a glimpse of Rhuvon facing the cathedral door, staring at the effigy of Teilo, before disappearing along the lane towards the river. No vision, no quest, just a riddle beneath the mute stones and the gaze of the heroes who knew the truth but could not say.

~~~

Dylan followed the road north towards the hills that were calling to him to undo the riddle of his thoughts, wandering from past to present like the pendulum of a clock moving back and forth through dimensions of time, overlapping the one in which we live and those of long ago. How could the vagrant and Rhuvon Bevre be one and the same? The one an unkempt drunk, expressing contempt for the superficiality of our time, the other a hero from the days of myth and legend. What did it mean to meet again outside the cathedral where he'd been flung back through time to the year 558? Why May the eighteenth, the same date as the invitation from Arthur?

Crossing the bridge over the Taff, he peered at the river below, calm but for the ripples of a rowing boat lapping against a shopping trolley wedged into the muddy bank like a tribute to the river goddess, whereas in the old days a simple coin would suffice.

He glanced back at the cathedral with the realisation that the Church had left a nation without a spiritual anchor, the flock without a shepherd, as the powers that be lead us to the slaughterhouse of the human soul. He turned his gaze toward a tumulus on a hill to the north with the surety that the person buried there knew that we are divine beings who incarnate for the sole purpose of knowing the miracle of life.

The Siege Perilous of Arthur's Round Table had become the challenge of modern man, for man's future myth is man's megalith. In a world of plenty, where entertainment consists of unlimited distraction diverting the mind from the simplest of thoughts, where sitting still means being stuck in traffic, or queuing at a supermarket checkout with a trolley full of food that not even the birds will eat whilst half the world goes hungry, and the latest gadget of upgraded technology pulls the mind hypnotically onto screens of pixels, creating photon images of excess to indulge and gratify the senses, humankind withers under the false god of gratification amid the dying embers of hope.

To lose our common bond with all that lives is to be devoured like a pancake of savoury meats that poison the mind with an avarice akin to cannibalism, and the Great Goddess throws down raindrops in ever greater cloudbursts to cleanse a despoiled planet, and the oceans swell and groan upon our shores, entreating us to be kind to the living creatures who serve nature with its right to exist alongside a pitiless race who abuse free will with an unthinking avarice in the name of the god of profit. Such were Dylan's thoughts as he grappled with the nuances of a multi-dimensional world.

15

Faganus

Dylan loved the land of his youth, the woods and fields, the rivers and streams abundant with life as skylarks sang above wildflower meadows. He recalled days of innocence, running through the woods to the river where fish swam amongst golden weed in clear water where he'd bathe and swim, and lie naked under the sun, obeying his own law, rebelling against a society intent on conformity.

Dylan retraced the old pathways through the woods, sensing the joy of those far-off days as the village of St Fagans came into view, with its thatched cottages and white-washed manor house. Crossing the railway and the river bridge, he paused by the old well of spring water famed for its healing properties, rekindling a dream of a fisherman who stood on the riverbank near a thatched cottage and an apple orchard, where he dug into the rich, dark soil, uncovering a white shell. Inside the shell were three ballerinas, which became three deep purple crystals. An elderly woman, tall and slim, came out of the cottage to hang washing on the line. The fisherman walked over to look at the purple crystals Dylan had found, before returning to the riverbank to fish.

Dylan deduced that the fisherman was Bran, the Fisher King, Arch-Druid and son-in-law to Joseph of Arimathea. The three ballerinas represented the Awen, the three rays of the flowing spirit, the creative force of the Universe. The old woman who hung washing on the line was the guardian of the ancient well, whose overhanging ash tree used to always be festooned with rags of many colours. The apple orchard was the *Insula Que Fortunata*, the Fortunate Isle of Apples.

Dylan entered the grounds of St Fagan's castle, now the Museum of Welsh Life, boasting one million visitors per year. Its walled gardens and Italian terraces overlooked two rectangular fishponds fed by a brook that ran alongside an ancient chapel, whose scant remains protruded sheepishly through the grass. In 1852, workmen searching for building stone discovered a crude stone sarcophagus there bereft of bones, with just a simple earthenware cup beneath an inscribed stone no one there could read, so it was broken up to build a wall somewhere in the castle grounds.

Dylan recalled an ancient document stating that: 'Faganus and Deruvian arrived at the Isle of Avalon'. The document further added that Faganus and Deruvian built a stone oratory dedicated to the Shepherd one hundred and three years after Phillip. Today, not even a simple plaque marked the spot where St Faganus, the Man from Italy, lived out his days.

Elvanus Avalonius returned from Rome with Faganus and Deruvian to Siluria, South Wales, at the behest of Pope Elutherius, in AD 187. Elvanus had taken with him to Rome manuscripts written by the Disciples of Christ during Joseph of Arimathea's lifetime. Dylan pondered the significance of Elvanus of Avalon returning to Siluria, which could only mean that Avalon was in South Wales.

All things conspire against the person who seeks the truth. The lie is strong and powerful. Thoughts create the desired vision of our dreams, that we have the potential to change what we perceive this reality to be, revealing in visions and synchronicities an adventure into the realms of matter, mind and time. An archaeological dig consists of a grid layout where dots are joined together. Human history is the river that cuts through the land, eroding barriers through creative endeavour to make new channels of knowledge and wisdom. *Footprints in the sands of time,* Dylan concluded, as he walked away from St Fagan's castle, whose memorial stone lay concealed in one of its many walls.

The Vale of Glamorgan beckoned, with its winding country lanes and green meadows. St. George's Church sat close to the River Ely. Its ancient yews were saplings when Christianity arrived to challenge the old ways. Its old name was Ufelwy, son of Anueirn, who wrote the *Goddodin*, an elegy to the fallen Celts at the Battle of Cattreath, warriors fed on the finest meat and mead for a year and a day, the Celtic way of living, sacrificial lambs to the sword of Fflamdwyn, the Saxon king. Their end immortalised; the Celts did not fear death. Arthur was mentioned, a throwaway line: *'Gwrgan was a great warrior, yet he was no Arthur.'*

The road wound its way north to the Church of Llanfihangel, set deep in a hollow by a flowing brook fanned by the sinewy branches of a yew. A Templar cross above the porch was no surprise to Dylan, as they venerated the Goddess of Wisdom, Sophia, who lives in a secret place, no one knows where.

No one truly forgets when the bell rings; they go to sleep, nothing more, waiting for the day of the trumpet call that will unite us all. No one goes there anymore, for now is the lost time, yet it is only a moment between breaths before the winds of change adorn the skyline with the verse of angels proclaiming the Second Coming, which is ourselves when we awake to the beauty of life, unadorned and simple, devoid of ostentation. Who are we to criticise and condemn? All are given a second chance, or a third, ad infinitum.

The road circled north-east, beyond the walls of Sant-Y-Nyll—named after an Irishman, a sainted Paddy, who dwelt above the Roman villa by a brook replete with trout, or trout replete with fly, as Rupert Brooke put it before his demise at Gallipoli. Fever took him, not some hero's death. Fate can be mean— the golden boy of English poetry, swatted by a fly.

Gypsophilia brushed his arms and honeysuckle oozed charm in the summer heat. Cottages hid away in their secluded escape from the world of plenty to a world where we are once more ourselves. A little way along, the Cwm, which measured the rain by its flow, though its source was deep and ancient as the barn atop the meadow fit only for cattle, was once a monastery, a Dark Age singularity among many. The Vale boasted deferentially of the famed, known only by name, of deeds done in defence of the land to usher in a future time of peace.

Dylan arrived at Capel Llanilltern hot and thirsty. Quenching his thirst in the brook below the remains of an ancient monastery, he recalled the time when he and his brother discovered in the brook a crown of silver filigree, a crown that only a Druid would wear.

A certain tranquillity returned as he followed the road to the derelict church, long bereft of parishioners, a sad sight with its graveyard of weeds, a dying ember of what was, its life-force extinguished by a joyless philosophy refusing to surrender its self-righteous pinnacle of limited vision. Yet it had once concealed a secret in the west corner of the bell tower: an inscribed stone of she who sparked a thousand tales on the nature of love, she who won a king but loved another.

The stone declared in its cold, factual way: 'Hic Iacet Gwenora'. 'Here Lies Guinevere'. A silent testimony to she who was crowned, who drowned the dream of Arthur in the muddy Usk at Caerleon. Here she lay, and the memorial stone testifying to the legend of the Round Table had languished in the Linguistics Department of Swansea University since 1894, concealed no doubt to perpetuate the myth of English supremacy over the Cymry and their history.

Guinevere, the white-skinned swan, lay beneath the land of her father, Gwrgan Mawr. The femme fatale, whose love affair with Lancelot lives on in legend. Dylan smiled with the knowledge of her present life at an ashram in India, exiled within the walls of a Buddhist sanctuary. They'd known one another a short while, a passionate affair that had tumbled into his life, a temporary fulfilment of what was. Truth hurts, redemption follows guilt like the hounds of conscience. A tangled web of deceit brought them to Capel Llanilltern long before he knew it to be her resting place. Time's loop often returns us to the place where first meetings occur, divided by centuries; time is the artist, and we are but phantom figures that come and go.

Facts were numerous and conclusions many, yet the riddle remained: where was the Circle of Prophecy mentioned by Melkin? Some say Stonehenge or Avebury, whilst others, who assume all roads lead to Glastonbury, say it is there.

Unfolding a sheet of A4 paper, Dylan sat on the church wall to read the Prophecy: *'Avalon's island with avidity, claiming the death of pagans, more than all the world beside, for the entombment of them all, honoured by chanting spheres of prophecy; and for all time to come adorned shall it be by them that praise the Highest. Abbadare, mighty in Saphat, noblest of pagans, with countless thousands there hath fallen asleep. Amid these Joseph in marble, of Arimathea by name, hath found perpetual sleep: and he lies on a two-forked line next the south corner of an oratory fashioned of wattles for the adoring of a mighty Virgin by the aforesaid sphere-betokened dwellers of that place, thirteen in all. For Joseph has with him in his sarcophagus, two cruets, white and silver, filled with the blood and sweat of the Prophet Jesus. When his sarcophagus shall be found entire, intact in time to come, it shall be seen and shall be open unto all the world: thenceforth nor water nor the dew of heaven shall fail the dwellers in that ancient isle. For a long time before the day of judgement in Jehosaphat open shall these things be and declared to living men. Thus far Melkin.'*

The Glastonbury myth of Ynys Avalonia still holds sway to the ineffable conclusion that Joseph lies there in a marble tomb, though marble in Latin is *mamore*, meaning a marble-like sea. Ynys Avalonia signifies an island or land between two rivers. Melkin's Ynys Avalonia lay concealed within the prophecy's hidden clues.

Dylan understood the Grail to be a metaphor for lost knowledge, the truth behind the revelations of a new spirituality that would unite all factions, dissolving differences, in the desire to unite with the Divine.

A picture of Joseph in Avalonia was beginning to emerge out of confusion, intermingled with snapshot images from dreams and intuitive insight. The lament of the seven maidens referred to the lost teachings of Christian gnosis, the Grail within.

Dylan walked the land seeking the answer to a fifteen-centuries old riddle. He followed clues revealed in dreams and synchronicities in a culture where things of this nature are mocked. He'd known many young people who'd been tempted into a drug-induced nirvana, a forgetful refuge amid a whirlwind of change.

Never in the history of humanity has there ever been such a time as now. No longer can a person be silenced by the Inquisition. Now is the time spoken of in the Prophecy when 'The rains of Heaven shall fall and the people will thirst no more', a reference perhaps to the fusion of the Gnostic teachings of Christ and Druidic lore.

He felt certain that the Circle of Prophecy close to the tomb of Joseph of Arimathea would be where Joseph had lived amongst the Silures in the Kingdom of Bran. Closing his eyes, he asked for guidance, though he felt unworthy compared to holy men who devote their lives to self-renunciation, whilst he wandered the countryside talking to angels in the ether who did not talk to fools, searching in the garden of dreams where lay the dead of centuries.

He smiled, thinking of Pamela, her beautiful face that radiated love in its purest form, unconditional and accepting the role she had to play, dedicated to revealing the true reality of Spirit. That was what had brought them together and bound their love.

He scanned the land until the image of a churchyard came to mind, close to a circular earthworks surrounded by oaks. He perked up sharply as a revelation revealed itself, just as a cricket's sharp sound masks a symphony of harmonics which human ears fail to discern, as so often we fail to hear the beauty of Nature's song.

Could the circular earthwork behind St Llid's Church be the Circle of Prophecy mentioned by Melkin? According to the ancient triads, Llid is named after the man from Israel, Joseph of Arimathea. Dylan wondered why he — or someone else for that matter — hadn't deduced this until now, unless it was Melkin's master plan that Joseph's tomb would remain hidden until the designated time when an evolved understanding would readily accept the 'true' relevance of Jesus' teachings.

Dylan thought it possible, in view of today's worldwide communications uniting people for the first time. The Church had silenced itself, but now there was no church but an inward reflection of our true divinity.

16
The Circle of Prophecy

Dylan splashed the water of Tre-Fran's well over his head and body. His muscles taut with cold, he shook the wet out of his long hair and gave thanks to the spirit of the place deep in the woods, of the spring that had quenched the thirst of Bran and Caractacus.

His feet firm on the wet earth, he strode toward the church, whose ancient yews yawned with the ache of time. A jaybird flew by as the outer ring of the cor came into view, its high bank crowned with oaks. He was convinced this was the circle where Joseph of Arimathea spoke the living words of the Prophet Iesu, whose birth was foretold by the Druids.

Standing on the earthen bank, he felt certain that this was the Circle of Prophecy mentioned by Melkin, the key to where Joseph lay in the heartland of Bran the Fisher King, whose mythic hero sons, Arviragus and Caractacus, stood against the might of the Roman Empire.

Quiet were the oaks that towered like sentinels around its perimeter, becalmed beneath a blue sky as the sun dispersed its light through the leaves. He stood in the centre of the cor listening to his own heartbeat, his breathing calmed to suspension between inhalation and exhalation, hearing sounds not of this world as his ears rang with the presence of those gone by, gathered in circles where wise men and poets sang praises to the Supreme Deity that lives in each and every one, healing and replenishing the weary with renewed vigour in the struggle for daily existence.

Dylan touched the soil beneath a sycamore and put some on his tongue, tasting bitter and sweet at the same time. Life after life we come and go, but the Earth that gave us birth remains. With the surety of inner knowing that spirit of place exists within its own reality, he sat against the sycamore tree as whispers from the invisible realm of the Goddess assailed his ears.

She appeared out of nowhere, the Guardian of the Threshold, fearsome and powerful, her movements swift as lightning.

"Who are you?" She commanded. "How strong are you? Where are you going? Whoever comes by me without a purpose perishes. I am the Governess, the Priestess. I know what comes by me. I am forever watching, waiting, holding, as I am now to you."

She vanished as quickly as she came, the protector of nature whose words had cut through all pretension to the core of his being. Was he strong enough? Was his integrity of purpose true or deluded by ego and false ambition? He felt certain that this was the circle mentioned in the Prophecy, hidden amongst the trees in the heartland of Bran's kingdom.

So long ago. How unreal it all seems to our twenty-first-century minds, that they lived between two worlds, but revering nature as the work of the Supreme Creator. No pagan effigy of a Celtic god has ever been found in Britain. The Romans brought with them their own gods, but the Celts saw the trees and the rocks, the birds and the animals, as part of one indivisible whole.

Dylan listened to voices and sounds not of this time: timbrels and harps, singing and triadic mantras. "The fire and the water, the air and the earth. Tasting the earth, drinking the water, divining the names in the fire." He saw maidens in white chiffon dancing around the trees as flames spiralled upward to the blue sky where white doves flew in a circle. The maidens swirled around him in a frenzy of revelation, whispering to the wind: "He lies at the bottom of the chasm. She calls on you to deliver him from Her womb."

He opened his eyes, but no one was there, no sound but his inner voice repeating the warning of the Goddess who guards the threshold. Why was he here? He was no pure and holy knight, no Galahad. Why did the snake woman challenge him? Did he truly hear the whispering, or was it the gentle breeze blowing through the leaves? Has the Goddess summoned him to deliver Joseph from Her womb, or were they his own thoughts giving life to his deepest wish? The feminine psyche lives in us all, the intuition of acute perception beyond logic and reason.

He raised his arms to pay homage to the spirit of place before retracing his steps to Trefran, the birthplace of Bran the Fisher King, pausing briefly in the churchyard where he and Pamela had often sat beneath the yew to enjoy the peace among the bluebells and the fairy-folk.

He walked on, his mind transported into the realm of transcendental thought, unaware of the nettles that stung his legs.

"Who or what are we if not a spirit in a body, living within a miasma of creation whose beginning and end no one knows?"

He returned home to his soul-partner, to a joy beyond daily cares.

"Welcome home, dreamer. What did you discover today — Homer's ghost or Joseph's tomb?"

He was used to Pamela's sarcasm and smiled, knowing that she loved his quirky ways. "It is definitely a Druidic cor. You remember when we were there last, five years ago, and you said that it was a very special place, that the spirit beings watch over it because it had an important past to do with Christianity."

"I remember, though back then you weren't sure, thinking I'd made it up. You should trust my knowing more, instead of believing you know all the answers."

"I honestly don't. It's just that I like to check things out for myself."

"Which takes you ten times longer." She kissed him lightly on the lips. "Shame you waste so much time in a daze of wondering over things that aren't relevant. Trust in Spirit, and you'd soon find the answer."

Dylan refrained from telling her what he'd witnessed at the cor for fear of ridicule, though the truth was he only half believed in his own imaginative impressions, that when in trance, what seems real was merely a projection of subconscious images.

"Tell me about your day at the shop?" he asked, as he helped Pamela prepare food.

"Quiet, so I decided to drill a hole in the ceiling on which to hang a light when a young couple came into the shop. She seemed nice, though subdued, but he looked a right nerd, an arrogant sod who said to me, 'My, aren't we the liberated woman?' I thought to myself, right you sonofabitch, so I got off the steps to look him right in the eye. 'Being liberated has got sod all to do with drilling a hole in the ceiling; being liberated is keeping spermatozoa in the deep freeze in case 'I' want to multiply.'"

Dylan laughed out loud. He knew how she could be when fired up. "So what did he say to that?"

"Nothing. The little fart backed off and left the shop with his tail between his legs; the little squirt couldn't take it, but his girlfriend stayed and spent all his money on books, CDs and jewellery. She got her revenge."

Pamela's fiery spirit and strength of character was hard won through circumstance, her independence honed on the sharp edge of many a masculine tongue who'd figured she was easy prey, as regional manager of a mortgage company, with Dylan as manager. Twelve salesmen under her, all of whom vied for her position, but she played them, using her forceful charm to convince them they were fortunate to have her direct their lucrative sales. She wasn't just good, she was the best. When the business went bust, and the head office in Carlisle demanded the return of the company car without paying what was owed to the sales team, she drove there and demanded they pay up or she'd be off to Scotland in their car to do a spot of fishing. They paid up there and then.

Hard to imagine such a fiery spirit sitting in circle meditating and channelling spirit guides along with Dylan and the other members of the group.

~~~

It was during their time in the circle that Min Sun Sang came to him once more in a dream to give him a warning.

"Exhortations! What is the mystery of this world that has no followers? Those that do follow pluck the flowers and eat them. You can partake not by eating but by believing only; thereby sparing life and denying death."

Dylan concluded the flowers to be the spirits that each took inside themselves during meditation, that it wasn't for him to channel the spirits, for whatever reason. She went on to say that love is gentle and lays about its brow an understanding, which is this: "Listen to your own heartbeat. There is a reason for this and a reason for that, but true judgement dwells in the heart. If the thoughts of man could be counted, then the sum of his knowledge would be thus: One finger pointing heavenward would undo the knot of his thoughts to lay about his neck as a string of pearls, and then with good reason, marry his thoughts to right thinking."

"The more you heed inner calm, the more it will come and succeed in its endeavour to wholeness. Liberation is a state of mind that gathers to itself the liberation of seeing and beholding a single truth of being which, though as still and as unmoving as a rock, nevertheless observes its place and purpose and is content."

17
The Doctor

A tall, distinguished-looking woman walked into their shop in Caerleon. Of graceful stature, she understood her own power as a bard and poet, harpist and weaver of Celtic tales.

"What do women want?" she asked boldly.

"Love? Children? To be admired?" he blurted, her question throwing him off kilter.

"Wrong answers," she replied. Her high cheekbones and generous lips radiated an aura of power and beauty. "What do women want? Think, what is it that women want? Come on now, you should know."

Dylan thought of the old Celtic stories. Rhiannon the Horse Maiden, Morgan, The Lady of the Lake, what did they possess? Power over men? He shook his head, unable to grasp the answer to her question.

"Shall I tell you?"

Dylan surrendered. "Okay, what is it?"

"Sovereignty!" she declared.

Her very presence proclaimed a woman's rightful standing. Mother Nature's power reigns over all, the giver of life that sustains our very existence.

"Perhaps you can tell me why women are reclaiming their birthright?" she asked.

"Because the Divine Feminine is returning to usher in a new age of love and understanding."

"Nicely put, Dylan. People like you walk the earth with eyes and heart open to the Creator's intent. Gaia has sent out her call for help, and the call has been answered. You know this, don't you, you of the vanguard race sent to proclaim the second coming of the wise women who will save the planet in its hour of need."

"We hope," he replied.

"Mere hope is dope to the mind. You must stand tall and say what you truly think." She liked Dylan, his naivety and open demeanour. "Here are some of my books, if you would be so kind as to sell them for me."

"Be more than happy to," concurred Dylan, knowing that she was one of a kind, a woman who knew her own mind.

She walked away, leaving Dylan with the germ of a new revelation: the Grail Maidens as guardians of the secret knowledge, yet they are nameless, unlike the seekers of the grail who are always named — Gawain, Lancelot, Perceval, Galahad, the list goes on. The Grail contains the hidden meaning of the feminine principle, therefore anonymous, an archetype, the anima that runs through us as it runs through all life. Its seekers are always male, searching for the hidden meaning of the anima, the mysterious other.

Dylan walked into the garden of the Ffwrwm to contemplate the Grail as a metaphor for the lost initiation into the otherworld of the Goddess Sophia, the Gnostic anima archetype. The Grail Maiden offers the cup of knowledge to the seeker. The Fisher King asks the question: "Whom does the Grail serve?" The question is known but not the answer, just as the mystery of physics remains concealed.

Rhiannon's suitor could not reach her no matter how fast or slow her horse galloped. The Lady of the Lake returned to the watery depths following her husband's failure to understand the true nature of divine love, of which she was the embodiment.

Dylan confronted the fearsome statue of Morgan le Fey, legs astride and holding a dagger, her piercing eyes challenging, saying: "l am a woman of power. Call me witch or an embodiment of dark forces, but I am you who made me in your image, I am what you deny, I am the angry Goddess who seeks justice for the rape of womankind."

The Grail is the chalice, the chalice is the woman who is part man. The man only thinks he knows who he is. The woman knows who she is because Nature ensures her role. The man serves her whether he realises it or not. The woman rules, and he dances to her tune. Mother Nature torments the man who rejects the other half of his androgynous soul. If men would return the power stolen from women and integrate their own anima, they would discover the Grail of knowledge and of their divinity, and the peace of gnosis would once more return to all who understand the question. Men would no longer reject their feminine quality, acknowledging that we are but equal parts of the whole.

Such thoughts flooded his mind. The Grail conundrum had fallen to his lot like some incurable disease, he thought. He touched the rough bark of the tulip tree, whose blooms in May are likened to the lotus flower, symbolising the awakened soul, and the rose as metaphor for spiritual wholeness. The

wounded Fisher King challenges the Grail seeker with
a question: 'Whom does the Grail serve?' To Dylan,
the meaning was clear, our heart and soul belong to
the natural world, which we abandon at our peril.

People wandered in and out of the little shop,
often bemused by imagery of Celtic knotwork and
zoomorphic circles and spirals, books on Celtic
history, Druidry and Arthurian legends. Dylan's
stone sculptures were mostly outside, where he
hammered away whenever business was quiet or
when Pamela was at the shop, persuading customers
to purchase pieces of silver jewellery or a Green
Man wall plaque, or just to talk, her open-hearted,
beguiling warmth and radiant blue eyes offering
loving advice to whoever needed it most.

By chance, they'd wandered into the Ffwrwm's
cobbled medieval courtyard fifteen years before,
awestruck by its myriad sculptures depicting
characters from the *Mabinogion*, life-size depictions
of Merlin, wooden thrones ornately carved with
figures of legend, of Arthur and Gwenhyver,
Lancelot and Galahad. The whole was an arena of
life, encapsulating the history of bygone heroes and
heroines of the Celtic era. Heliki, the dryad of the
willow tree, sat cross-legged, playing a flute on a
branch of the hundred-foot tree rooted in a Roman
wall, out of which a dragon spouted water into a
stone trough.

They ventured further along the cobbled walkway
flanked by craft units in bright yellow and green,
past the open doors of a cafe selling ice cream and
vegetarian fare, next to a shop of homemade lace and

cushions of soft pink, adjoining Rafi the Goldsmith, an Israeli-born child of the kibbutz.

Dylan was following the Roman wall which once had encircled the City of the Legions, when something caught his eye, an image from his long-ago vision of the dancing maidens, whose lament of the Rose and the Lion haunted him still. Peering closer, he saw an embossed rose on a tile and above that a lion. He wondered if who'd placed them knew of their significance to the Grail.

Dylan sensed the magic of the place with its imaginative plethora of symbol and myth, and Pamela, sensing the energy of the courtyard, closed her eyes to tune in to its vibrant healing energy.

A renovated barn doubled as a restaurant and tourist information office full of antiques.

"Hello." A dapper, great-haired man greeted them. "Welcome to the Ffwrwm. Bear with me while I finish telling the story of Kilhwch and Olwen to this American gentleman." He turned to a bald man in a bright orange shirt and blue trousers. "Kilhwch encounters the wild boar, Twrch Trwyth, and Arthur chases him out of the Preseli hills and across Wales. The fighting was bloody, and Arthur gathered his army from Scotland to Cornwall to confront the enemy, proclaiming: 'No longer shall I follow the Pig, but will oppose him life to life.' Arthur confronted the boar at Mount Baedan, which is north of Bridgend in Glamorgan, and Twrch Trwyth is driven into the Severn Sea, never to be seen again."

"The invasion of the Vandals driven out of North Africa," cut in Dylan. "They wore boar-tusk helmets, Gormund their king is Twrch Trwyth, the boar that lies."

"Stay here while I fetch Doctor Rhys," exclaimed the host, who left, reappearing moments later with a bull-like man, a cross between Winston Churchill and Sitting Bull with his tied-back silver mane.

Scanning them with knowing eyes, he sat upright in an ornately carved kingly throne. "Speak," he commanded. "Tell me your version of Kilhwch and Olwen."

Dylan reiterated his telling of the tale, followed by a thoughtful pause.

"Hmm, interesting," he replied, looking up at Dylan as if to measure the man. "You appear to know your stories on Arthur."

"I know a little."

"Would you be interested in having a place here, a unit in one of the converted stables?"

"A shop?"

The Doctor shook his head, "No, no, a craft unit. The Ffwrwm is home to the arts and creativity in all its forms."

"The Ffwrwm?" inquired Dylan.

"Welsh for forum, a meeting place." The Doctor arose from his throne as if to go. "Might I suggest that you go away and think about my offer?"

Dylan had already decided. The wall plaques connected to his vision were enough to convince him that this was a special place, for such synchronous signs had always figured largely in his and Pamela's lives. Both sensed its special energy, lively yet radiating a certain tranquillity.

Two weeks later with borrowed money, they filled the space with all things Celtic: jewellery, CDs, sculptures and jewellery. That was before Dylan bought a hammer and chisel to carve rock in this place so steeped in history it squeaked the presence of ghostly heroes long gone.

He dreamt of a thatched hut in the garden, where a knight lay on a bed of straw, attended by a beautiful woman in a white gown. Turning around, she said to Dylan, "To heal the wounded knight."

He soon realised what she meant when many patients from the nearby St Cadoc's hospital for the mentally ill wandered into that courtyard of pagan imagery, of Green Men and nymphs, dryads and Blodeuwedd the flower maiden, to which many responded, sensing the imagery to be a part of their split-off selves. The Ffwrwm offered a refuge of peace and understanding for those too sensitive to withstand the rigours of modern society, who often found solace in alcohol or drugs.

Jung concluded that the cause of schizophrenia was often a failed initiation into the otherworld, which without the guidance of the shaman of psychic awareness, causes the soul-mind to be cast adrift in a storm of uncontrollable thoughts and irrational behaviour divorced from reality. Jung knew the dream world to be more real than the one in which we live. Dylan soon realised that many of these patients were not mad, but in need of spirit doctors to help integrate their fragmented fantasies into the wholeness of psychic well-being.

The Doctor, as he was affectionately known, had recently retired. In eloquence and intelligence, Dylan had not met his equal. He was fluent in seven languages, including Yemeni; his fund of humorous anecdotes could out-do Oscar Wilde on a good day. Often in company with visitors from afar on the trail of King Arthur, his portly body seated on a throne of oak, inviting passers-by to join him in a glass of wine.

"*Yn Siarad Yn Cymraeg?* Do you speak Welsh?" Welsh was his first language, its history his passion — hence the sculptures of Taliesin and Morgan le Fey, Arthur, Merlin and Lancelot. He declared the Ffwrwm to be but a small enclave of Welsh culture, which he'd created during the early 1990s, merging ancient remains in honour of the Celtic past.

"Come now," he would say with a gesture of invitation to passers-by. "Join me in a glass of wine. Are you from these parts? Welcome to Wales, *Croeso Y Cymru*, be my guest. We Welsh never exclude foreigners from our table. We are gloriously famed for our hospitality and conversation enlivened with an occasional beverage." Putting them at their ease, if only temporarily, his eyes twinkling in mischief, the catch having seated, he'd lean forward ever so slightly with a purposeful look. "Would you mind if I ask you a personal question?" His shrewd gaze pierced the shell of the person sat opposite. "Sat as we are in Camelot" — at which point the guest would shift uncomfortably — "a city of wonders, the sun city of the ancient world... Do you know how many brothels have been excavated here? More than is proper in any civilised society, but that is how the Welsh defeated the Romans." A chortle and a raised glass would soon put them at ease, the conversation covering various topics and anecdotes, real or imagined, playful as the birds and squirrels skidding in the trees above their heads, such was his uncanny ability to breathe life into suffocating conformity.

Engaging a young woman in conversation, he said, "Come, partake a glass of wine with an old man whose only enjoyment left in life is to engage in conversation with such an attractive lady as yourself. You see before you a failed romantic who listens to the wind and walks the way of long-forgotten heroes. But hush, here is the best kept secret of all... Caerleon is Camelot." Never put off by the silence that would inevitably follow such a declaration, he would pursue the claim by adding, "Those more knowledgeable than myself testify with emphatic eloquence that this city of a thousand tales was Camelot, which is why I had the audacity to place a plaque on the outside wall declaring: 'Camelot, The City of the Legions'. Furthermore, you have it from my lips, that the Once and Future King shall return to Wales. Truth is, my dear, he never left it. We Welsh are good at keeping secrets. *Diolch!*" His belly-laugh wobbled his large abdomen, for jolly was his humour and sharp his wit.

A full-blooded Renaissance man and one-time Communist, socialist politician, and physiotherapist to the Royal Ballet Company with a practice in Harley Street, he moved to Caerleon to become the local GP, having fallen in love with the place. Russell was a man of means, rubbing shoulders with politicians and people in high places — rich or poor made no difference, just his curiosity as to what made them tick, what stories they had to tell, for storytelling was his great love, enchanting audiences with tales from the *Mabinogion* with expressive gestures and belly-rumbling chortles, possessing the magic way of child and man.

He was often mocked by the locals for his outspoken thoughts on the Cymry and their history. "There goes King Arthur!" was a common jibe from those who derided their own history, but the Doctor was a rock against all that was false and low.

It was enough for Dylan to be part of this magical place where people intermingled in a melee of lively activity in homage to the Celtic spirit of living in the now with generosity and humour. It soon became apparent that the shop was something much more, whose real purpose was to help others reclaim their lives from the restrictions imposed upon them by a society that placed wealth above spiritual wellbeing.

Fifteen years had come and gone, and Dylan sat forlorn on a roughly carved wooden throne, for the battle between the forces of light and dark had claimed the lives of many who'd fought for the dignity and freedom of the human spirit.

"Who is here now?" he mused, surrounded by images of kings and statues of angels with frozen lips. "What truths lie ice-bound in their hearts of stone?"

Nymphs danced on the wall, a parody of a journey to this courtyard of dreams. What did the Doctor know, what truths did he hold, what stories untold, who stood like a monolith to a dream of Wales? A dream rooted in socialism, or a throwback to an age of benefactors to the arts and linguistic skills of the bards?

Taliesin and Merlin vied for poetic honours, Talhearn composed his Druid prayer in the halls of Caerleon's many colleges, though no trace remains but the ghost of a city asleep beneath the grass. Yet their footprints remain, for words never die, for whoever repeats them rekindles a name. No more will they be silent, no longer will the Cymry fade away into the forests of the uplands. Many legends fade away, only to be reborn into a new age when their truth will rise like the sap of a tree. Such are the stories of the Holy Grail that grow fondly in our thoughts as we seek its hidden meaning.

Dylan's ambition to discover the Holy Grail seemed as contraband washed up on a distant shore, pounded by storms and dashed to pieces on the rocks of circumstance. Yet life is full of surprises, offering the antithesis of what we expect.

A woman walked into the shop. Dylan sensed her aura of aliveness, a visible energy that intrigued him, physically young yet mature, possessing a somewhat innocent quality.

"Pre-Raphaelites are my favourites," she said, staring at *Circe* by Waterhouse.

Dylan watched her intently. She stood tall, yet wasn't, her bold posture revealing an aura of light and quick intelligence.

"They were the Romantics of the Victorian era, their depictions of the Grail Knights quite profound as their profiles are all alike, as if to say that they are everyone who searches for what has been lost, which is true. They possess a wonderful mystery... don't you think?" She stared openly at Dylan. "Why do the men and women always look the same, as in Burne-Jones' *The Arming and Departure of the Knights*? Doesn't that tell you something of the male-female conundrum, that the two are really one?"

"Hadn't thought of that," mumbled Dylan, awed by her delightful manner.

She gazed around the shop, taking everything in as if feeling what could not be seen, then left, saying she would be back.

18
The Talk

The hall was hushed as Dylan stood on the rostrum, anxiously shuffling through sheets of notepaper. The local Women's Institute had invited him to give a talk on the Celtic Church, to which he'd agreed, but now wished he hadn't as he fumbled nervously with his notes. His head hot and his throat dry, he coughed to clear his throat.

"St Illtud, son of Bicanus of Brittany, cousin to Arthur and a soldier in his army, left his wife and family following a discourse with St Cadoc of Llancarvan. He became a hermit monk, and years later the Bishop of Llanilltud Fawr. It was not compulsory to abandon your wife to join the Celtic Church. Like many aspects of Celtic society, it was a free choice.

"Illtud was known throughout Britain as a wise man, well versed in theology, philosophy, mathematics, astrology, herbal medicine and the healing arts. He, like Merlin, could also prophecy the future. Not a done thing in the Church as we know it, but this was the Celtic Church, deeply versed in Druidic lore. There is an account in the life of St Samson of Dol, a pupil of Illtud, of a boy bitten in the groin by an adder. Samson pleaded with Illtud to use his knowledge of the Arts of Stipho to cure him, but Illtud said, 'It is forbidden for me to do so now that I am a man of God.' He did however relent and the boy survived. So, who is this enigmatic Illtud, if not a fully-fledged Druid? Truth is, there was never a time when the Druids opposed the teachings of the Prophet Iesu, which is how they referred to him.

"Arthur and many of his knights were taught by Illtud. We know that Maelgwn Gwynedd, who succeeded Arthur, was inculcated there during his youth. Also St Patrick, before he was carried off by Irish pirates. Two thousand four hundred monks sang in relays around the clock. Perpetual choirs called bangors existed only in Wales during the Dark Ages. The Celts do love to sing.

"Thirty-seven monastic establishments between Caerleon and Swansea have been located. Llandough, west of Cardiff, discovered by chance during a house-building project, produced a Roman villa and eight hundred and seventy-five burials from the fourth to the eighth century, the vast majority being Celtic Christians. The building of houses went ahead and continues to this day. What are we losing when connections to our past are being bulldozed into oblivion before our eyes?

"The Celtic Church was a strong and independent movement whose structure and discipline was along the lines of the Druidic, which included worship in the open, under the Eye of God. The Druids believed in One Great Spirit, the Creator God, and many claim that their modes of ritual were identical to the Hebrew. The Gold breastplate from Llyn Carrig Fach in Anglesey is identical to those worn by Hebrew priests. The Druids themselves claim they were taught by Enoch in the Vale of Hebron.

"Were not the Druids and Celtic Christians one and the same? Druid derives from the Sanskrit word for oak, *druin*, or from *druthin*, meaning 'servant of truth'. Bran, the Fisher King of the Grail legends, was the Arch-Druid of Siluria, converted by Joseph of Arimathea, having married Enygeus, Joseph's sister.

"The wise men of India referred to Britain as a great centre of religious learning. Druidic universities were the largest in the world, accommodating over sixty thousand students, to quote Gildas the Historian, affirmed by Greek and Roman testimonies which state, 'The nobility of Rome and other nations sent their children to Britain to study law, science and religion.' Yet the Welsh were often mocked as ignorant barbarians, an insult to their ancient legacy."

Dylan sipped water from a glass, relieved that the audience were beginning to respond favourably.

"As for the origins of Christianity in South Wales, the Tudor Church historian, Polydore Vergil, states: 'Britain, partly through Joseph of Arimathea, Faganus and Damianus, was of all kingdoms the first that received the Gospel.' In AD 44, Roman Legions arrived under Claudius and swiftly conquered England, whilst the Silurians, under the leadership of Caractacus, stood firm against their all-conquering might. Thirty years of warfare ensued, hence the building of Caerleon in AD 75. Wales was never truly conquered, and as a province of the Roman Empire, retained rights of governorship with powers to elect their own kings.

"The Cymric Welsh were not the barbarians supposedly subdued by the all-conquering Romans, but a highly sophisticated society whose laws became the English laws of England, derived from those perpetuated by Hywel Dda. Let anyone look into our history and decide for themselves the truth of the brave dignity of their forefathers and the Druid priesthood, whose wisdom survives to this day."

Dylan took a few deep breaths before continuing. "Joseph arrived here in AD 37, in the last year of the Emperor Tiberius, to quote Gildas's *De Excidio*, written in the sixth century. Joseph and many of Jesus's followers fled from Roman persecution to Bran's kingdom of Siluria following Claudius's edict to exterminate all those of the line of David. The Romans condemned the Messianic bloodline of Christ, afraid the new religion would topple their gods, and with it the Roman Empire.

"Here's where a fascinating sequence of events occur. Caractacus, the Pendragon, is betrayed by his mother-in-law, Cartamanduau, Queen of the Coritani of Shropshire. She handed him over to the Romans in chains, and he was taken to Rome to face execution. Three million lined the streets of Rome to catch a glimpse of the formidable unconquered hero of the Silures who defied death with a bold speech to the Roman Senate. Emperor Claudius, impressed by his courage, pardons Caractacus on condition that he and his family remain hostage in Rome for seven years.

"Claudius adopts Caractacus's daughter Gladys and renamed her Claudia. She then marries Rufus Pudens, Senator and aide-de-camp to Aulus Plautius, Commander of the Roman legions in Britain. Aulus Plautius then marries Eurgain, Caractacus's sister, who is already Christian. She was tried in Rome for following a foreign superstition, but the judge, her husband, declared her not guilty.

"Saint Paul was half-brother to Rufus Pudens on his mother's side, and often visited his niece Claudia and her family at the Palatium Britannicum, renamed the villa of Saint Pudentiana, famous for its mosaic depictions of early Christians. She is the daughter of Rufus and Claudia. Claudius was a frequent visitor, even though he'd sworn to exterminate followers of the Messiah. Doubt even Hollywood would come up with such an unbelievable story, which happens to be true."

Dylan paused to catch his breath and drink some more water. He felt that the audience was with him now, so he took his time, smiling at the chairwoman of the Women's Institute, who'd invited him.

"Absurd as it may seem, whilst the Roman armies were seeking out followers of Christ all over the Roman Empire, Bran, brother-in-law of Joseph, was in Rome with his son Caractacus, whose daughter was married to the half-brother of St Paul. She was already Christian, having being converted by Joseph years before. So where was Joseph, the Nobilis Decurion, the merchant of metals so invaluable to the Roman war effort? Imprisoned in Jerusalem by the future emperor, Vespasian, who would use him as a peace envoy to the Silurians, knowing of his connections to Silurian royalty. Who says life isn't sometimes stranger than fiction? This configuration of circumstance did occur, as in AD 59, when the son of Caractacus, Prince Linus, was elected first bishop of Rome by St Paul. The first Pope was a Welshman! These revelations were common knowledge in Wales a hundred years ago.

"Incredible as it may seem, what took place right under the nose of the Emperor Claudius was that Christianity went from Siluria to Rome, not the other way around, because Joseph came to the kingdom of Bran in Siluria. Joseph's tomb isn't at Glastonbury, but here in South Wales."

Dylan paused. He knew he was skating on thin ice as, while many in the audience were beginning to take an avid interest, others shook their heads or murmured disapprovingly.

"Joseph's sister, Anna, the Enygeus of the Welsh Bruts, the wife of Bran the Blessed, the Fisher King, was Arthur's ancestor, which makes Arthur of the bloodline of Christ. All that I have told you today was common knowledge before the treachery of the Blue Books of 1851, forbidding the teaching of Welsh history.

"So what of Arthur and the inscribed stone found on Caer Caradoc, with its inscription 'Artorius Rex Fili Mauricius'? Or the cross of electrum also found there under archaeological supervision, inscribed with the words 'Pro Anima Arthur', 'For the Soul of Arthur'? Or the stone at Ogmore Castle which states: 'Be it known to God, that Arthur gave this land to Nertat, to Eglwys, and to Bishop Fili'. A land grant on which to establish a monastery, of which thirty-seven have so far been located in South Wales, all were up and running during the turmoil of the sixth century, the Saxon invasions, the northern Picts and the Irish raiders, indicating the violent background of Arthur's time.

"We may have discovered his burial place up there on the windy hillside, now renamed Mynydd Y Gaer. We may have found Merlin in the form of Illtud, and the Holy Trinity in the three rays of the Awen, integral to the Druidic Christian belief. But it doesn't end there, for we have also in the liturgy and sacramental methods used by the Gnostics of Alexandria and the Coptic Church, recognised today to be the closest existing connection to early Christianity. St Anthony, the desert hermit, father of

Celtic Christian monasticism, hailed from Alexandria. And here in South Wales, we have the Roman city and trading port of Caerleon, with its influx of new ideas from across the Roman Empire."

Dylan sensed the audience were becoming very attentive, as no one coughed or went to the loo. He felt he could only go so far with his talk, as many of his conclusions were based on legend and personal insight.

"One thing is certain," he continued, "the Celtic Church was not born during the closing years of the Roman Empire but during the first half of the first century, during the time of Caractacus and Arviragus. Glastonbury was not known by that name until the twelfth century. One hundred excavations in a hundred years have produced nothing earlier than the eighth century when Ina, a Saxon king, built a hut there.

"That the British Church sat predominant at all church synods until the nineteenth century is proof of what I've told you, facts supported and confirmed by Cardinal Baronius, Virgil Polydore, Clement of Alexandria and the Roman historian, Tacitus, as well as the testimony of early Christians, whose works were dismissed by the political Roman religion, which turned Jesus into a god to supersede their own gods for fear of the collapse of the empire.

"I believe that Joseph and his followers came to South Wales and were given land by Arviragus, the regional king. Not just any land, but the sacred burial ground of Neolithic settlers who chose to live and die in an area close to the sea. Ynys Avalonius is in South Wales. *Ynys* not only refers to an island, but to a sacred sanctuary where relics were kept and important people buried, such as Joseph. Avalon was also the sanctuary of Morgan le Fey, where Arthur was taken to be healed of his wounds.

"So what of the Holy Grail you may say? Where is it and what is it? Is it an object or something far more profound? The first to mention the Grail was a sixth-century Welsh bard named Melkin Avalonius, or Maelgwn of Llandaff, both one and the same. The Glastonbury myth is based on Melkin's prophecy, which describes in obtuse Latin the whereabouts of Joseph's marble tomb. X marks the spot, but the spot remains a mystery. Marble in Latin is *mamore*, which means the marble-like quality of calm water, such as a lake or the sea, indicating the location rather than a tomb of marble.

"Melkin composed his prophecy during the middle of the sixth century, when Glastonbury was under Saxon control. Melkin would never have placed Joseph's tomb as being there, because he knew it to be in the heart of the Silurian kingdom of King Arthur. His prophecy describes what he knew of the true location of Joseph's burial. He probably visited there many times, as it would have been common knowledge to such as Arthur and the elite of his day. Maelgwn, a Welsh king, would have been familiar with the stories of the Roman invasion, and of Joseph of Arimathea's return to the family he'd known for years: his brother-in-law Bran, Bran's daughter Eurgain, wife of Aulus Plautius, who together with Joseph, set up the Achan Y Saint at Llanilltud Fawr, possibly the villa built to house Caractacus following his seven years hostage in Rome.

"Melkin states that the Grail or *Gradalis* refers to steps to enlightenment, just as Jesus conveyed to disciples capable of understanding the true meaning of his words, such as Mary Magdalene, which is why he loved her more than the others."

"Do you believe they were married?" asked the chairwoman.

"Most certainly, as you could only become a Rabbi if you were. The Nag Hammadi's Gospel of Phillip states that 'He kissed her on the lips', though the Church will never admit that he was married, as that would undo the fabric of Christianity as we know it."

"Wouldn't that be something," she replied with obvious delight.

"Wouldn't it just," confirmed Dylan.

"So the Grail, or *Gradalis* as you call it, is a way to enlightenment?"

"The Grail is the lost knowledge the Knights of the Round Table were seeking. The quest was to find the *Gradalis*, the lost knowledge, since the Celtic Church was being forced to succumb to the doctrine of the Roman Church, which sought to destroy the teachings of the Druids and the heresy of Pelagius which refuted the doctrine of original sin.

"I believe that the true Grail is hidden somewhere in South Wales. Melkin is quite clear about that. Can you imagine what would happen if it was one day discovered? The repercussions would be as profound as the Grail itself. So with these thoughts I will leave you, even though there's so much more to say, perhaps at some later time, if you will have me."

Low-key handclaps quickly erupted into enthusiastic applause. The chairwoman congratulated him on his revealing aspects of Welsh history of which she was unaware. Dylan felt inspired by the response, though there were many die-hard Christians present who'd give him the go-by, believing that the origin of British Christianity began with Augustine in AD597.

Dylan left the building to walk alongside the Usk, pondering the question: why did the Britons defend their land so vigorously? Why were they willing to die for their beliefs long before they became Christian? The Druidic doctrine of the immortality of the soul? Perhaps there was something special about the land itself. Earth energies and ley-lines were everywhere, criss-crossing arteries of telluric forces, similar in function to our own arteries. Stonehenge and Avebury were erected on nodal points, vortices of earth energies moving in and out of other dimensions where shamans experience visions of future events, a place of no time where all things connect in the underlying matrix of the web of life.

Dylan had delved into his past for clues given by unseen forces whose instrument he was, examining threads of evidence that baffled common-sense perception.

He wished for a swift conclusion to a quest that was pushing him to the edge of reason; fortunately for him his soul-partner was the anchor that held him to the here and now.

19
Beautiful People

The Pre-Raphaelite woman returned several weeks later with a poem about a grieving widower, which she read out to Dylan, whose eyes were red with tears.

"I lost a good friend last week," he said. "Her funeral was yesterday. Your poem has lifted my gloom, cheered me up."

"Glad of that. Just had a feeling. Who was she?"

"Lynn Lauren was the most gifted spiritual medium I ever met, apart from Pamela. A very gentle soul, true-blue as they say."

"Don't know why, but I had a feeling to bring it to show you."

"Thank you. You're very thoughtful."

He noticed how young-looking and full of energy she was, that the light was still with her, extending far beyond her petite form like a living flame. Her flashing blue eyes radiated intelligence, not of the academic kind, but of mind and spirit. Such sensitivity had its price, which only the bold and brave know, an acute vulnerability combined with a deep inner conviction of the true meaning of life, a true warrior of the spirit. He invited her to stay, but she said she had to go.

She left in her wake an aura of peace as Dylan sat back in his chair to recall the euphoria of midsummer at Glastonbury Tor the year before when the wind lifted the Druids' cloaks like birds' wings flapping to the beat of drums as feet danced to the rhythm of Irish pipes. A circle of Druids two-hundred strong bound the summit tight with intent, blessing the land with well-aimed arrows of thought carried by swallows to the four corners. The Cornovi spoke of this, as grove after grove mimed words into the ether where only the spirits dwell. The mimed gesture worked well and caused their archaic selves to join the sacred dance.

As a master of the art of mimicry, Professor Sutton expounded upon Saint Bloody Cochlan's over-zealous popery to the rustic dwellers of that place: "No, no, no, to life, to breath, to singing in the trees, laughing in the sun, playing in the water, living in Nature's heart. No, no, no, to joy, to life—just stern death. We always vote the wrong people in, thinking they know something we don't. A verbal creativity extolling virtues not of a purest heaven but of flagellation, taut sex and choking vowels, exclaiming no gods, no pagan fun. Don't they know that you do not get out of life until it has been enjoyed to the full? Hedge your bets if you must, but the winners' enclosure is for the brave few, and who would know them but their own?"

Many spoke, many danced, many sang the oaths of their creed as the Awens flew in the wind with chalice offerings of wine and water, evaporating into the air like a conjuror's trick as Irish pipes played the Druids down the tor's well-worn slopes. Such is the beauty of these people who stand for humankind, not those sleek-suited ones in grey sitting on a pot of gold having won the wrong prize, but those who were born to win, who recognise their common humanity.

Lucy's brave but cheeky smile, sitting on the slopes, blue eyes twinkling in the sunshine, at peace beneath her restless exterior.

"I am home again," mused Dylan. "After many years in the wilderness, this is where I belong. Oddballs all, but gifted human beings, and I'm happy to be counted amongst them, for sweet joy lives in the hearts of the innocent, whose hard-won knowledge lights a torch for all to see."

Dylan held on to such memories linking the past to the present, as the Kalahari Bushmen carry their past in their stories as a continuity of existence. Our connection to the Earth slips away as mankind moves at the speed of light towards a technological whirlpool of artificial intelligence like runners who see only the blue sky and not the cliff's edge.

Dylan was shaken out of his reverie by the dinging of the shop doorbell.

"Did you get those tarot cards for me?"

Dylan looked into the shining eyes of Wesley, whose perpetual smile would melt the heart of Attila the Hun.

"The lady said she'd get some for me, the tarot with the basic images of the Kabbala, the Tree of Life."

"I expect she's forgotten," replied Dylan. "But I'll get some for you to choose from."

"Thank you, Dylan," he replied. "Just to work with the Kabbala Tree of Life. I'm studying Hebrew at the college—beautiful language, you know. Have learnt so much already of its healing powers. I don't listen to the news any more. Worse than pubs open twenty-four hours a day, the news around the clock, twirping birds in black telling of bad times and death, of sorrow and torture, before rounding off with the cricket news and grinning at the grim weather bulletin—winds across the country, tree-felling gales. Nice-guy weatherman smiles pitifully at the anchorman reeling off the death toll of floods in India."

"Are you still up at St Cadoc's?" asked Dylan, knowing Wesley was often on medication, though nothing quelled his soulful smile and gentle manners.

"I don't believe everything David Icke says; sometimes he's off-beam. UFOs. Had an experience near Caldicot—that's where I'm from. Green stuff by the side of the road. It was this big." He stretched his arms wide. "I put some on my hands and took it to the police station. It made me loopy. I ran around without clothes. That's why I'm here, sectioned."

"Are you still doing the ayahuasca?"

"No, I've given that up since the foo-fighters episode over China."

"Probably the wise thing to do, not good doing it on your own."

Wesley looked at him with wide-open watery eyes innocent as a seal pup, reminding Dylan of Sian who'd come by the day before and sang a Janis Joplin song like an angel, her Mona Lisa smile obviating her private hell. She told him with tearful eyes why she was forbidden to see her nine-year-old son, and how her father left her when she was fifteen. She'd begun taking drugs, which got worse, and she likened herself to a mermaid, her father also, and her third eye, which he plucked out along with her future lives. "The Masons want this," she'd said, even though her father wasn't one of them but a Labour Party organiser who suffered from a cognitive brain malfunction. She'd told her psychiatrist that her cat speaks to her. The psychiatrist asked in what way, and Sian said, "He comes to me, or I to him, because he's feeling cold, so I give him a hug to warm him up." The psychiatrist said she was schizoid because of the way she talked. So she said, "When an athlete talks to himself to psyche himself up for an event, is he schizoid too?" She said the psychiatrist didn't answer.

Dylan wondered what it was they did to people like Wesley and Sian at St Cadoc's and other institutions. Casualties of war, the sensitives who are often healers and seers, clairvoyant and wise, drugged and suppressed with chemicals instead of love and understanding. Sian told him the drugs were meant to shut down her chakras, but she wouldn't let that happen because she knew what they were trying to do.

So many young people with insight were looking for a new way, exploring their own inner dimensions, such as Juliette, the art student, who expressed the feminine in art through her own experiences, saying how the Aborigines could manifest dreams into waking existence, seeing their ancestors or visions of anthroponosis. Jung understood this phenomenon.

"Why are you studying Jung in art?" asked Dylan.

"Because of the images," she replied. "The whole series of paintings and artwork that I have done, I never dreamt I could have when I see them. The ones on greed, fear, superficiality, I use lots of glitter—Glam Rock, it does work too—and slate for despondency. And the others, the paintings on positive things, blues and reds, a picture of the Virgin Mary and Child. Also I found I used alchemical symbols. I don't know how—shapes, lines, I only knew later on after I'd read up on the subject. Jung, Freud, but Jung, oh Jung, yes! I know how they came about into my paintings; the fox woman emerging through, coming out of the feminine psyche, the femme fatale, the powerful woman who destroys. The image is life-size, eight feet tall."

Dylan listened attentively to her words, how she expressed herself in an animated manner. Her dark hair and brown eyes, her slight but dynamic physical form.

"I know that you like to come here to talk, and I enjoy listening to you. You love your art, how you illustrate your emotions. You dig deep, not many do that."

"I do," replied Juliette. "That's because of my pain. My parents think I'm strange. My son Charlie doesn't think so, though his behaviour does worry me sometimes. He's only eight and he says obtuse things that upset people..."

"You mean he's honest?"

"He will say whatever comes into his mind without thinking if he should or not."

"That's to be admired, not worried over."

She smiled. "Thank you. I like sitting with you and talking about my life, my work, my son Charlie. I have my past, negative life in Newport. I have this now — my memories, my time then, my troubled past. Now I know I have these things because of that. Tomorrow is today. What I do, think, breathes tomorrow awake. This is what I do, how I think of me, how I am living now. These layers of my life — oh it's good to talk. Some things must be kept hidden, not for public consumption. I was taken on a journey. I don't know why. My life changed, I took up art, and here I am now. The alchemical aspects of art."

Dylan would never let the memories of these people go. They were just as he, individuals on their own path, seeking answers by looking within. Struggling against conformity, they had one thing in common: they smiled a lot and gave out a loving warmth despite the turmoil of their lives.

20
Llanilltud Fawr

Richard and Dylan descended the steps into the precinct of St Illtud's Church at Llanilltud Fawr. Its fairy-tale setting close to the sea invariably conjured up images of chanting monks, of smoke filtering through thatch and acolytes cultivating the fields.

"Welcome to the greatest monastery in Britain during the Dark Ages," declared Dylan, "where two thousand four hundred monks sang in relays in the perpetual choir of Llanilltud Fawr."

Richard sniffed the air like a dog on the scent. "Wax lyrical all you like, but I don't feel at ease here. I told you on the way of the past-life flashback I had of you and me at the mercy of Illtud."

Dylan was puzzled by his remark. "Difficult to imagine the famous Illtud to be that way."

"Trust me, I know what I saw," replied Richard, puffing on an e-cigarette. "Being back here's like revisiting a crime scene."

Dylan ignored his remark. "This place holds many secrets, this is where my vision of the seven maidens took place fifteen years ago."

"Tell me then," urged Richard.

Dylan related his vision as they sat on the steps of the Pilgrim Cross.

"Some vision," responded Richard. "Now I know where your quest for the Holy Grail comes from. But why seven maidens instead of the nine who guard the Celtic cauldron?"

"Because seven is a sacred number to the Gnostics—seven chakras, seven gateways to alchemical knowledge through gnosis."

"The monk who took you to the two rivers, was he Gildas or Illtud?"

"Gildas," affirmed Dylan. "You've read his *De Excidio*, where he rants on like a madman, hurling biblical reprimands at the kings and warlords..."

"Especially Maelgwn," laughed Richard. "And I know the reason why."

"Why?"

"Gildas was in love with you, infatuated, he and Illtud both. Holy saints? Just human beings with certain sexual preferences."

Dylan frowned, unable to grasp Richard's meaning. "If it was Gildas, then why did he take me to where the treasure is hidden?"

"Because he knows that it was you who wrote the Prophecy."

"But why did Gildas lie about Maelgwn killing his uncle in order to seize the throne of Gwynedd? Was it Gildas the monk who wrote the *De Excidio*, or was it Anselm of Yarrow who wished to derogate the Cymry?"

Dylan felt dizzy and held onto the Pilgrim Cross to steady himself.

"You okay, Dylan?" asked Richard. "You don't look too good."

Dylan shook his head. "I'm alright—just thinking about what you said."

Richard slapped him on the back. "Wake up, Butty, don't let the monk get you down. Been dead fifteen centuries, can't still be pissed off with you."

"Why were you so reluctant to come here today?"

"Past life replay. You and me monks together, Maelgwn and Derfel."

"Okay, so tell me what the hell went on?"

"Maybe it's better you don't know," asserted Richard.

"What crime?" insisted Dylan.

"Buggery! He liked boys."

"Who, Gildas?"

"Both," corrected Richard. "Mad sonofabitch Illtud believed that it was the only way to exorcise the devils out of them. Had his eye on you the moment you arrived, with your long fair hair and body of a Greek god."

"Tell me what happened?" insisted Dylan.

"Sorry to shatter your dreams about the past, but he took you into what he called the hut of initiation. I knew I had to act fast, so I banged my fist on the door, shouting to you to get the hell out of there. Illtud opened the door, yelling into my face that he was doing God's work, that I'd do well to stay away, or he'd have me thrown into the black pool of the sinners..."

"I recall the black pool below the brook, where all the gunk collected and stank like a cesspit."

"That's right, what he referred to as the hell of the damned. And if we didn't bow down to his obedience, to his exorcism of the demons, that would be our fate. Didn't fool me though, I knew his game, what he was up to, believing his own lies, deluded mad buggerer, standing in front of me naked, his scrawny white body scarred by scourging, his black eyes and scraggy beard. Always dunking himself into ice-cold water to suppress his sexual appetite or whipping his body with brambles and nettles. A real nutter, but gifted with an intelligence that was scary. He was scary alright, God's right-hand man who had a penchant for boys."

"What did Maelgwn do?"

"You grabbed your cloak and ran outside."

"You saw this?"

"Clear as day. Not your fault for thinking it was some kind of purification ritual, unaware of what he was about to do. He used his powers of persuasion to convince innocents that this method of initiation had God's blessing.

"Illtud," continued Richard, "son of Biicanus of Brittany, cousin to Arthur and a captain in his army. St Cadoc, who stopped his troops from pillaging his monastery of Llancarvan, persuaded Illtud to become a monk. He abandoned his wife and children to live the life of a hermit in the woods, foraging for food like a wild man. Years later, due to his Druidic training and forceful personality, he became abbot of this monastery, which in those days was called the College of Theodosius."

"I know that he was trained in Brittany by St Germanus, who sent him over here to oust the Pelagian Heresy, yet he fought in Arthur's army."

"Perhaps he thought to dodge the religious task allotted to him by playing the soldier."

"I've no recollection of any of this."

"Why should you?" empathised Richard. "You were far more inclined towards religious studies than personal friendships. Gildas had been 'initiated' long before your arrival..."

"You mean buggered?" cut in Dylan.

"So you made enemies without even knowing it."

"But Gildas accused Maelgwn of buggery also."

"Wishful thinking on his part, as it was you that he wanted to bugger, so he got his revenge that way."

"Bloody hell!" exclaimed Dylan. "So his vituperous accusations were his way of exorcising his own demons."

"You got it," affirmed Richard. "Welcome to the real world of monastic life. Not the golden age of the saints, but a mishmash of individuals with all of their personal baggage and hang ups. Just human beings, Dylan, trapped in their own desires."

"But that doesn't answer the question as to why Gildas chose me to find the treasure."

"Because you were born gifted, whereas most struggle to find their way on the spiritual path, but you were assigned to graft Christianity onto the Druidic tree of knowledge to prevent it from being lost altogether. That's why he's come back to you, to help show the way to the truth of Joseph of Arimathea, which isn't what you think at all, but Joseph made sure that the secret buried with him would stay hidden until such time that it would be accepted by all with open mind and heart." Richard threw a rock into the brook, splashing water over Dylan. "Shatter your illusions, Dylan. They'll only get in the way."

"Okay, I got the message."

"Well, here's another one: find the true meaning of the seven maidens and you will find the true Joseph and the true Christ."

Dylan was beginning to see Joseph in a new light, one that would change his view of the 'Nobilis Decurion' of the Bible. "The White Castle is the mind of Spirit, and we are that mind; it is the mind of humanity that is going through this Great Awakening right now. All the peoples of the world are waking up to a new dawn of love and compassion. You and I have our parts to play. Day by day we plough through self-doubt, searching for the meaning to our lives. We reach out to Spirit, who says, 'Only follow and the rest will follow.'"

"Seems we didn't bump into one another by chance."

"No such thing. So what other memories do you have of that time?"

"Llandaff Cathedral."

"Yes, you told me about that. Any others?"

"Flying over Wales like an eagle, witnessing armed conflicts, warfare between the kingdoms and the Saxons. Opposing armies about to engage and a Druid standing between them, calling on champions from either side to resolve the dispute. Then going north to Anglesey, where the vision ended with the words: 'Marcellinus, the third fateful expedition to Skye. Marcellinus, he who counted hands. Marcellinus Agrippa, the contentious period, sullied by the Church, sore and unhappy years. Marcellinus, Maelgwn Gwynedd, the Servant, Lancelot of fame, from whose bloodline Robert Fitzhammon came. The third fateful expedition to Skye. The hooded priests of Llancarvan.'"

A stony silence followed Dylan's recollection of the vision, declaring himself to be Lancelot.

Richard eyed him questioningly before breaking into laughter. "Why not? Someone had to have been the greatest knight in the world. We've got Merlins on every street corner between here and Land's End. Convincing though, the wording, but who's Marcellinus?"

"Marcellinus was a fourth-century saint who lived on Anglesey, whose name he's assumed for its spiritual connotation."

"What's the ill-fated Skye refer to?"

"The Irish had taken over the island, they were raiding the north into Scotland, and it was the end of the road for Maelgwn."

Richard paused, realising what that meant.

"I was shown where he was buried. Just an ordinary place, nothing special."

"Sullied by the Church?"

"Gildas."

"Of course," confirmed Richard. "But you said the hooded priests of Llancarvan."

"Cadoc's monastery, which isn't far from here, where I've one recollection of facing three men in grey woollen habits sat behind a table, who were reprimanding me for leaving Illtud's monastery to fight the Saxons. I told them that it was my duty to protect my people, not to pray for my own soul but to fight to save all of our souls who would die at the hands of the scum who honour their blood-loving god with murderous ferocity. Pray for the souls of the dead if you must, but barricade your doors, for they are surely coming. Cadoc then accused me of housing devils at Deganwy, referring to the twenty-four bards at Deganwy."

Richard laughed out loud. "Bloody pagan, that's what you are."

Dylan shrugged. "Damn right I was. Still am. So I told them that we are at war, that my bards could prophecy the enemy's movements."

"Bet that went down well."

"They all did it, even Cadoc. They were trained Druids who'd scry the crystal bowl, usually a naturally formed granite bowl."

"Have seen such perfect cups filled with rainwater."

"Merlin prophesied that way." Dylan paused. "I said to Cadoc that we fight or die, that the Saxons have no law but that of blood sacrifice, that we are nothing but forest game to them."

"Was Illtud among them?"

"He was there. So was St Samson, Arthur's nephew, a truly spiritual man who understood my predicament and gave me his blessing. Illtud predicted that the Saxons would overrun the Britons along with the heretics, but he underestimated Arthur's prowess as war leader, so he returned to plan A."

"The Church?"

"Of course," confirmed Dylan. "Illtud was anti-Pelagian and pro-Church of Rome. Maelgwn was Celtic Christian, an initiated Druid, pagan and a Pelagian."

"Just about sums you up now, Dylan,"

"Except I don't have twenty-four bards in our little shop in Caerleon, though the occasional musician or poet performs there, and we did once host a busker's eisteddfod."

"I know the place well. Loved my time there, my artist's studio, meeting people from all over, a regular Piccadilly Circus."

"Tell me about it. No other place in Wales like it. Should be there today, but Pam said to come here with you to hopefully conclude my quest because it's beginning to obsess me."

"You and me both, buddy. I like this ultra-time-travel detective work. Take this fragment of history here — that ruin, just stones, but they have a story to tell." Richard peered inside the ruin. "Done thing in those days, you know."

"What is?"

"The young pupil and his older teacher, what the Druids called suckling from the teat of the wise one."

"Surely that meant receiving knowledge and spiritual nourishment?"

Richard smiled. "You're a great guy, Dylan, but naive. Look at it this way: quid pro quo, no student fees, just buggery. Instead of money, you gave the guy a huggy. So quit dreaming about a golden age that never was, and live life now, because that's what we're here for."

"I do tend to romanticise, but why not? Because when things are gone and done and time leaves a trace of good or bad, I choose to remember the good."

"You think a woman scorned is bad news?" said Richard. "What about a monk screwed by the master, convinced he was Illtud's successor in all things, who slandered Maelgwn to destroy his reputation, even though he knew Maelgwn to be a benefactor of Christian churches in his kingdom?"

"A Druid Pelagian," interjected Dylan, brushing his hands through his hair. "Crazy what we do."

"I was Derfel, and you were Maelgwn. What's mad about that?" Richard laughed, his missing front tooth accentuating his piratical demeanour. "The answer's inside you. That's what the maidens were telling you, because you wrote the prophecy."

"Spiritual Law, the Biblical version of Heaven. The Church teaches that we only have one shot at earthly life, but the Druids say that you have an infinite number to attain spiritual perfection."

"Course you do," said Richard, slapping him on the shoulder. "Loosen up, relax, enjoy life a little."

"The Rose and the Lion conundrum, the lament of the seven maidens calling on me." Dylan stared at the lion carved above the church doorway. "Why couldn't I be searching for Pan's Pipes or a holy cabbage, or some other relic?"

"You carry on wrestling with the ghosts of the past. I'm going inside the church to look at the Arthur stone."

Richard wandered off in the direction of the church, leaving Dylan with his thoughts of ghostly maidens whose voices begged to be heard. The Rose, the gnostic symbol representing the flower of the spirit within, just as the Lion represented the life-force and the courage of one's beliefs. The ancient walled garden stood for ancient values, protected knowledge concealed within the feminine psyche. The maidens dancing along the wall of the white castle displayed meaning by graceful movement, just as the Celtic cauldron contains sacred knowledge of Druidic initiation and Christian mysticism.

Drawn once more to the ruined building he knew so well from long ago, with crumbling mullioned windows, constructed from Roman capitols salvaged from an age of conquest where the heroism of a people defending their land against the might of the Roman Legions, welcomed the incoming tide of Christianity.

From the rubble-filled interior he retrieved a crumpled page from a Bible which was Psalm 45: *'Gird your sword upon your thigh, O mighty one; ride on and prosper in the cause of truth.'* It was a clear message to get his act together.

The Hodnant brook rippled rainbow colours in the dappled sunlight. Tranquillity, meditation and prayer—feelings all too brief in our troubled and often frantic lives, yet he recalled that other life, hungry for soul-food, a banquet of words displayed in colourful exaggeration. Gildas's illuminated book of the Gospels was Llanilltud's prized possession, alongside Plato and Aristotle, Virgil and Homer, Anaxagoras and Aristophanes.

He imagined Maelgwn staring at him through the mullioned window, commanding he put on his sword in the cause of truth, for fear is the smoke that blinds.

Richard approached with an easy gait and upbeat manner. "Found the bugger."

"Arthmael?"

"The very same."

"Except that the stone has been misdated to the eighth century on the premise that the Welsh were incapable of carving stone before then."

"What a joke," said Richard, pointing to the meadow west of the church. "Over there lies the ruins of the monk's dwellings, and no one will ever be allowed to dig unless someone writes a book about the whole thing. People are hungry for the truth."

"You're right. Maybe I will do just that," affirmed Dylan, splashing brook water over his face.

"Good man," said Richard, slapping him on the back. "What's up? You look like you've the troubles of the world on your shoulder."

"I'm okay. Just thinking about what Owain told me years ago."

"Go ahead, I'm listening."

"He said it's very important for the evolution of the whole Universe that our Earth becomes a planet of light, that our planet is a backward little place of no consequence if you compare it to the millions of others in the Universe, but it is still a very important planet, and if this transition fails to take place, it will affect the cosmic evolution of the entire Universe. That's how important this time is, and that's why we

must go through with it and on to the next stage of
the evolutionary process. If we lag behind, then the
rest of the Universe cannot go forward, and the whole
structure could collapse, which is why the success of
the Divine Plan is so important."

"That's true," said Richard. "All life is connected."

"There are millions of highly evolved souls who
are waiting for this transition, the Indigo Children
who are born knowing what to do, waiting for this
planet to begin its journey towards the light."

"Well, let's hope it happens soon," said Richard
wistfully. "We're in a race against time and the
clock's ticking."

"Which makes my quest to find Joseph a mere
distraction."

"All of us have a bit part to play," said Richard.
"All you have to do is allow Spirit to guide you."

"Even though I feel like a puppet on a string."

Richard laughed. "So what do we know, we who
fail to see the big picture? Which is why I consult
Silver Birch, a Native American, whose teachings are
my guide. True knowledge is universal, no matter
what language it's written in."

"The Lion without the Rose is a tree without
roots," said Dylan, pointing to the lion carved high
up on the west chapel. "The present that disowns the
past is a ship without an anchor. Man has delved too
deeply into the nature of things, but not deep enough
into his own psyche, preferring to feed the intellect
with an insatiable quest for the fruit that fell from the
tree in the garden of our origins, where death first
claimed the spirit of man trapped in a never-ending
cycle of incarnation."

Dylan looked closely at the effigy of the lion as
images flooded his mind of the tribulations of the

Druids and the Church of Rome's agenda to destroy the Celtic Church, which went into hiding, disguised in the myth of the Once and Future King, prophesied to return what was lost to the people of the Isle of the Mighty.

"Where will you go from here?" asked Richard.

"Caer Caradoc and the church of St Peters, where the Pro Anima Artorius cross was discovered by Blackett and Wilson. You're welcome to come along."

"Love to, but I'm going to have to take a back-seat for a while."

Dylan looked surprised and disappointed at the same time. "Sure, I understand."

"As I said before, family commitments and the Cwmbran Society. I'm also an artist who has little time to paint."

"You must follow your own star, Richard, as I have to follow mine."

Dylan still felt that he was nowhere near the goal as they drove off. He looked again at the Psalm and knew there was no way out, that he'd no choice but to continue, but to where and in what direction he did not know.

That's when he asked for a sign to show him the way.

21
The Sand Dunes

Dylan returned to their home in Rhiwbina to find Pamela lying prone on the settee, looking pale and forlorn.

"What's the matter?" he asked. "You don't look very well."

She looked up at him. Her blue eyes had lost their usual lustre. "I'm not feeling too well. Had to sit down—my breathing."

He joined her on the settee. "Is it like before?" he asked, thinking of the time she couldn't breathe and he'd called emergency services, who arrived within minutes to give her oxygen—just in time, it seemed.

"Sorry to be like this, I really am." She tried to sit up; Dylan put a cushion behind her. "How was your day with Richard?"

"Good, fruitful, told me things about the past I did not know. We were both there at the same time, it seems, and it wasn't all roses."

She smiled. "Oh, you. You are such a romantic, dreaming your life away."

Dylan frowned. "I try to remember the good and not the bad. Enough of that around as it is, so I focus on the positive to engender that."

She looked at him knowingly. "Some of us have to deal with both. You can't just go off willy-nilly and leave me to it, as you've been doing."

"I know that, but I feel I'm getting close now."

"You said that after your visit to St Llid."

Dylan shifted uncomfortably. "Let me make you a coffee."

"That would be nice."

"Might be a good idea to stop smoking," he said on his way to the kitchen. "I mean both of us."

"I can't, not now," she answered, "not while I feel like this."

"Glad it's Sunday and you weren't at the shop," he said, knowing how much she gave to people who needed her help, talking for hours, often to her detriment. Frequent visitors needed a fix of her energy, which she gave freely. This concerned him, the takers who drained her life-blood. Now she was paying the price.

Dylan handed her a coffee and sat next to her. "It's how it's been all these years at the shop—so many who require our time. Most give as well as take, but some just take. I have tried to warn you."

"I know, but what can I do? I can't turn them away."

"Of course not, and I don't expect you to, but you give so much, often beyond what's necessary, especially to Carol—"

"Whose husband virtually keeps her prisoner," interjected Pamela, "and doesn't even allow her money to do the shopping. He's a mentally abusive control freak, and she's a nervous wreck."

"Yes, I know, but the problem is she comes too often."

"She doesn't mean to; she's desperate for help."

"She is, but she doesn't take your advice and nothing changes. All she knows is that you make her feel better."

"No more, Dylan," she pleaded. "I need to rest."

Dylan walked into the garden to clear the stress of concern. What could he do to make her alright? Sitting on a garden chair, he relaxed and smiled at the birds and butterflies. On a small table rested the book she'd been reading on Edgar Cayce, the trance medium who could heal people who lived thousands of miles away. Pamela loved people enough to know their inner turmoil. She had a natural grace, the poise of inner peace that so many wish for. They saw it in her and wanted it.

"Damn them!" muttered Dylan. "Why can't they leave her alone?"

He walked back into the house to see Pamela sitting upright, smiling. "Thank you for all you do to help; I know your concern for me sometimes gets you down. I don't want you to stop doing what you're doing, as I know how important it is to you..."

"Nothing is as important to me as you," Dylan replied. "I want you to know that."

"I do know, and I do miss going places with you."

"How about we go somewhere tomorrow and forget the shop?"

"We can't afford to take time off when we've bills to pay."

"It'll do you the world of good."

Pamela pondered his suggestion for a little while. "Alright, where to?

"You suggest," said Dylan.

"Merthyr Mawr." Her bright-eyed reply caused Dylan to smile. "Be lovely to go to our favourite place in the sand dunes."

"By the big scots pine?"

"Yes, where the flowers are." Her eyes brightened as she took his hand in hers, the love between them requiring few words.

They headed west, turning south at Pencoed towards the coast. Following the turning lane and crossing the humped-back bridge over the Ogmore, they entered the village of Merthyr Mawr, with its thatched cottages and St Teilo's Church, whose ancient crosses languished in a lean-to, one of which was dedicated to Paulinus, son of Meurig, Uther Pendragon.

"I do love you," Pamela declared as they walked hand in hand away from the car park. "Thirty years, and it seems like a day."

"That's how I feel too."

"So good to be here. The peace."

"Yes." He smiled. "Always the peace."

"This place is very special. You've no idea how special."

"The perfect place to restore our equilibrium."

"That isn't what I meant," she replied. "I'm talking about something quite different."

"It's most definitely a special place," he replied, unable to grasp her meaning.

"Will you look after me when I'm unwell?" she asked.

"You know I will," he replied, his consternation causing him to squeeze her hand.

"Do you mean that?"

"You know I do."

"No matter how bad things get?"

"I promise. But why do you say that? You're feeling a bit weak, that's all."

"I see things. Intuition, call it what you will."

Dylan glanced at her as a feeling of trepidation swept over him.

"Here we are," she smiled. "Let's put the blanket down amongst the flowers."

Dylan placed the blanket on the moss-covered sand by a scots pine. Pamela inhaled its scent, relieved to relax among the tiny blue and yellow violas popping out of the sand.

They lay in the warmth of the late-afternoon sun, but Dylan was troubled, wishing that being here together would last forever. Pamela smiled and held his hand to soothe his misgivings.

"Tell me your thoughts," she asked. "Are you happy being with me?"

"You know I am. Why do you ask?"

"You seem a little distracted of late."

"That's because I've been wrestling with the Melkin Prophecy."

"Then let it go, and allow Spirit to guide you as they always have."

"I do, but it's down to me to figure the spiritual conundrum of the Grail."

"Have you thought that perhaps it isn't the right time, that it might be better to wait a little while?"

"I don't know." His agitation was obvious. "Can we not talk about this just now? It's good just being here, the healing."

"Yes, it's lovely."

They lay side by side, allowing the tranquillity to wash over them. Pamela slid into a delicate sleep as Dylan stared wide-eyed into the future consequences of ill-health. Pamela had been slowing down for some time, a gradual regression that went unnoticed at first.

Walking from the shop to the car was taking longer, and she would occasionally stop, gasping for air.

Pamela awoke with a start. "You okay?" he asked.

"Thought I was somewhere else. Funny old world; one minute here, another minute there."

Dylan smiled with relief. "Don't know where I am half the time either."

"You do live in a dream world most of the time."

"They keep on coming," he replied. "What else can I do?"

"Keep a grip on reality?"

"Which one?"

She smiled. "The one we were born into." She sat up to sip water from a bottle. "You dreamt about me, and I dreamt about you before we met. I saw your face hovering in the bedroom. 'Take it away!' I said, 'I don't want to know.'"

Dylan frowned at the thought of rejection. "Why was that?"

"I'd just come through a terrible relationship and couldn't handle the thought of another one. 'But you will,' said a voice. 'You will.'" She clasped her knees tight and glanced lovingly at Dylan. "And the rest is history."

Dylan chuckled. "Spirit's got a great sense of humour. What a wonderful, amazing life this is. So many levels. It's not surprising we, you and me, wander into dimensions unknown to most, yet accessible to all."

"We are the Law of One, the Power is One. There is only one Power, one Source, one God. We are the Children of Light, Love, Truth and Harmony."

A robin came close to perch on an overhanging oak branch above them, chirping its sweet song.

"Do you remember that dream you had about us?" asked Pamela.

"Which one? There have been so many."

"The one where we're on a rooftop."

"The Etheric Travel Agency?"

"That's the one. Do you remember it?"

Dylan thought hard for several minutes. "We are looking for the goddess of the fish in the water, the trout I tried hard to catch—nimble fellow, swift like a torpedo, luring us ever on. Everywhere a hue and a cry; after us, those blasphemers of the cross, naked, alone and vulnerable on the rooftop of the old Sunday School, and you putting a mantle of gold mail over my chest and shoulders as the only honourable thing to wear, and I place one on you as well, for we are sorely tried for our beliefs..."

"Wonderful!" She smiled.

"Well here's part two," he replied. "For we are sorely tried as the hue and cry goes up ever more strongly as we search for the fish in unknown waters—and then a spark of peace overwhelms us from the azure blue, and we sit atop a flat roof surveying the view between heaven and Earth and the Soul of Man, which in Christ was born to you all, for Christ is the reaper of the field and the catcher of the Goddess fish, a sleek brown trout who goes hither and thither, as swift as the wind and nimble as a zither. Christ came this way, and we are looking for His path."

Pamela clapped her hands. "That's us to a tee."

"We were sat on a flat roof holding up a sign which said: 'The Etheric Travel Agency'."

"That's so funny," she responded, gently touching the delicate petals of a viola in their sanctuary of peace, as she thought of those first days when Spirit brought them together. "I love being with you, Dylan. Feels timeless being together, from the day we first met, sitting in circle holding hands, always a warm feeling. They were jealous of us, the way we were. They said things during the channelling sessions they shouldn't have. So sad."

"My Native American guide, Red Arrow, was angry. I recorded our sessions, as you know, and in one of them was the definite sound of a rattle, not once but twice."

"To ward off negative energy, which is what they use them for. Our time in the circle was bound to end sooner or later because of the jealousy that arose when you and I became close friends."

"Close but apart, that was the way you wanted us to be. It was nine months later that things changed."

Pamela smiled, amused by what had happened next. "We were chaperoned. Whether we were out walking, or sat on a bench talking, they'd be there."

Dylan laughed. "I remember at the time you telling me that they were there."

"Do you remember when we were sat on an old rickety bench in Cefn Onn gardens, and we talked about us being together, and we both agreed to see more of one another so long as there weren't any strings? And before you know it, we were tied in knots with family complications and all kind of things."

"I do remember the no-strings bit. What a joke that was."

"As for being chaperoned, they wanted to make sure our energies wouldn't expand too quickly."

"You sense these things more than me."

"Walt was there with them."

"Walt the healer?"

"Who operated on my thyroid—when he was alive, of course. He ran his finger along my neck like a scalpel and took out my thyroid, which looked like a slug. He squeezed the stuff out of it and put it back, then ran his finger over it to close the wound without leaving a scar. I'd be on thyroxin for the rest of my life if he hadn't done that. So overactive, I was down to six stone, no matter how much I ate."

"I remember you telling me he was a commando who took part in the raid on Peenemünde during the Second World War."

"Yes, they came under heavy fire, and his friend Tommy was killed. Walt was stood against a wall when Tommy appeared, shouting at him to get down. Walt ducked as machine gun bullets raked the wall."

"And how, when they were training in Iceland and he'd be on sentry duty, a wolf would stand on a rock and howl. A woman in the village told them that the wolf only appeared when someone psychic is around. Only he didn't believe it was him and he fired at the wolf, but it kept on howling as the bullets went right through it."

"Not the end of it either. He was captured at Peenemünde and twice escaped the prison camp, so they smashed his feet with their rifle butts to stop him escaping. When the war ended, the surgeons wanted to amputate both feet, but he wouldn't let them and healed himself enough to be able to walk. He became a healer, never charging, only donations, which few gave, but that didn't bother him, as that's the way he was."

"I can imagine," affirmed Dylan.

"The night he died, I was standing in my kitchen making a cup of tea when there was a loud knocking on the kitchen door. I opened it to see Walt standing there with a big grin. He said, 'How's about a cuppa, luv!' I dropped the teapot which smashed into a hundred pieces."

"We truly are such stuff that dreams are made of," said Dylan. "Would've loved to have met him."

"You will one day, in Spirit."

Dylan looked up at the sky. "Why is the world of Spirit so real to us, I wonder? We are dreamers, you and me; we are what we are and nothing more."

"Which is everything," she said, sinking back onto the sand and looking up at the blue sky, feeling happy just lying there, yet a certain discontent fell upon her like a cloud. "What will you do, Dylan? Will you help me when the time comes?"

"How do you mean?" Disconcerted, he looked at her, her eyes misty with emotion.

"You won't go wandering off as you have been, even though I know how important it is for you?"

"You mean Llantwit Major, or Llanilltud Fawr, as I prefer to call it?"

"The vision you had of the maidens was a long time ago."

"Fifteen years to be exact."

"Do you really believe it was the Grail they were referring to?"

"I do."

"And your past life as Maelgwn, is that true also?"

"I'm certain of it, though I wish it weren't."

When the sun dipped below the treetops, they drove away, stopping at Chrissie's market garden at the edge of the village to buy some fresh vegetables. An unusual woman, tall, lithe and beautiful, Chrissie's melodic voice and quiet smile radiated an inner peace.

Continuing on through the village, Pamela reminded him of the time they'd visited the open gardens there on the day of his birthday, when the sun broke through the clouds and they'd meandered about herbaceous borders and walled gardens, reminding him of the ruin hidden amongst the trees close to a chasm.

Crossing the bridge, he glanced at the river, which joined the Ewenny a short distance downstream before entering the sea. Perhaps he felt tired and overly concerned about Pamela's wellbeing, but he was unable to see what was right in front of him. All things happen in their own time, as all things pass on the journey — love, hope, the joy of being alive — but he could not have known that this was the last time they would go to the dunes together.

22

The Garden of Dreams

Dylan wandered about the Ffwrwm sculpture garden, where ivy draped the reliefs of Arthur and Gwenhyver. Opposite, a stone plinth displayed a life-size statue of Mordred inflicting the fatal blow on the Once and Future King. The willow tree draped its greenery over the head of the bull of fertility. 'Do not touch', said the sign, 'for its magic is potent'. The willow would one day split the indomitable Roman wall in two. Nature has its way with empires, which come and go, and we place ourselves before its generative power or perish.

On the pillar between the gates, the Doctor had dared place a plaque declaring Caerleon to be Camelot. His friend, Paul Flynn, the local MP, of great integrity, had once declared to Parliament that Arthur was Welsh. On another occasion he addressed the MPs in what the Speaker deemed to be Welsh, a language forbidden to be spoken there. Ordered to leave by the Speaker, he continued reading before handing to him Chaucer's *Canterbury's Tales*. Paul Flynn had succeeded in bringing to their attention that the indigenous language of the Cymry was forbidden in the hallowed halls of British democracy.

The Lost City of the Legions boasted Taliesin and Talhearn, Merlin and Lucius, the Great Luminary, who taught alongside Druid Christians in a trading port with an influx of people from all over the Empire. It was here that Arthur was crowned by Dubricius, who sat predominant at all synods in recognition of Britain being the first country to declare itself Christian under King Lucius in 179 AD.

Dylan sat beneath the tulip tree to contemplate the spiritual dilemma of those times. Druidism readily accepted the teaching of Christ. Druidism was a way of life that held the soul to be immortal. Celtic warriors fought to uphold their beliefs in the face of pagan Saxons, whose gods demanded military allegiance and blood sacrifice, a culture that would never produce a Taliesin, whose insightful poems astound to this day.

Dylan visualised Excalibur winding its power, serpent-like, around a city famed for its Druidic knowledge, driven deep underground where slept Arthur and his knights. But what if that knowledge awaited the return of the Celtic Spirit, the Golden Age of Saints and Grail Knights who fought to discover the true hero within, whose light became a beacon of illumination in the chapel of the soul?

Dylan wrote down his thoughts along with names and places, creating a map of possibilities regarding the whereabouts of Joseph's tomb, determined to follow the clues to whatever end, though a man alone is prone to the subjective dictates of his own mind.

He closed the notebook and turned to see the Pre-Raphaelite woman standing there, who'd sensed something about this man who was gentle and reserved, serious even.

"Do you know why we feel what we feel? she queried. "We talk of many things, but it is the feeling that counts."

"Can't answer that," replied Dylan. "Though I knew a man who went to Canada as a young man to teach an Ojibway Tribe in the remote northwest. He waited three days at a trading post until two Ojibway arrived in a canoe and beckoned him to go with them. He returned five years later, an honorary member of that tribe, his most profound recollection being when he sat with the chief on a quayside for three days and neither spoke a word."

"How marvellous!"

"He performed the snake dance for us here. A big man who danced as if on air, his gentle movements conveying the grace of a swan in reverence for the snake. The way people move can say much more than words. Our primitive sense of knowing is always with us."

"What is ballet if not the harmonics of movement?" she said, moving her arms in sinuous motion. "I dance every day, and practise yoga. I think the human body is our temple endowed by nature. Why people should abuse such an amazing miracle is beyond me."

"Discontent?" replied Dylan. "Without joy of life, you have nothing."

"I love life—I love everything." She stretched her arms, looking at Dylan watching her. "Don't get me wrong, I have my ups and downs, but deep inside I like myself. It's just other stuff gets in the way."

"Tell me about it," he replied with a chuckle. "It's called life, and life lived to the full is the only way to discover our own strengths."

"That's not what I'm saying. Of course that's so, but something's missing in people's lives, or they wouldn't go about chasing shadows." She sat and stared him straight in the eye. "Anyway, what about you? What are you doing here?"

"The shop— what else?

"But what do you do?"

"I sculpt stone," he said, pointing to the carvings outside the shop.

"I'm impressed," she replied, scrutinising the smooth finish on the head of Bran. "How did you learn to do that?"

"Bought myself a hammer and chisel and just bashed away."

"What do you think this place is?"

"The courtyard?"

"What is it about?"

"What you see—sculptures depicting the legends of Arthur."

"But what else?" she asked, staring into his blue eyes. "There's a kind of energy here. Can't put my finger on it, but I can feel it and it's quite dynamic."

"You really feel that, the healing energy, which is also creative if harnessed properly?"

"I can tell by all the beautiful sculptures that are everywhere."

"Beneath the courtyard is the Praetor Pretoria, gateway to the City of the Legions, intended to be the capital city of the Romans in Britain, except that this was the centre of the most ferocious tribe they'd ever encountered."

"Can just imagine hairy beasties crawling over the walls to pay homage in kind to the Beast of Rome."

Dylan laughed at her humour. "Except those so-called barbarians were highly civilised. Many of them spoke Greek and Latin, even Hebrew. This city exudes knowledge of the ancients."

"I definitely feel it," she replied, warming to his enthusiasm. "Also a gentle vibration."

"Many sense a special quality about this courtyard. The Doctor knew that, which is why he chose this place. A great man, was Russell—sadly no longer with us, though his presence is often quite tangible. Lord of the manor in many ways, having a natural nobility that commanded respect. He was also a very unorthodox doctor reluctant to prescribe pills. I'd often rib him by saying, 'You're a closet Druid on the quiet, aren't you?' He would just smile and walk away. He had a big standing in the community, so orthodoxy was the stance he took, even though he was a deeply spiritual man. You could not be as magnanimous and generous as he and not be, even though he shunned the Church like the plague, calling it Churchianity."

"I also avoid the Church like the plague. Twenty years in the Salvation Army taught me that most of it was based on lies and hypocrisy, so I spent the next twenty years researching the origins of Christianity, determined to make sense of it for myself as I felt confused and betrayed. It was my passion, my goal in life to read everything I could on the Celtic Church. I discovered that today's Christianity is based on falsity and half-truths, denying everyone the truth of what Jesus actually said. You've no idea what real Christianity is until you dig deep into the archives and think for yourself. It is not what they say at all. Jesus was a man, albeit highly evolved, probably an Essene."

Dylan stared at his sandals, listening to her views on the Druids and the Celts, of how the legend of Joseph of Arimathea had little to do with Glastonbury. Her integrity of spirit was alive with an intelligence that searched for indications of hidden truths. He sensed her peace was the path she walked, her passion to know the truth of the past, driven by an inner knowing that was her birthright.

"My name is Gail."

"I'm Dylan."

"Pleasure talking to you."

"Likewise," he replied. "Do please come again, and we shall talk some more. What you say echoes my own thoughts on the subject."

"Yes, I shall." She smiled. "Would love to."

She walked off with a wave and a skip to her step. She had been hurt and was hurting still. An acutely sensitive person, yet she had retained the open innocence of a child. He wondered if she would come again.

With an inward smile, he picked up his mallet and chisel and hammered away on a lump of stone that was destined to become the face of the Grail Maiden.

Dylan arrived home to find Pamela wrapped in a blanket listening to Mozart and reading Edgar Cayce, whose prophetic insights into the human condition are only now understood by acknowledging quantum physics.

They invariably greeted one another with joy, but he could only smile wanly as he dumped his rucksack on the floor, glancing at her sideways, wondering how she was. Her breathing had worsened since their trip to the dunes.

"Smile, Dylan, all is well. It doesn't matter what happens to me, my main concern is you—always has been. We pass through the clouds on wings of fire.

What we believe we are fades away like the petals of a flower, and what is left is what we are."

He could see that she was in a reflective mood and sat silently by her side.

"Let me tell you a story. It is the story of a smile. It isn't the smile of Leonardo's Mona Lisa, serenely enigmatic as it is; it is the smile of unconditional love." She paused to sip some mineral water. "When we first met and sat in circle and we all held hands to pray for guidance from our spirit helpers to help raise our consciousness to be in alignment with theirs, the warmth of your hand in mine was the same warmth of their love for us."

"I remember that well," added Dylan.

"So what is there to be afraid of knowing what we know? We come, we go, we meet and we part, but the love remains. Remember that when I am gone, and you will never be alone, even when guilt and remorse lie heavy on your conscience. We are what we are, Dylan. Even before you are born, you know that you will do things you ought not to. Conduct unbecoming happens to all but the saints who pray for empty vessels to be filled with God's love, especially to those of us who gravitate to the edge of the abyss, curious to know what lies in the depths."

She lit a cigarette even though it wasn't wise for her to smoke, but like Dylan, it afforded her a moment of tranquillity in which to gather her thoughts. "I went there once to rescue a soul from Hell. I took his hand to lead him out, but on the way I saw a bookies and couldn't resist popping in to peek at the horseracing results—because there you can see into the future—but I was pulled back sharply and told off."

They both laughed at the farcical side of a spiritual journey, aware of the dangers that accompany ventures into other dimensions.

"I recalled a few of the results but knew I'd better not follow it through. 'Naughty, naughty,' they said. Tell you what though—I did dream a horse once, Century City, won at twenty to one, helped a lot at that time. So try not to be so hard on yourself; we all fall now and then, it's what makes us the way we are, spurs us on to be good."

Dylan looked downcast, his conscience flickering like a faulty torch.

"So be of good cheer. You have a book to write, a story to tell. They are telling me this because they find it hard to get through to you, except in your dreams, to show you things like a map of the soul. They wish you would wake up to the truth of who you are. Not the soldier king or the slave pauper, but the real you hidden behind the smile of knowing how love is apportioned to levels of understanding."

Dylan stared at a cat on the window ledge looking at him with big eyes, unemotional, yet seeing everything. A cat knows well if you are friend or foe, and sees in the dark at what is hidden. Who is the cat? The cat is he who slumbers through the day when there is work to be done. The cat is he who walks by night when everyone is asleep and he has no one to talk to and he isn't seen, except by the moon, who watches over the pale reflection of the sun. The sun is light and life and the cat is death.

"We smile," continued Pamela, "because our inner light responds to love, which is our essence. All else is illusion, the *maya* of desire, the pit or the candle, or the candle to see inside the pit. All we need to know is already inside us, and it is the smile which is the candle that illuminates our soul, the spirit within."

Sat side by side on the sofa, his reflection in the mirror above the fireplace he'd made from the fallen battlements of a castle, he saw himself on the battlements of his own castle, a psychic facsimile of a man who knew what it was to be a warrior king, a protector of land and its sovereignty, with a soul-deep care for its people. In the simplest terms, he had chosen then, as now, to nurture the fruit that fell to the ground, the golden orb given by the Creator as a salve to heal the wounded spirit of humanity, one that would open the doors of perception to the light that will show the way home.

23

The Grail Maiden

Richard called by at the shop over the ensuing weeks, curious to know how Dylan's Grail search was progressing and to offer his art for sale. One painting in particular caught Dylan's eye. It was of a cross, but what was unusual about it was that its elongated shape, entwined in typical Celtic style, looked more like a female form. Its original, dating from the sixth century, formed a window ledge inside St Brynach's Church at Nevern, next to the inscribed stone of Maglorius, meaning the 'Great Hound', Maelgwn.

Dylan noted its distinct Gnostic flavour, particularly as the brook running alongside the church was named after Arian, a Gnostic Christian, outlawed at the Council of Nicea in 325 AD, when Nicholas of Smyrna objected to Arian's claim to free will and independent thought and punched him on the nose, and that was the end of Arianism.

Nevern rested in a valley close to Carn Ingli, the Hill of Angels, where Brynach experienced visions akin to Moses on Mount Sinai. Carn Ingli's reverse polarity engendered the unusual, as did the Nevern Cross, an Excalibur lookalike.

Richard said he was sorry to hear that Pamela was unwell, and offered to give her healing if she would allow. Dylan said he would suggest it to her, and gave him incense for his healing sanctuary.

Midsummer brought many visitors to Caerleon during its ten-day sculpture symposium, featuring sculptors from as far away as Argentina and China, who'd hack away at three-metre tall tree-trunks to be displayed around the ancient city, once described as a mini-Rome with gold gabled roofs and temples. Gifted sculptors all, but none so gifted as Ed Harrison, the barefoot bear, who'd allow the tree-spirit to guide his adze and chisels to produce an exquisite Rhiannon or a Flower Maiden in oak or white chestnut.

Gail called by as he was putting the final touches to the Grail Maiden, and sat watching his diligent tap-tapping. She seemed like a little pixie, lively and chatty, a welcome relief from worry and care. A frequent visitor during the weeks that followed, divulging more of her knowledge on religion, not always of the Christian kind, she encouraged Dylan to open up his own thoughts, including his efforts to discover the tomb of Joseph. She agreed that the Glastonbury mythos was fake, that Joseph was somewhere in South Wales.

Between the shop and caring for Pamela, they managed excursions to St Fagan's and Llandaff, Capel Llanilltern and St George's, whose two-thousand-year-old yew tree she climbed like a monkey, quite at home in the natural world, playful and humorous, fun-loving one moment, serious the next, a curious mixture of adult and child.

She was keen to know more about the Circle of Prophecy, asking if they could go there. She needed to know if it felt right and was not some daydreamer's fiction caught up in a miasma of wishful thinking. Dylan wasn't sure either, which was why he needed a Grail Maiden to help attain the vision necessary to maintain a balance between fact and fantasy, airy Gemini that he was, a walker between worlds.

When the clouds roll in from the east and the snow begins to fall, where are we then? Do we stand alone against the blizzards to come? Are we ever alone?

She walks through the snow; Her smile melts the snow. We think we feel Her warmth, Her heat melts ice, She is the spirit inside us. She gave us life—She walks with us always—She is the Mother—She is the season of winter, spring, summer. She hides Her face from men of power. She is illusive. She is the love in the eyes of a child. She is our Mother, She is the Universe, She is the Goddess of Creation, She is the First and the Last, She is Sovereignty.

There were no bells this time, no harps or voices, no sound but the rustle of leaves dancing to the gentle breeze, the oaks of the cor touching one another, enclosing the circle.

Gail came and stood by his side. "Look," she said, pointing upwards to the arms of the sycamore tree which grew in the centre. "Do you see what I see—the branches spiralling clockwise? What kind of energy could do that?" She looked around at the circle of oaks. "What is this place?"

"A sacred *temenos* of the Druids, a circle of prophecy where no man dare lie, where kings were crowned and marriages took place beneath the Eye of God."

"Magic, then."

"Maybe."

"This place is special," she said with an awed smile. "And the church is named after Joseph of Arimathea?"

"Llid, the Man from Israel, who the ancient Bruts call Joseph. Not only he, but Aristobolus, son of Herod Antipas, and Simon Magus, and Mary Cleopas. Siluria was the heartland of Bran the Fisher King whose son, Arviragus, gave them Ynys Witrin, the 'Isle of Glass'."

"Do you know where it is, this Isle of Glass?"

"Yes, a monk told me that there was a treasure buried there."

"A monk?"

"Yes, in a vision."

"A dead one then?"

"Fifteen hundred years dead."

"So you do know where it is."

"Not far away," he answered. "I'd been there several times without realising its importance."

"Many times and did not know it?"

"Haven't told you the whole story. I needed to know how you felt, that you didn't think I was deluding myself."

"I'm here, aren't I? Seeing what you see, feeling what you feel, standing in this ancient earthworks that whispers to us of times past."

"Do you?" asked Dylan.

"What?"

"Hear the trees?"

"Yes, something here has been shut away for a long time." She stood still, listening intently. "The trees stand guard, watching over us. We must be careful. They say this ground is sacred. It is a miracle it is still here. No one knows about this place. They say that you alone have the insight, that you must treat it with great respect. The wheel of the sun points to where you have been in the past; that this is how they communicate with you."

She broke off suddenly, looking around as if for danger. Dylan smiled at her dramatic posture as he scratched a cross on the ground with his staff.

"Rabbits burrow for a reason, to keep warm and protect themselves, and you must do the same. The journey will take you where your feet walked in the past. Your intuition is your divining rod. The demon of doubt will laugh if you imagine that love lives in every corner to welcome strangers such as yourself. They say you know but are afraid. What are you afraid of, Dylan?"

"That I will fail, as I failed once before."

"But you didn't. You did what was necessary. There would be no story to tell otherwise. If it isn't lost, it cannot be found, and if it cannot be found, it cannot be written about."

Dylan was shocked to hear those words again. "Who told you that?"

"What?"

"What you just said?"

"I don't know—something came over me. I thought it was the wind." She held on to the sycamore tree. "I feel dizzy. What's going on? Why is this place so alive?"

"We know why."

"Do you know?"

"Know what?"

"That you're right to believe in your intuition. You've been given something special, even though you don't feel special. Will you go to the other place where the treasure is and look around you? Not just look, but see? Because the answer lies in the trees."

"Are you okay?" he asked anxiously. "You've gone quite pale."

"I need some water," she gasped, hugging the tree of Isis.

Dylan gave her water he'd collected from the spring. "Take it easy, Gail. I didn't bring you here to lose you to the spirits that haunt this place."

"You saw them, didn't you?"

"Who?"

"The maidens, when you were here last."

Dylan refused to believe that she knew.

"There's something that you need to tell me, the link from then to now, your past, who you were."

Dylan pondered her question, knowing it would be difficult to answer without losing all credibility in her eyes, yet she was open minded and trusted him. "I've had many dreams and visions, some relating to past lives. Peeking through the gateway, as it were."

"I'm listening."

"Like a bird, I fly over Wales. I see armies facing each other on opposite sides of a valley. A Druid walks between them, tells each side to choose a champion to fight single combat to decide which side wins. They fight and he goes away. Druids had the power to do that. They are peacemakers.

"I go further north, over hills and mountains. Many battles, the Saxons, the Irish, much bloodshed and turmoil. I continue on my journey to the Kingdom of Gwynedd, then on to Anglesey, where I board a ship bound for the Isle of Skye. The Irish were using the island as a base to attack the Scottish mainland."

"What else?"

"Words."

"Tell me – I want to know."

"Marcellinus, the fateful third expedition to Skye. Marcellinus, he who counted hands. Marcellinus Agrippa, the contentious period, sullied by the Church and sore and unhappy years. Marcellinus, Maelgwn of Gwynedd, the Servant, Lancelot of fame, from whose bloodline Robert Fitzhammon came. The fateful third expedition to Skye. The hooded priests of Llancarvan."

She looked into his eyes. "I believe you."

"You do?"

"Of course." She smiled. "Always knew that there was something about you."

"Which could apply to millions of others."

"Don't think so," she replied. "You possess a certain quality, something indefinable, except I know you to be a blithering idiot as well as brilliant."

Dylan laughed, delighted by her version of himself. "You've got me sussed."

"Not really," she said, "just a woman who sees what a man dreams — only she knows that it's mostly a load of old cobblers. We keep the world going. Men see only their own egos."

"Do you put me in that category?"

"No, you passed through that gateway long ago. You are who you say you are. You have come back to finish something. We are together for a reason. So tell me more about Maelgwn, aka Lancelot?"

"Maelgwn was King of Gwynedd. L'ancelot is Norman French for 'The Servant', as Maelgwn served Arthur with his army in North Wales. Taliesin wrote of him, 'It was Maelgwn that I saw with piercing weapons before the master of the fair herd, and severely did the embattled warriors pierce in the bloody enclosure.'"

"Were you really the bravest knight in the whole world?"

"You joke," replied Dylan. "I am who I am, whoever that is."

"Stop playing it down; this is serious. It's who you are now that's brought us here."

"Just trying to make light of nonsensical circumstance... except you don't think it is."

"How many have a purpose such as yourself? How many know what to do with their lives to make it worthwhile for others to benefit from?"

Dylan shook his head. "I don't think like that, I just do what I do."

"Then consider yourself fortunate."

Joke as he might at the absurdity of who he was, she saw in him a noble bravery in a world at war with the truth of Spirit, a world of military power and the pillaging of human dignity, measured by percentage of use in the Dow-Jones Index.

"Thank you for not laughing."

"You fear ridicule too much. You shouldn't. I'm sure others have stranger experiences than you."

"Most of them are at St Cadoc's, sedated."

"So who was Marcellinus?" she asked, ignoring his remark.

"A Gnostic Christian who lived in Anglesey during the fourth century. Maelgwn adopted the name."

"Why the Isle of Skye?"

"The Irish had massacred its people. No mercy, no god but glory in battle, even though Patrick had set the Christian torch alight many years before."

"And who were the hooded priests of Llancarvan?"

"Followers of St Cadoc, who was more radically Roman than Illtud. He opposed the teachings of Pelagius, denouncing Maelgwn as a heretic and abuser, though it was they who were the abusers by forcing the doctrine of original sin into the hearts and minds of the innocent."

"Does time not heal? she asked, sensing the anguish of his past.

"We came here many times, me and Pamela. Always the peace, something not quite of this world." Dylan walked away to sit beneath an oak tree to reminisce about those happy times.

"So what are we doing here?" she queried, sensing his change of mood.

"I believe it to be the Circle of Prophecy mentioned by Melkin."

"You told tell me a bit about him, this Melkin, but who was he?"

"A sixth-century bard who prophesised the location of Joseph's Tomb. '*Insula avalonis avida funere paganorum preceteris in orbe as sepulturam eorum omnium, sperulis propheciae vaticinantibus decorata.*'"

"I know a little Latin, but what does it mean?"

"The Isle of Avalon, greedy for the death of pagans more than all other places in the world, decorated beyond all others by portentous spheres of prophecy."

"Feels pretty portentous to me," she said, sweeping her arms in a circle.

"Stonehenge or Avebury are the usual suspects, as so many conclude, when it's so obvious it isn't Glastonbury, which wasn't even built until the twelfth century. Melkin wrote the prophecy when England was Saxon. Not only that, but Maelgwn was many years at Llanilltud's monastery, a mere seven miles south-east from here. I think he knew all along where it was."

"You're right. It must have been familiar to him."

"Also the Prophecy is couched in barely translatable Latin, a deliberate ploy intended to mislead its reader."

"Very clever."

"More than clever if you consider the time-frame."

"How do you mean?"

"By constructing the wording in such a way that it could only ever properly be understood by someone who was intimately aware of its underlying clues, someone so familiar with the locale that they would have had to have lived then."

"Such as Maelgwn?"

Dylan's enigmatic smile unnerved her.

"Do you think Maelgwn would have known Melkin?"

Dylan smiled like a cat who'd got the cream.

"After all, both of them were bards."

"Yes they were," he acknowledged.

"Druids then?"

"Undoubtedly."

"Stop smiling, you're playing with me."

"Melkin was also known as Maelgwn of Llandaff."

She blinked hard. "What?"

"Melkin and Maelgwn were the same person."

"Hang on, let's get this straight—you mean it was you who wrote the Prophecy?"

"Yes."

She sat on dead leaves under the sycamore tree, trying to make sense of Dylan's declaration. "Why didn't you tell me?"

"No reason, other than I find it hard to figure myself. It's enough to have been one of them, never mind both."

She smiled at his confusion. "I'd find that pretty difficult to come to terms with also, even though it simplifies your quest somewhat, the fact that you wrote the Prophecy under a pseudonym."

"I didn't, it's just the name got changed through mistranslation. Maelgwn is Welsh, Melkin is English. Sort of thing that happens when semi-literate monks tackle a language other than their own."

"Intimately aware of the clues, the underlying meaning, isn't that what you said?"

"Yes, which is why I know this place to be a very important pointer to the whereabouts of Joseph's burial site."

"And the whole of the vale is your territory, so to speak?"

"I've lived in Glamorgan all my life; I know practically every inch of the vale. Has always fascinated me, even though I'd assumed King Arthur to be either a myth, or that he was from the West Country."

"Me too. The English did a good job usurping our history."

"Which most still believe." Dylan leaned against an oak tree in deep thought. "Here's a question for you. Why this place? Why is that church, situated next to this prehistoric earthworks, named after Llid the Israelite, who the ancient records say is Joseph of Arimathea?"

"Because he was here with Eurgain."

"The Harleian Manuscripts record Joseph arriving here with Eurgain, sister of Caractacus, from Rome. The same Eurgain who married the commander of the Roman armies in Britain, Aulus Plautius. Claudius, the Emperor, hoped to wed the warring Silurians through marriage to resolve the conflict."

"Makes sense," said Gail.

"The manuscript states that she founded Achan y Sant near Llanilltud Fawr, whose original name was Caerworgan, the Cor of Eurgain, which I believe to be Caermead, the Roman villa."

"Isn't Llanilltud where your vision of the maidens took place?"

"Yes, it is. Which is why I believe early Christianity was deeply Gnostic. Eurgain was a princess of the ruling family of Siluria. She would have received a good education. Her sister, Gladys, who married a Roman senator, spoke fluent Greek. Roman poets called her Pomponia Graecina."

"So much for ignorant barbarians, as they would have us believe." She slapped her hands on her knees in anger. "Makes me so mad, the lies they teach us of history. Of course, the Romans were highly civilised — so much so that the slaughter in the Colosseum continued for a further two hundred years after Constantine made Christianity the official religion of the Roman Empire, and it was the so-called barbarians who shut it down after capturing the Eternal City."

"Makes you think, huh? About the rest of the lies we've been taught."

"Reminds me why I turned away from my own indoctrination."

"You surely did," he laughed, observing how overwrought she'd become.

"So if it was you who wrote the prophecy, then you must know where he's buried?"

"No, it's never as simple as that. Past lives are a locked door through which you are only allowed to peek, and only then when it is of worth not to yourself but to others. It's like being born the son of a millionaire—you don't have to work for a living, it's all there for you, but you'd rot inside because life is meant to be full of challenges, it's how we grow. So no, I recall very little, because that's how it's meant to be."

"You're right about past lives being a locked door. They'd only get in the way of living truly in the now." Gail laughed. "Your memory's crap anyway, and I know how muddle-headed you can be."

"Have difficulty recalling what I did yesterday, let alone fifteen centuries ago. We stumbled upon this place by chance, being off the beaten track and invisible from the road. Pamela's always been the guiding light of my life. We'd picnic on the grass as parishioners passed by, curious as to why we were there. The lady vicar even invited us in one time."

"Did you?"

"We politely declined her invitation."

"The Circle of Prophecy, how does it relate to Joseph's tomb?"

"Only indirectly, as an indicator to its location."

"Which you deduce to be close to where we are now?"

"I do."

"Do you know where that is?" she said, staring up at the twisting branches of the sycamore tree. "Have you seen the spiralling branches of this sycamore? Is that normal? Is this place normal? Is anything you or I do normal? I don't think so."

Dylan observed numerous long-dead oak stumps lining the perimeter, as if replacement oaks had been planted in succession over centuries. Who else but the Druids would ensure its continuity as a sacred *temenos*? Dylan deduced that the old wise ones were still around, keeping their age-old flame burning.

Gail looked thoughtful, and wore the crown of serious contemplation. "Listen to me, Dylan. All my life I have asked questions — who am I, and suchlike. I grew up in the Salvation Army and walked away when I was twenty-one. Couldn't take the hypocrisy any longer, so I just left, and I've been on a quest ever since to discover the truth behind Christianity. I've read and thought my way through a maze of conflicting notions as to what the blooming church is all about, and, like you, I've come to the conclusion that the first church was the Celtic Church. Many disciples came to Wales, possibly to this very place. That's why I know what you say is true, that you know where it all began."

Dylan absorbed the meaning of her words, her soulful purpose to discover the truth despite her past so fraught with obstacle and contradiction, the way of the crooked path of discontent that questions the whys and wherefores of our lives.

They stood staring at each other for a full minute, their gaze locked in mutual understanding.

"When we go to the two rivers," said Dylan, "I shall tell you what I know, but we need to proceed with caution, as there are certain elements who will stop us in our tracks."

"I'm very much aware the uproar the discovery of his tomb will cause. The Church—"

"Not to mention the Vatican," interjected Dylan. "We need to be careful, is all."

"When we go to the rivers, I'll collect some pebbles."

"Pebbles?" queried Dylan.

"I like pebbles."

"You're so funny," he replied. "Here we are talking about Joseph of Arimathea, and the repercussions that will surely follow if we discover his tomb, and you want to collect pebbles?"

"I do—I love pebbles."

"Come on, Grail Maiden," he said, touching her affectionately on her shoulder. "Time to leave this place to its guardians."

"I am your guide, you know."

"Yes, I know."

"I will follow you all the way."

"I know you will—you are the Grail Maiden."

"Every Grail Knight should have one," she said.

She ran around the cor waving her arms and dancing like a child full of glee, yelling "yippee!" and touching the trees.

Dylan sat on a tree stump, watching a creature of nature dance with joy. She ran up to him, her eyes bright with passion. "We've been to Llandaff Cathedral, Capel Llanilltern and St Fagan's. Loved it there by the lagoon under the yew tree. Shame no one knows about the ruin by the lakes, no marker to say that it is the site of an ancient chapel."

"It isn't the historical remains but what they convey, such as touching a stone that someone long ago carved."

"You mean like vibrations through time?"

"There was once a shrine to Joseph at St Fagan's, long gone now, of course. So much of our past destroyed. So many dreams I can't recall, hanging over me like ghosts, haunting my days and nights. I wish I were free of them; they give me no rest..."

"But what an adventure."

"An adventure into madness."

"You're looking at it the wrong way up. You've been called to do something important."

"But what if it's all hooey?"

"Only one way to find out," she asserted.

"What, to prove Christianity was established here by Joseph and Eurgain in 59 AD? Though Gildas stipulated 37 AD, which could refer to when Joseph's sister, Enygeus, married Bran."

"And if you believe this to be the Circle mentioned by Melkin, whose prophecy you've yet to properly explain..."

"Wish I could," he answered with a gesture of surrender. "It's a baffling riddle, even to me."

"Then put on your armour and your sword and battle alongside this wild Celtic woman you call your Grail Maiden, and go forth to find what has been lost."

"Grail Maiden's what you are," affirmed Dylan humorously. "So let us part from here with a prayer of thanks and leave this cor in the care of the guardian spirits."

"When will you take me to Avalon?"

"Soon."

They left the earthwork to the squirrels and badgers sniffing for nuts and worms around the oak trees, whose roots reached downward to the roots of the sycamores, touching one another like brothers and sisters in a sacred dance. Imprints of the past are like the flickering images of an old movie, whose garbled soundtrack muffles the voices of actors long gone. What gossamer-like threads do they leave behind for us who follow in their wake?

24
Lady of the Lake

Dylan had long since left the world of the Druids, yet longed to be with them at Beltane and Samhain, or Imbolc in February with snow on the ground and ice on the water, trees stripped bare as the earth sleeps and the first buds of spring appear, green shoots peeping cautiously out of cold soil. Bodies huddled around a fire, bright eyes joyful to be together again, talking of the coming spring, waiting for the ceremony of Brigida to begin in the wooded hills where streams cascade over rocks, gurgling over dead leaves and fallen branches, clearing remnants of the past, just as we let fall the outmoded in ourselves. What Nature accomplishes with ease, we often resist, wishing to hang on to insubstantial memories that block the way to the new and the now.

He missed them one and all, under the sky and the all-seeing eye, naked and vulnerable, willing to stand alone if need be, knowing the joy of joining and the pain of separation that inevitably follows, seeking out quiet places in the hills and valleys beyond the sound of progress that tramples the land with ever more modes of destruction.

Pamela had recovered sufficiently to allow him more free time. She seemed not to mind Gail taking him on his Grail-hunting jaunts, a kind of taxi service as he didn't drive. Prior to their visit to the Cor of St Llid, he'd dreamt of a lake in the Rhigos Mountains and felt an urge to go there, as if something was calling him. As it was a Sunday and the shop was closed, he caught a train to Hirwaun, the nearest stop to the Rhigos. Pamela and Dylan had discovered the lake by chance some years before. It was only a small lake, yet it felt special, set deep in the Rhigos Mountains of Hirwaun. Walking through forestry land of pine so thick barely a sun's ray hit the ground, suddenly there it was. Llyn Fach, as opposed to its big sister, Llyn Fawr, three miles to the east, which when converted into a reservoir a century before, produced swords and shields, bronze armbands and cauldrons, Druid offerings to the Goddess of the Lake.

They'd peered over the edge of the escarpment to the lake below. It was a long way down, but they skidded along a narrow fissure, holding onto roots and heather. They loved their adventures into the unknown. They say a little danger is good for the soul, an antidote to day-to-day existence.

Pamela and Dylan had slid on the mud until they hit the bottom. The lake had looked serene. Pamela had smiled. Swallows skimmed the surface, a poet's delight. Dylan pointed to two nearby cairns some nine feet tall. Kingly burials, he thought, and went to investigate.

Pamela was always good company as they walked together in silence, fullness of feeling always with them. Words—what are they but superfluous phonetics at such times as these?

They circled the lake to its outflow, where conifers partially shielded the Plain of Argyngroeg, sloping gently upward towards the Brecon Beacons. Flowers were abundant; heather and gorse had shed their offering to the future.

Pamela, awed by the view, looked at Dylan and said: "God is saying, 'Love me, for I create beautiful things.'"

He dreamt of a beautiful maiden with long fair hair who stood at the water's edge, a sword concealed beneath her white gown, barely touching the water which was clear and deep. '*Rex Omni Gloria*', 'Glory to the King' — so the dream told him, before she pointed the way to King Arthur's treasure, which was over boggy ground towards a castle, now a well-known landmark to the south, frequently visited, built atop a Roman fort.

Ten days later, Dylan pushed through the dense forestry to stand on the escarpment overlooking the lake. Nothing had changed, though sections of trees had been cut, leaving stumps protruding from the soil like amputated arms.

The escarpment enclosed a semicircle of rock and heather, stunted oak and mountain ash. Cascading waterfalls tumbled over craggy outcrops into the lake two-hundred feet below. Dylan descended down a narrow gulley, whose running water threatened to tip him into the lake of the Goddess, hungry for an offering to her sovereignty. Holding on to roots and heather, he slid to the bottom, where the cairns concealed the bones of the lords who once ruled this land.

Dylan skirted around the lake to where a wall of dressed stone served as a barrier and also a causeway leading to the centre of the lake. The hot summer sun made him sweat as mosquitoes stung. A peregrine falcon nesting on a rocky ledge swooped by, its prey vanishing into the conifers.

Dizzy from heat, he splashed water over his face and neck, wondering what had caused his sudden shaking, when a feminine voice told him to "Go to the centre of the lake and see the broken chariots and the vessels of silver and gold, and then the chains that bind the soul to that time shall be broken." He did not know if they were his own thoughts or someone else's; it mattered little, as such promptings were his way of venturing into metaphoric deep waters.

Wading naked along the causeway just below the surface, he paused halfway and asked the Goddess to protect him in his search for the truth of the past that so many had fought and died for. At the bottom of the lake, pebbles rippled in the sunlight that glinted on the silver scales of small fish, revealing objects protruding through the silt, some oval, others round as misshapen chariot wheels and pointed weapons, barely visible after two thousand years lying undisturbed in the silt.

Llyn Fach offered its secrets to Dylan, but would he accept them to prove the validity of his quest and so mar the beauty of this place? The Druids had come and gone, their beliefs long submerged with their treasures into the silt of time, offerings to the Goddess of Wisdom, for whilst they believed in one androgynous Great Spirit, they also believed in a multiplicity of deities imbued with the living essence of the One, reflecting Mother Nature's diversity as a reflection of life in all its forms.

Dylan stood in the centre of the lake to offer up a prayer: "Nature is beautiful. The people were beautiful, what held them together was beautiful. Their knowledge of the true dignity of man was beautiful. This day by the water of the lake is beautiful."

25

Ynyswitrin

The third day of the new moon arrived, when swallows gather for their long journey home to Africa, when the sun falls low in the sky and waves lap the sand where the river flows into the sea, and swans and Canada geese proclaim their riotous chorus and dunes shelter the sinking sun to balance the moon rising in the east on this autumnal equinox day.

A ruined castle tottered on the banks of the Ewenny, a reminder of the power and authority of the once-mighty Norman lords. An inscribed stone standing between the west wall and the river boldly stated: 'Be it known that Arthur gave this land to God, to Nertat, to Eglwys and to Bishop Fili'. It was discovered lying face down, the stone over which had walked the usurpers of Arthur's kingdom. On the hill flanking the valley to the east, Celtic warrior burials had been unearthed with armour, swords and shields, whose helmets of gold and silver surpassed in beauty those of Sutton Hoo.

Over to the west, mighty dunes sang hymns to pagan burials in sandy hollows and mounds clustered around a spring welling up from deep below, forming a lake for wildfowl in a sandy desert. The Ewenny

ran smoothly alongside the castle where the White
Lady of legend kept a watchful eye on those who
came searching for the treasure, but the man and
woman who stood at the confluence of the Ewenny
and the Ogmore were looking for a different treasure,
perhaps not even of this world.

"Welcome to Avalon," declared Dylan.

"This is Avalon?" responded Gail. "But isn't
Avalon an island?"

"Ynys Avalonius refers to a sacred enclosure
where the relics of a saint are kept, or the burial
place of a very important person. Here where the
rivers join forms the 'V'-shaped sacred enclosure of
the Divine Feminine. It can also mean a rising dry
spot, such as sand dunes."

"You said Merthyr Mawr means Great Martyr...
Do you think it refers to Joseph?"

"Who knows?" Dylan shrugged. "The Ewenny
once joined the Ogmore upstream by the footbridge,
where two standing stones stood by the Roman road
leading to the lost Roman city of Bomio."

Gail gazed at the surrounding meadows on which
horses grazed and teepees were pitched below the
Pelican Inn.

They crossed over the stepping stones to the
opposite side of the river, where a path meandered
towards the village of Merthyr Mawr, where ancient
inscribed stones set into the floor of a lean-to behind
the church of Teilo gave credence to the founding of
a monastery on land bequeathed by Arthur.

"If this is Avalon then where are the apple trees?"
asked Gail.

Amused by her question, Dylan said, "Glamorgan
was once known as the Garden of Wales, whose
apples were sent to the king's table in London."

"You're full of surprises, aren't you?" she replied. "Apart from apples, what else makes you think this is Avalon?"

"Firstly," said Dylan, plucking a piece of pottery from an earthen bank, "Avalon's not just this place but the whole of Glamorgan. Do you remember what I told you the other day about the twelve hides of land given to Joseph by Arviragus, whose original name wasn't Avalon but Ynyswitrin?"

"Which means?"

"Isle of Glass."

"Okay, but where's the glass?"

"The sand dunes — Look, what do you see?"

Gail stared at the dunes sparkling in the evening sun.

"Silica!" he said, triumphant. "From which glass is made. Witryn derives from the Latin *vitrium*."

"They do look glassy," she concurred, now with his train of thought, but careful not to make things fit out of whimsical notions.

"You see this," he said, handing her the piece of pottery. "How old do you think it is?"

"No idea," she said. "Nice brown and yellow colours though."

"Slipware, from the time this bank was constructed in the sixteenth century when the Ogmore was diverted. What we require is a different method of dating, one based more on conjecture than radio-carbon dating, one that relies on a fifteen hundred year old prophecy, the first line of which reads: 'The Isle of Avalon, greedy for the death of pagans, more than all other places in the world.'"

"Which means?"

"A pagan cemetery, such as the hundreds of Neolithic burials in the sand dunes, cremated bones in grooved-ware urns, complete skeletons and artefacts."

"Makes perfect sense — except this isn't Avalon?"

"Ynys is a mutable word that can mean either an island or land between two rivers forming a 'v'-shaped sacred enclosure or *temenos*. A calm sea can also appear glassy as in the Latin word *mamore*, generally interpreted as meaning a marble tomb, hence Joseph is buried in a marble tomb in the Glassy Isle."

"Glastonbury?"

"Don't shatter my illusions just yet. The words of the prophecy are difficult to tie down to any single location. Avalon is the healing sanctuary of Morgan le Fey and her twelve sisters. Llantarnam Abbey also has the 'V' shape between two rivers, but that wasn't it, being so far from the sea."

"You seem certain this is where the monk took you."

"I am," affirmed Dylan. "Two months ago, Pamela and I went to our favourite spot in the dunes. She reminded me of the open garden day, and what we'd seen that day, and the more I reflected on it, the more I was convinced there was a mystery there waiting to be uncovered."

"Where is that from here?"

Dylan pointed to a wooded copse on a hill to the north. "There."

"And what do you think is there?"

"Do you recall when we were at the Cor of Llid and you went into some kind of trance, and you said to me, 'look to the trees'?"

"Vaguely."

"Which makes sense now that the pieces are beginning to fall together."

"All seems to fit, the dunes, the rivers forming a triangle... but if the river was diverted then the sanctuary could be further upstream."

"The standing stones stood close to the Roman road just beyond the castle, so it might well be further upstream, but rivers change course over the centuries, especially one so close to sand dunes."

Put off by her unwavering gaze, he looked away. "What have we got? The Circle of portentous prophecy, which is the Cor of Llid. The burial place of the pagans, which is here. Topographical clues five miles apart, which leaves a lot of unexplored territory, except..."

"Except what?"

"Conjecture's an unreliable master when convinced of its own conclusions." He pointed to a group of submerged megaliths in the river opposite the outflow of a sewage works discharging its waste like an impudent intruder with bad breath. "They're what's left of a stone circle that once stood here before the river claimed them, just like us in a world of shifting sands that threaten our very existence. What we are doing will be lost if we don't put the pieces together. Others have tried and been way off the mark because Glastonbury draws them like a magnet."

"So is the treasure here or somewhere else?"

"Sorry, you've lost me," he said, preoccupied with his thoughts.

"The treasure," she repeated. "Is it here?"

He shook his head. "I honestly don't know. If I knew, I'd know what the treasure is. It isn't earthly treasure—that I do know."

"The monk told you, but you forgot to listen because of the maidens."

He thought he knew what she meant, that the maidens were a distraction, which was why the monk had taken him to this place, because the treasure was the important thing, that the meaning of the maidens' lament of the Rose and the Lion would be resolved when the treasure was found.

"Avalon!" Gail yelled, scaring Canada geese downstream towards the sea. "You were a bard and author of three books relating to King Arthur and the Round Table, whose prophecy of Joseph was supposedly received by an angel?"

"Which may well be true, as angels—or what we nowadays refer to as spirit guides—have told me things."

"I have a thought," said Gail, fingering her chin.

"Okay, but don't give yourself a headache," joked Dylan.

"Funny," she replied, mocking his jibe. "Avalon is associated with Joseph, yeah? And Arthur, who was taken to the Isle of Avalon to be healed of his wounds by Morgana le Fey. So am I right in thinking Arthur could be buried here as well?"

"But not by Morgana, but by Illtud, if Nennius's story is true."

"Make-believe myth surely?"

"Rumours plus time create myths and legends," he answered. "They always contain a kernel of truth."

She sat on the grass, hugging her knees to her chest. "Everyone knows the story of Morgana, who lived on an island of blue glass."

"Which cannot possibly be real." Dylan sat by her side and offered her some chocolate. "Allow me to tell you a story from the historian, Nennius, written in the ninth century, of Illtud living in a cave at Ogwr, which is Ogmore, when a boat with a white sail approached the shore. In the boat were two men and a third lying on a bier. They said to him, 'This man of God commended us that we should bring him to you, and that we should bury him with you, and that his name should be revealed to no man, that men should not swear by him.' And they buried him, and the men returned to their ship and sailed away, and Illtud built a chapel about the body of the holy man. '*Anoeth bid bet y Arthur*', 'The world's mystery the grave of Arthur', ensuring that no one should swear by the Once and Future King."

"So where did Illtud hide Arthur's body, in a chapel or a cave?"

"In a cave, of course, hence the legend of Arthur sleeping in a cave until his return. Always a core of truth in the old legends, if you know where to look."

"As I'm beginning to realise," concurred Gail.

"The monks of Glastonbury transplanted the Arthur story from Wales to England; so effectively that even the English think Arthur was an Englishman."

"But why was he brought by two men in a boat instead of by Morgana?"

"Because Arthur was beyond healing, so Morgana's services would no longer be required." Dylan sensed her scepticism. Old stories die hard. "It is well documented that Illtud chose to live in a cave at Ogmore, a hermit who immersed himself in cold water every day, mad monk that he was, one time soldier, a man of his times—as was Arthur, who staved off the Roman Empire in the guise of religion, which employed Saxon mercenaries in an act of genocide against the Celtic Christians, whose deeply gnostic ways were a threat to the Roman Church."

"You believe the Church of Rome wished to destroy the Celtic Church?"

"The reason why Arthur forged alliances with the northern kingdoms to join forces instead of fighting one another, why Maelgwn stood alongside Arthur, knowing that if Catholicism won the battle for men's souls then the war would be truly lost."

"You mean he knew of Joseph's role in establishing the Gnostic teaching of Jesus?"

"Whom they regarded as a great prophet who wasn't the Son of God, but an enlightened human being."

They sat on the riverbank where the Ogmore joined the Ewenny, two rivers and two parallel lives, weaving a web from the flower of life over the earth and all living things.

"Enough of history," said Gail. "My head's spinning, the sun's low in the sky and the tide's about to cover the stepping stones."

Retracing their footsteps they crossed over the river as a horse and rider splashed through the water like a phantom, its black mane adding to the drama against the backdrop of a castle standing like a broken sentinel over this place of secrets.

"You okay?" he chuckled, as Gail shook water off her coat.

"Just a bit."

"Do you know what that reminds me of?"

"No, but I'm sure you're going to tell me."

"'The Dream of Rhonabwy', the *Mabinogion* story of the gathering of Arthur's army before the battle of Baedon. Just imagine Arthur standing here, conferring battle plans with Owain and Rhuvon Bevre, when a young knight gallops through the river and they all get soaked, as if they'd immersed themselves in the river, so is said."

"Make-believe tale it may be, but I am truly wet."

"You don't get it, do you?"

"What don't I get?" she retorted.

"It was here."

"What?"

"Where they gathered before the battle."

"Shush! You're having me on. Badon's in the West Country."

"No. Check your OS map."

Gail fished her map out of the rucksack and opened it up.

"There!" said Dylan, pointing to a hill north of Bridgend. "What does it say?"

"Mynydd Baedon."

"How far would you say that is from here?"

"Roughly seven miles."

"Which is the distance given in the story."

"So it is true!" she exclaimed in disbelief.

"Though few know, apart from the people who live there. You see that place name close to the summit, Maescadlawr?"

"What does it mean?"

"*Maes* is field and *cad* is battle."

"The field of the battle?"

"Conclusive, wouldn't you say?"

"Were you at that battle?" she asked, and Dylan shook his head. "Maybe it was you who got wet."

Dylan laughed. "Come on, let's go eat."

"This truly is a magical place," she said, gazing at the dunes bathed in golden sunlight as swans sailed upriver towards a lost city amongst the woods and fields of an enchanted land where

Joseph may have lain, alongside the Once and Future King.

"The magic of stories gilded with an aura of legend," Dylan mused, sitting on the castle wall.

"So glad you chose me to be with you. I do feel honoured, you know," she said with a delicate smile.

"Well you needn't be," replied Dylan. "I'm not someone who needs to be honoured, just a person like you searching for the truth of those times, trying to piece together something of the real history. Who knows if this was the place of his burial? Who knows the effect that might have on the people of Wales, who have been denied their true history all this time?"

"I sometimes feel so frustrated I just want to shout it out in the streets: Wake up, all you people! Don't you know who you are? Don't you know you've been lied to? Can't you see that your rightful heritage has been stolen from you?"

"Might as well shout to the four winds, Gail, no one wants to know anymore," replied Dylan with a playful smile. "What say we go to the Pelican for a wee drink and bite to eat?"

"Whatever your lordship commands," she said with a curtsy.

"I like that, do it again." He laughed. "Long time since I was curtseyed. Don't overdo it though; I'm just a man like any other."

"Don't think so, somehow, not after what you've told me." She pushed a white feather into his hat. "Thought you were different from the first time I saw you."

"Nonsense! I have the same problems as everyone else."

"Yes, but there's something about you."

"Yeah, like crazy off the charts and plagued by doubts."

She smiled as they passed by the Arthur stone with its weathered Latin inscription, pleased that he'd acknowledged their mutual journey.

The garden of the Pelican Inn overlooked the rivers and the sand dunes in the red-gold sunset that cast a magical aura over the 'Avalon' of a thousand tales, yet none so true as the tale of the two who sat eating veggie curry and enjoying the view.

Gail nibbled and chatted. She loved conversation as others enjoy a sunny day.

Dylan blinked at the setting sun.

"To Ynyswitrin!" he declared, raising his glass of cider to the dunes.

"More beautiful than all the Avalons put together."

"Ask yourself a question and observe the images of your dreams. Do they illustrate the past, present or future, before disappearing into thin air? We are two halves—conscious, subconscious, male and female. If you let go of who you think you are, you will see the lost child, for our true kingdom belongs to the world within. Our ancestors built bridges and causeways into the waters to place offerings to the Goddess, the Divine Feminine, whose image reflects in the deep."

"Not exactly normal chit-chat we have, is it?" she said, nervously fidgeting with her glass of water before releasing the clasp on her hair, allowing it to cascade over her shoulders. Dylan admired her auburn hair and well-defined features that never saw make-up, her electric persona visible in her vivid blue eyes.

"You know what I think?" she said.

"No, but I'm sure as night follows day that you're going to tell me," he responded, amused by her boldness.

"That happiness comes from acceptance instead of trying to control things such as when a man tries to control a woman—and I know all about that, allowing someone to control you, to take over your life, turn you into a quivering wreck." She turned away to hide the fear in her eyes.

Dylan sensed the pain of her past, glad that she trusted his sincerity enough to tell him this.

"I have all my life suffered for my beliefs," she said with a sharp intake of breath. "How hard it is for me to open up to a relative stranger. I know I'm only a small person, but I want people to reclaim who they are. Not crutches that can be kicked out from under you—we don't want crutches now—we need truth, solid truth, not illusion. We need internal transformation not external falsehoods parading as truth, otherwise the vortex in which we are stuck will diminish any hope for mankind. The secret of love and the true joy of life deserves more."

Dylan listened intently to her words. He knew this was the person he was meant to be with on this quest, male and female combined by divine chance to unravel an ancient mystery.

"I know," she continued, "that if there's one person on this planet to see this through, it is me, because with you it's easy. I don't take prisoners. For me spirituality is my heartbeat. I'm just a messenger; I'm Joan of Arc since a little girl when I had a comic book of her who got burned at the stake. It's time for the dogma to be burnt at the stake, not the truth, otherwise there will be a hollow void which nothing can fill. I've the passion to see this through. The

passion for the truth within is the Universal Truth."
She paused to wipe a tear from her eye. "What is
truth but our own discernment which lights up like
a light because our eyes are open?"

He touched her hand gently to ease her pain.
"But there's always a price to pay, seeing things as
they are, uncensored and full on."

"There are many who would pick up the books we
read and throw them to one side because it disturbs
them, because the gap between where they are and
where they should be is so wide it unsettles their
illusory peace of mind. Our passion for the truth is
what drives us on, because it upholds the ancient
tenet: 'Man, know thyself.'" She wiped away another
tear and smiled. "Soon as you ask that question you
tear the veil, and then the connection to the higher
power can begin to communicate, and by invocation
and soul-guidance, lead us on, and hopefully a
journey of transformation will begin."

Horses nudged one another in the castle field
where a group of people drummed and danced by
a teepee close to the river swollen by the incoming
tide in the valley of rediscovered Avalon, home to the
inheritors of a long line of seekers, whose concept of
love was akin to the spectrum of the rainbow whose
colours are revealed in the light of the sun.

26

Dylan's Dilemma

Dylan was a soul in torment as hope faded in the obscuring mist of a dilemma. His love for Pamela and his growing affection for Gail threatened to cut him in two. He was at a loss as to what to do to resolve his inner conflict. Did the Grail Knights who fought the Black Knight of their own shadow face such a challenge? What code of ethics did they abide by? What parameters of courtly love did they uphold? What codes of chivalry drove them onward to an otherworldly goal more important than life?

His meeting Gail was for a purpose, their separate pathways converging due to their commonality of beliefs, impelling them forward on a quest beyond personal feelings and into the realms of a Celtic Otherworld, the birthplace of beginnings and the home of unconditional love.

He meditated often beneath an oak, gaining comfort from its strength. He wandered through woods and veered off well-trodden pathways to where brambles scored his skin, nettles stung, and horseflies bit his naked body, where he bathed in a brook chanting Awens to the wind.

He longed to hear the voice within where megaliths stood to mark the solstice and equinox of spring and autumn. He placed coins as offerings in the roots of trees, vowing to see the journey through to the end.

One day, a jaybird perched on a branch above him and called out three times. Dylan wondered if nature was trying to tell him something. The next day, Gail rang his mobile to tell him that she was coming to see him, that she'd discovered something very important.

Gail knew the moment she saw him sat on the wooden throne in the Ffwrwm courtyard that the strain of caring for Pamela was taking its toll. She was worried about his physical and mental health, wondering if her intrusion into his life might be making things worse.

He looked up at her and smiled. "Hello, little lady. Welcome to the abode of legend, of kings anointed and heroes praised within the walls of a once-mighty citadel, where warriors' footsteps resound an urgent call to arms on these courtyard stones. What news have ye, Lady of the Wishing Hour? Is it me you've come to see, or the image in your eye that deems me favourable in your sight?"

"Oh shut up," she said, laughing at his playfulness. "Poet you may be, but pleasing to my sight you are not. You look ill. What's going on?"

"Just the usual."

"I know what's happening. You need help and you're not getting it."

"What is it you want to tell me?" he said, ignoring her concern.

She sat on a wooden throne opposite, put down the bag she was carrying and leaned back, shaking her head. "You're not well. If you'd rather I wasn't around, just say."

"That's not what I said," he replied swiftly.

"What did you say?"

"I don't know, I'm confused. We go off, she stays. She must think—what are we doing? Going to places she would love to go to, places we investigate, searching for the Joseph connection; Llid, Ogmore, St Fagan's. She knows you know."

"What do you mean?" she said, suddenly defensive. "We are platonic."

"No, not that. The other dimension, she sees things—spirits from that past. We have lived many lives together: Egypt, American Indians, here, the Celts. She was with me as Maelgwn. That's what I mean."

"I know what you're saying," replied Gail. "She is aware. Oh, I feel not a part of this anymore. You must go on alone without me."

"No, she doesn't want that. This is a spiritual obligation we've all signed up for. We've come back to do this one thing. Spirit talks to her. They say that it's right for us to do this. Thirty years we've been together, thirty years and many lifetimes. We are all spiritual warriors now. The past is done but for its spiritual legacy. That's all there is, the treasure, the truth, what initiates know. Taliesin, Merlin, Arthur—me, you—we've joined in a pact to reawaken the connection to the Rose and the Lion. It is here in this place, Siluria, Glamorgan, Llanilltud Fawr. The treasure is the legacy of the Druids, their truths profound, their origin unknown. Egypt, Mesopotamia, the Indus valley—all knew the golden pathway to self-knowledge, dispelling fear of death as the chiming of a bell resonates within us. We need this. The world needs this, the gold. Maelgwn and his wife Sandd gave the gold of the land to the monks at Llanilltud, the knowledge, although Illtud passed it on at a price. Maybe he considered sexuality to be an important part of initiation, expressed freely, not oppressed or subjugated. But then Illtud was a disciple of Germanus, a bishop of the Church of Rome, where oppression of sexual energy was doctrine."

"The truth?" interjected Gail.

"Sexual energy should be sublimated, not denied or oppressed. The Kundalini is the gateway to higher forces. The life-force of the Universe is sexual energy. Procreation is pro-creation. Nature profligates itself that way, but we humans have been endowed with a gift, a magic formula with which to escape repeated incarnation by rising the spirit up through the chakras to the crown of light, the dove of peace and love. Once there, you are free and no harm can come to you." He glanced at her with her head down. "You with me?"

Taken aback, she could only mutter, "I think so."

"The Gurus know this — Paramahansa Yogananda, Sri Yukteswar, Buddha, Jesus."

She looked at him, his blue eyes intense as sapphire. "You know so much more than I in these matters, even though I know a lot of history and theological points of view relating to enlightenment. What you say about the Druids, I do not know, apart from the little you've told me."

"Follow my way, Jesus said. But what is that way, do you know? Does anyone know? Why did He say to the Pharises and the Sadduces, 'You have the secret but you do not practise it yourselves, nor do you allow others to share the secret and you shut the door'? Or words to that effect."

"Paraphrased out of recognition," she replied, amused.

"For the Pharises read the Vatican."

She sensed his fire, his urgent passion, his conflicting emotions. He had to reclaim his centre of gravity. He believed he knew what the secret was, though no one had told him, he'd been born with it, life after life, an indestructible force that never dies, that cannot be lost, even if thrown away.

"Is that a yes, then?"

Startled, he came to. "Sorry, what?"

"That we continue?"

Dylan relaxed and smiled. "You could say."

"Good," she replied, relieved. "Now I can tell you why I called you yesterday."

"Go on, I'm all ears."

"David Nelmes."

"Yes, I know David," he said eagerly. "He lives here in Caerleon."

"You introduced me to him at the Hanbury."

"That's right. Loves history, grew up near Ogmore."

"Very knowledgeable," she affirmed, relieved he'd exorcised his inner daemon. "Bumped into him at the supermarket day before yesterday. Told me about Caer Caradoc, Mynydd y Gaer, the mountain fortress of Caractacus north of Bridgend. As a young man he'd befriended an old man. He told David that on the mountain close to the ruined church of St Peter, he'd seen a big stone with Arthur's name on it."

"Rex Artorius Fili Mauricius."

"You know?"

"A dig took place up there thirty years ago. That stone was discovered and a cross of electrum which read: '*Pro Anima Arthur*'. 'For the Soul of Arthur'. Both were rejected by the Oxford-Cambridge fraternity as forgeries."

"Why?" asked Gail.

"Because this is Wales," replied Dylan in disgust. "The historians who found them, Blackett and Wilson, campaigned for years for the truth of Arthur to be known, but the academic establishment slammed the door in their faces. Threats, even had their house set on fire. Da Vinci Code stuff."

"Where does that leave us?"

"On the edge," laughed Dylan. "Ecclesiastical history would have to be rewritten. The Church will deny the truth of Joseph, but we Welsh are born heretics who don't give a damn for the orthodox view."

They both laughed.

"You are an awkward so-and-so," she remarked. "Which isn't surprising, considering your background."

"What do you mean?"

"Difficult to grasp, elusive as—"

"What else did David tell you?" cut in Dylan.

"That the sighting of the Arthur stone predates the archaeological dig by thirty years."

"Did he tell you about the Grave of the Warriors and the Night of the Long Knives, when the Saxons under Cerdic, during a peace conference, slaughtered three hundred unarmed Welsh princes with knives concealed in their boots."

"That's terrible."

"The *Saesneg*'s code of honour is measured by gold, and the Cymry's by blood." Dylan raised himself off the throne to stand in front of the statue of Arthur and Mordred locked in mortal combat. "You know where this might lead, what the repercussions might be."

"Does that mean we stop dancing?"

"Never!" he said in deference to her defiant attitude.

Stretching his arms, he took a deep breath before re-joining Gail at the table. She was reading a poem glued to its surface telling of the magic of the courtyard, of warriors' ways and visions of yore, a dreamland conjured by sculpture into a living landscape of the past.

"Twenty years ago, Pamela suggested we go out for the day. I said no because it was raining."

"You can be a miserable moaner on times."

"Whatever," he replied dismissively.

"Quit waffling and get to the punchline, Dylan."

He enjoyed winding her up. "We saw a sign which said 'Open Garden Day', so we wandered about the gardens and chatted with the owners who were fairly elderly, good people. He was a quiet, thoughtful man; she possessed an air of regality without a whiff of superiority."

"So, where's this leading?" asked Gail.

"A sign which said, 'To the Chapel', indicating an uphill track through woods which led to a roofless ruin."

"A chapel?"

"And a chasm."

"A chasm?"

"Yes, and banks and ditches of a prehistoric caer, and megaliths half buried in undergrowth."

"This chapel in the woods, does it have a name?"

"I only remember being there, awestruck by its presence."

"Does it have anything to do with Joseph and the Prophecy?"

Dylan produced a sheet of notepaper from his pocket. "You recall the first two lines of the prophecy: 'Insula Avalonius, greedy for the death of pagans'?"

"Yes, which you presume refers to the sand dunes."

"And the second line referring to the Circle of Prophecy?"

"Yes, but what's the connection?"

"*Tredicem.*"

"Please translate."

"Thirteen."

"Thirteen what?"

"Degrees, derived from *sperulatis*, meaning small spheres. '*Sperulatis locum habitantibus tredicem.*' 'There he lies at thirteen degrees.'"

Suddenly their quest had become almost too real for comfort, despite the tingling anticipation of an adventure to come.

"Please explain."

"Allow me to read the Prophecy: 'The Island of Avalon, coveting the death of pagans, above all places for their entombment there. It is before the circle of portentous prophecy and in the future adorned shall it be by those that give praise to the most high.

"Abbadare, mighty in Sapphat, noblest of pagans, has fallen asleep there with one hundred and four knights. Among these Joseph of Arimathea has found perpetual sleep by the sea, and he lies on a line that is two-forked between that and a meridian in an angle on a coastal tor, in a crater that was already prepared, and above is where one prays, which is at the extremity of the verge. High up in Ictis is the place they abide to the south at thirteen degrees."

"Ictis?"

"*Ictis* is Latin for fish."

"I know, but who is they in 'they abide'?"

"It's a reference to the pagan burials of Neolithic people whose remains are all over the sand dunes."

"So that's the prophecy on which the whole Glastonbury myth is founded, their claim to be Avalonia?"

"If you tell a story long enough, it becomes the truth."

"The prophecy states that Joseph is buried near the sea, on a coastal tor, which is before the Circle of Portentous Prophecy, the circle being the Cor of Llid, which is seven miles north-by-north-east of Merthyr Mawr."

She peered over his shoulder at the map and the line he had drawn. "What is that line?"

"That's where it gets really interesting. If *tredicem* is thirteen, and *sperulatis* refers to the little spheres of degrees as in latitude and longitude, and the direction given is south..."

"South from where?" interjected Gail.

"From the Cor of Llid."

"I see," she said, peering closely at the map.

"Follow the line south to Merthyr Mawr and you will see that goes right through..."

"The chapel?" she interjected, staring at him wide-eyed. "Oh my giddy aunt, what are we going to do?"

"Go there of course."

"When?"

"Soon as possible, but we need to ask permission as the chapel's on private land."

"What land isn't?"

"Sure, but we have to respect the landowner's privacy."

"Probably think we're a couple of crackpots."

"Wouldn't be the first."

"Unless they're aware of what's there."

"A well-guarded secret doesn't surrender itself lightly."

"Perhaps not," said Gail. "Only one way to find out. What are you afraid of?"

"Nothing," he lied. "Sixth-century Latin's like translating Chaucer into modern English. No one's yet cracked the code of Melkin's obscure Latin, a deliberate obfuscation to ensure that the secret would remain so until the right time."

"Do you think that time is now?"

"I do."

"If you were the Melkin who wrote the Prophecy, then that's why the time is now."

"If only it were as cut and dried as that, like translating a Keats poem into the reality of living off the land," he replied. "It's important we remain objective about this."

She subdued her passion sufficiently to see his point of view. "Sorry, got carried away. Please continue."

"*Sperulis*, or big sphere, refers to a circle of stones, or earth, such as the Cor of Llid, which we know to be a valid location in the heartland of Bran the Fisher King..."

"Who is brother-in-law to Joseph by marriage to his sister, Enygeus."

"Maelgwn would have been aware of Joseph's connection to Siluria."

"Simple logic wins the day," she said, clapping her hands.

"I wish all three of us could go there together," he said sadly. "If we're given permission, that is."

"I'm sorry she's unwell. I know how much you love her. I've no wish to be in the way, but this isn't about personal relationships. We're both on a quest of sorts. With all that you and I have read over many years to do with our individual journeys, maybe we've met to fulfil some kind of purpose. So never think I don't know how painful it is for you. I just want to be of help by being your Grail Maiden."

"You give me strength, and I thank you for it," he said, placing a reassuring hand on her shoulder. "We'll see this through together. I can't do this alone, but together a hundred devils won't stop us."

He stared at her, his bright blue eyes filtering reality's painful edge into the fiction of his dreaming, creating his own reality, transcending what they knew into what could be.

"Dammit!" exclaimed Dylan. "Why is life so cruel?"

"No one has it easy. If life were always on the up, we'd float about like disconnected angels looking for somewhere to crash land."

"True, a calm sea in a storm doesn't happen. We see the big picture, the purpose of our life, you, me and Pamela. We are the lucky ones, even though it's like living in a cauldron."

"Can say that again," she said with a wry smile. "The cauldron of spiritual awakening."

"But what an adventure."

She seemed somewhat nervous, apprehensive, out of place in his life as she glanced at the windows of the shop, displaying intricate Celtic designs. The wind-chimes' soft sound blew in the gentle breeze.

"When are we going?" she said suddenly. "I mean, when do you think we'll be able to go?"

Dylan shrugged, reticent to answer.

"Shall I just go away and never come back?"

"Hold on," he said, thrown. "Be patient. I don't know what might happen today, never mind tomorrow."

"I think it's best I go, don't you? What am I doing in your life? Not that I mind running you about like a taxi service, taking you places in your search for a treasure that may or may not exist."

Dylan reeled back in shock. He'd never seen her like this. What had he done wrong? It seemed as if some kind of twisted fate had conspired to prevent the culmination of a quest to reveal the truth of a two-thousand-year-old mystery.

"Why does that sculpture look like me?" she demanded. "Is it me?"

"Yes, it's the Grail Maiden."

"And I am that, a figment of your imagination?"

"Symbolic is all."

"I am real, I have feelings. Don't insult me by categorising me as a Burne-Jones stereotypical Grail Maiden without personality, a man's idea of heavenly virtue, a whimsical female to do his bidding, to serve his imaginary dream world and adolescent fantasy."

"Wow! Didn't see that coming. If you want to back off, that's okay, I understand. I never wanted to impose myself into your life, it's just that I thought you'd be interested in what I'm doing, the Grail thing. You did say—"

"I said a lot of things," interjected Gail. "Maybe I was under some kind of spell. Maybe you were as well. This myth and magic stuff has connotations that can be far reaching. My life has been topsy-turvy, relationships that turned sour, turning me sour, being psychologically abused in all manner of ways. I'm pretty vulnerable, you know, and easily hurt, and when I am, I retreat into my shell. That's what I'm doing now, pre-empting being hurt by pushing you away. It's all getting a bit too complicated for me to handle."

Dylan rolled a cigarette to calm his nerves, avoiding any self-justifying retort, waiting for her to calm down and be reasonable.

"You and Pamela have been together a long time, yet you seem quite happy to be with me, albeit as a fellow colleague searching for the truth of our history."

"That's what I thought..."

"Is it?" she said. "Or is it something more?"

"No!" he replied emphatically. "I've no desire other than to be friends."

"But what does Pamela think?"

Dylan looked at her pleadingly.

"I'll tell you what she thinks. She thinks, 'Who is this other woman?'"

"But I've explained to her —"

"What? That I'm just your sidekick, like one of your male friends?"

"No, of course not."

"Exactly."

Dylan walked off into the garden. "This is no good. We'll have to call it a day. I can't handle Pamela being unwell as well as trying to keep the shop going and searching for the bloody Holy Grail as well. It's a joke."

"You're right it's a joke, which is why I'm off."

Snatching her bag, she walked hastily out of the courtyard and into the street, leaving Dylan to lick his wounds in the garden of shattered dreams.

"There, by the Grace of God, I fall flat on my face," he muttered, pacing up and down the courtyard.

Reality had hit him hard. Why had she turned on him? Was he that naïve that his trusting nature could be turned against him? He'd been hoping to ask her if she would help him out in the shop for a day or two a week to ease his burden.

Perhaps it was inevitable that she should back off. After all, he didn't really know her, as was obvious by her remarks. He'd unwittingly taken her assistance for granted. Also, did he have ulterior motives beyond liking and respecting her as a person? They'd hugged, but then he'd embraced many women friends over the years out of deep affection. He loved women who were strong-minded, who knew deep down their role in life wasn't to be a man's slave, but an equal, despite the differences essential to a true and meaningful relationship.

The truth, of course, is that women in general will not tolerate or allow another woman to intervene in their life, no matter how innocent. Dylan had assumed Pamela was fine about their occasional jaunts into the Vale, knowing how important it was for him.

Caught in the middle of a female power struggle, he thought it best to drop the whole thing and take care of Pamela and the shop—not that he hadn't given his all to that end, but what he was doing he couldn't justify to his conscience, pursuing the Grail conundrum as if all was well, which it wasn't, far from it. Dylan decided to let it go, that it wasn't meant to be.

27
The Chapel

Dylan spent more time with Pamela over the ensuing weeks, only going to the shop three days a week, enjoying being together, released from his dominating drive to find Joseph's tomb that had not only alienated the love of his life but Gail as well.

"How could I be so blind? he asked himself, knowing nothing truly succeeds without love and compassion. He'd torn himself in two by not listening to his inner voice, cursed with an unbridled ambition to achieve something without the consent of those he loved most.

Self-flagellation and introspection dissolved his glory-seeking quest, leaving a vacuum he filled with walking, gardening and creating sculptures. Even his friends seemed to have dropped away. Richard hadn't called by for months, and his family members hadn't been in touch because he'd often ignored their phone calls, being too preoccupied with himself, like the archetypal flawed hero who worships his own self-image.

Three weeks passed before Pamela suggested that he and Gail go to the chapel. He hadn't told her the whole story of why Gail had walked away, only that she had important things to see to. Pamela knew anyway; very little escaped her attention, as his mood swings pointed to a serious disagreement between him and Gail.

"Only if you come with us," suggested Dylan.

"Don't be silly, how can I with this oxygen canister?"

"We'll all go in Gail's car."

"I'd love to, but I can't, so why not give her a call? I'm sure she'll be pleased to hear from you."

Dylan was surprised by her suggestion, but then she was like that, empathic and unselfish, knowing that in some way his quest was his life's mission.

"I need to drop this now," he said. "You being unwell, it's best I let it go and wait for a more favourable time."

"Or another life?" She looked at him with a smiling compassion. "I know how you feel, I trust you, so why not give her a call?"

"Not just yet." He couldn't face further rejection, his low self-esteem couldn't take it.

The very next day, he received a text from Gail requesting they meet at the Ffwrwm on Saturday. He replied, affirming that would be okay. Pamela said it was better than him being a misery around the house, though she meant it good-humouredly. Dylan felt strangely relieved to be taking one more step into the unknown—only this time, with Spirit's help, with a little more humility.

Their differences resolved, Dylan and Gail set out for Merthyr Mawr the following Tuesday, parking outside the Church of St Teilo in Merthyr Mawr.

"What an amazingly beautiful village," said Gail, venturing into the churchyard.

"Would you mind not picking the flowers?" snapped Dylan. "Not here, not today."

"Look," she said, holding up a purple rose. "Haven't seen one this colour before."

"Neither will anyone else if you have your way."

"Alright," she replied like a smacked child. "Just three then."

"Three, no more. We're not here to pick flowers,"

"But I love them," she pleaded. "I want them all."

"What do pebbles, purple roses and the Holy Grail have in common?"

"Avalon?"

"And where is Avalon?"

"Here."

"And why are we here?"

"To ask the landowner's daughter for permission to go to the chapel."

"Who lives just there." Dylan pointed to an old mill-house. "So let's be on."

"Alright, mister serious," she said, placing the purple roses on the car roof. "You're not very happy today. What's the matter with you?"

"Nothing."

"Yes there is. I can sense it."

"Just nervous about asking, that's all."

"Have you met her before?"

"Once, years ago," replied Dylan. "Her name is Iona."

Dylan stared at the church, unwilling to surrender his conviction about the chapel. "Maybe we should phone first to ask if it's convenient to call on her?"

"Let's just knock on her door. I'm sure she won't mind, as she's probably a really nice person."

"She's more than nice, as you'll find out for yourself. She uses the old smithy to create works of art. Pottery too. Very gifted."

"Fingers crossed then."

Dylan clocked the image of a fish on the gate of the Old Forge.

"Best let me do most of the talking, seeing as how nervous you are," Gail said. "Then say something about your findings."

"Be careful not to say too much," cautioned Dylan. "We don't want to alarm her about its possible connection to Joseph. All I'll say is that there may be a link to early Christianity. We don't want her thinking we're going to be crawling all over her land with picks and shovels, along with hordes of treasure hunters searching for a gold goblet on which are inscribed the initials JC."

Gail laughed. "Glad you've got your humour back. Never known such an up-and-down person as you. Just as well the ups outdo the downs, or you'd be travelling alone."

A millrace ran alongside an old sawmill before entering the Ogmore River. Cut logs were piled under a makeshift awning, and an oval lawn given over to wildflowers.

Gail tapped on the door, which was opened almost immediately by Iona, wearing a potter's smock.

"Hello." She greeted them, with an inquisitive look.

"Hello," said Gail. "Hope you don't mind us calling on you uninvited, but we were wondering if we might have a quick word with you about something on your land?"

"Oh?" she said, intrigued. "If you'd like to come inside and tell me about this something?"

"Very kind of you," replied Gail, following her into the open-plan kitchen of the smithy's cottage.

"Would you like some tea?"

"If it isn't too much trouble."

"No trouble, I was just about to pour one for myself."

"Lovely, thank you," said Gail, looking at pieces of Montefiore-style pottery and iron sculptures of intricate design. "Did you make these?"

"Before the forge closed. Now I make pottery. What is it about, this thing of such importance?"

Gail patted a Labrador that had wandered in. "The chapel."

"Oh? What about it?"

"There may be a connection to early Christianity," said Dylan, "and it may possibly be of great importance regarding several early saints."

"The chapel," said Iona, placing mugs of tea on a large oak table, "used to be a pilgrim's stopover en route to St David's."

"Two visits to St David's equalled one to Rome."

"So they say," replied Iona. "Please, sit with me at the table."

Gail raised her mug to thank Iona with a winsome smile. "Do you know much about it, the chapel? Does it have a long history?"

Iona's brow furrowed, concerned, but her interest was clear. "The old chapel's a ruin. No one goes there anymore."

"Did you know that the hill on which the chapel stands is a hillfort?" asked Dylan.

"Yes, but there's not a lot left to see now."

"And the stone circle?"

"Is there one?"

"Maybe I need to explain how I know," said Dylan. "You held an open-garden day here twenty years ago; you were on the gate that day. I was with my partner, Pamela, we visited the chapel on the hill—"

"Yes, I was there, though we don't do that anymore."

"There's also a chasm close to the chapel."

"Yes, but it isn't safe to go down there."

"Of course," concurred Dylan. "Steep sides and a long way to the bottom, as I recall."

Iona wondered why they imagined a roofless ruin with its ancient crosses could be so important. Were they wishing to disturb the peace of the place with their investigations? She knew how these things worked with the authorities when it comes to protecting ancient monuments.

"You know, of course, that Cadw won't let you near the place. You may look of course, but they won't allow an investigation of any kind."

"I am well aware of Cadw's control over these things," replied Dylan. "It isn't our intention to dig but to look."

"Should really ask my brother, he's in charge of things now."

"How do we get in touch with him?" asked Gail.

"He's away at the moment," said Iona, sensing their disappointment. "Though I'm sure it would be alright if you go and have a look."

"Thank you," replied Dylan, with a smile of relief. "That's very kind of you."

"Do you know the way?"

"Through the main gate?"

"No, it's best you follow the lane up and to the right and over the style, then across the field to the woods on the far side."

Dylan reminded her of an astrology reading she'd given him. She recalled that she had, but that was a long time ago. He liked Iona, her sense of who she was, her lively intelligence and quick wit, gifted and half-wild in a Celtic way. Though he was prone to categorise people, he was convinced the Celts were imbued with a wry sense of humour and the ability to laugh at life. He was also delighted that she empathised with their request.

Thanking her for her hospitality, they walked away with a feeling of anticipation. Dylan suggested they look at the ancient crosses behind the church before continuing their journey to the chapel, but decided otherwise as the sun was beginning to sink low in the sky.

"You were right, Dylan, she is a lovely lady."

"Yes, indeed," he replied. "Really good she said it's okay for us to go there."

"She said to follow this road to the top and bear right..."

"Then over the gate and across the field."

"I'm excited, aren't you?"

"Sure," he replied, his mind on the goal. "What she said about Cadw is true. There's no way we'll be allowed to scratch its surface, even though that isn't our intention. What we're about is to feel our way and look at what's there. Who knows what conclusions we'll come up with in the heartland of Bran the Fisher King, the Arch-Druid who married Joseph's sister, Enygeus? Makes you wonder if the Druids really needed Christianity?"

"Go on, I'm listening," she said, enthralled by the magic of the place, the birds, the horses in the fields and the snug cottages along the way.

"Druids were Gnostic, same as Jesus. Gnosis simply means to experience divinity from within."

"How did we find our way here?"

"Instinct?"

"Of a sort." Dylan looked up at the blue sky. "Been here many times on a cloudy day, invariably greeted on arrival by a circle of blue sky. A beautiful day in a beautiful place where all things seem possible, but where does this reality end and the Otherworld begin?"

"Right here." Gail pushed a bottle of water into his hands. "Drink, or you'll end up in the Otherworld sooner than you think."

Dylan swallowed a mouthful. "'Drink from my words,' said Jesus. I'm no orthodox Christian, but he's right."

"You do know what we're going to find, don't you?"

"No," he replied, eyeing her askance.

"Yes you do, but you're afraid."

"No I'm not."

"Oh yes you are," she said as though reading his subscript. "Not too late if you want to quit."

"Let's be on; we haven't much time before it gets dark."

"Alright, Mister Druid, but I know I'm right."

"So you keep saying."

"Do you ever ask yourself why you are doing this?"

"How do you mean?" queried Dylan.

"What do you hope to prove?"

"That we live forever, that the soul is immortal?"

"But what else?" Gail persisted.

"That we do not live just one life but many, that each time we return we pick up where we left off on the soul's journey towards spiritual perfection. That's if we follow the soul's blueprint, and allow our intuition to point the way in accord with our inborn attributes."

"True, everyone's born with certain gifts."

"Sometimes we are given insight into our past to signpost what we came to do, which is to help others rekindle knowledge of who they truly are. Does that make sense to you?"

"You mean like the Grail?"

"The light of the human heart."

"So why are you afraid?"

"I'm not," he said, trying to convince himself.

"I am," she said, touching an oak tree. "Afraid of where it might lead, because when reality bites, dreams take on a different hue."

"This tree knows its place but isn't consciously aware of its need to give us oxygen to breathe, or caring for the environment, or the burden of free-will to choose."

"What will it matter if nothing's there?"

"So then we just make fools of ourselves," replied Dylan. "Everything evolves, religions change or stagnate. Gospels carved in stone turn hearts into stone. We live in the now, you and I, moment to moment. Things change, and everything is renewed. Each morning is a not only a new day but a new beginning."

"That's what I do every day—say thank you for everything, for my sense of well-being and joy."

"Me too," said Dylan, clambering over a gate into a field of sheep.

"You!" she mocked. "Who lives on coffee, cake, tobacco and cider... Do me a favour. It's a miracle you look the way you do."

"All in the mind," he said, helping her over the gate. "You may laugh, but I once met a lady who by chance happened to dine with the Dalai Lama's physician, who ate meat. She was shocked, assuming he was vegetarian. 'Why do you eat meat?' she asked. His reply was simple. 'The mind can transform anything.'"

"I wish people would realise that the body's a temple instead of gorging on sugar and fat and chemicals that kill you."

"Let's be on, and mind the sheep shit."

They strode quickly across the field towards a wooded area on the far side, as the sheep gathered into a tight circle, watching the intruders who'd invaded their meadow, strangers who might take them to market or the slaughterhouse. Sheep know these things in the unspoken words in their hearts—that life for them is short—yet their lambs gambol and bleat for their mothers, as do all children of the One Creator.

"We're almost there," said Dylan.

Confronted by a barbed-wire fence, he raised the upper strand to allow Gail through, whereas he simply legged over it, being so tall.

"Good to be on the road with you once more," he said. "I'd given up thinking it would happen."

"Feels good," she replied. "And I am sorry for all the things I said."

"Don't be. It was inevitable. We're here now, that's what matters."

Gail followed him into a wooded interior where nothing stirred, not even a leaf.

"I remember this arboretum from twenty years ago," he said, reaching into his pocket for tobacco.

She put her hand out to stop him. "You don't need that. Put it away."

"A puff or two and I'll be fine."

"Do as you please," she snorted. "I'm going to explore."

As she disappeared into the greenery, he thought back to that day twenty years before when he'd first seen the chapel, and standing in front of a cedar of Lebanon, he said a thank-you prayer to Pamela for allowing him to follow his passion and his dreams.

"You're not going to believe this, but there's a huge hole in the ground over there," Gail said pointing to a low wall of rough stone half-circling what could not be seen.

"That's the chasm. Be careful not to go too close."

They stood still, embracing the silence as the evening sun imbued an ancient yew in a dark purple glow, its serpent-like roots and feathery foliage an abstract work of art.

Dylan stepped forward towards the chasm to peer into its opaque grey depths. Although familiar with the place from long ago, he'd forgotten the impact it had on him then: a realisation that in the depths of the chasm, there lived something not of this world.

Staring as if hypnotised, seeing through the eyes of a parallel universe frozen in time, Gail sensed in the tangible stillness something waiting to be revealed. Their eyes were drawn downward by the movement of water, a rivulet moving east to west at the bottom of the chasm. A tawny owl flew out of a crevice on silent wings, distracting them momentarily.

Gail stared silently, feeling the strange otherworldly vibrations.

Dylan had never known her be so quiet for so long and smiled. "Seems it's really got you, the awesome fascination of it."

"What is this place?" she whispered. "What is here?"

"I don't know," he said, allowing the subtle energies to wash over him like a warm waterfall, his gaze fixed on a cave halfway down whose entrance was blocked by a boulder, as if deliberately placed there.

"Oh, Dylan," she said, holding onto his arm. "I feel something. I can't describe it; it's telling me... I don't know. I've never felt like this before. There's a magic here not of this world. What should we do?"

"Stay here," he said. "Wait and listen. This place is holy and sacred. It is hidden, and no one knows."

Dylan prompted her to follow him around the perimeter wall. "This was put here as a barrier to prevent unwary animals from falling into the chasm, including any two-leggeds who might stumble about in the dark to suddenly find themselves in another world."

Dylan took a camera out of his rucksack and photographed the rock face and the cave, the flash startling a blackbird in a yew tree. Gail trod cautiously on brambles in the rough woodland, occasionally glancing into the chasm's dark depths that summoned up archaic fears of the unknown.

"This is one of the Ancient Wonders of the Celtic World called Anoeth, the place where past and present meet, or the place where time stands still. *'Anoeth bid bet y Arthur'*. 'A world's wonder the grave of Arthur'."

"That's what you think, that Arthur could be buried here?"

"The Stanzas of the Graves say that he is buried in Anoeth."

"This is Anoeth?"

"Such a chasm is described by Clement of Alexandria: 'that in the Island of Britain there is a cave situated under a hill, and a chasm on its summit, and when the wind falls into the cave and rushes into the bosom of the cleft, a sound is heard of clashing symbols, and when the wind is in the woods a sound is heard like the song of birds'. That's from his 'Stromata', which he wrote in 147 AD. This Wonder of Britain is located in the district of Brehant, according to Wormonoc, 884 AD. Brehant was the name given to this area long ago, which means 'windpipe'."

"How do you know all this?"

"I've done a quite lot of research on the chapel these past few weeks."

"So the legend of Arthur sleeping in a cave might well be true."

"Legends contain truth. They always do."

"Do you think we should try to go down there?" suggested Gail.

"Too dangerous without ropes, and the rock face on the other side isn't climbable. Besides we're only here to look at the chapel." He moved away from the chasm into a circular clearing bounded by a low wall, within whose centre stood a roofless chapel.

She sensed straight away the chapel was twin to the chasm. One above and the other below, the upper world and the lower, whose juxtaposition Druid and Celt saw as a gateway to the meeting place of both worlds.

"There's running water at the bottom of the chasm," said Gail.

"Yes, it runs through a cave system all the way to the Ogmore. The ancient name of the chapel as recorded in the Book of Llandaff as Merthyr Buceil, is dated 862 AD."

"Who is Buceil?"

"It isn't a name but a title, which means Shepherd."

"In other words, it is the Chapel of the Shepherd."

"That's right. *Buceil* or *bucalis* is the Greek word for shepherd. And Merthyr Mawr means the place where the shrine or the relics of someone of great importance are kept."

"The shrine of the Shepherd," said Gail. "So who..."

"That's the puzzle," interjected Dylan.

"How do you know all this when it was only recently that you remembered your visit here?"

"Like I said, I've spent these last weeks researching its origins." Dylan ran his hands over the weathered doorway. "As for who the Shepherd is, there can only be one claimant for that title."

"Who?"

"Who else but 'He' is the Shepherd?"

"Possibly, but might not the Shepherd also refer to the Arcadia of the Cathars?"

"Although this was once a Templar stronghold, and Fitzhammon's daughter married Hugh de Payens, I think it unlikely, even though they connect through their Gnostic beliefs."

As Dylan wrestled with the origin of the chapel and its possible connection to an unsolved mystery of early Christianity, Gail was drawn to fonts placed either side of the doorway.

Dylan stepped inside, ducking beneath its limestone lintel to be confronted by a weathered memorial stone protruding five feet out of the earthen floor, its intricate lacework and faint lettering barely visible after millennia of rain and frost.

Touching him gently, reassuringly, Gail went to another Celtic cross standing in place of an altar. Taller, its shoulder cross was half-missing, its interweaving lacework and faint lettering barely visible.

"I wonder what the words say?" she said, running her fingers over its worn inscription. "That this is the magical place where Joseph and Arthur lie buried until the time mentioned in the Prophecy has been fulfilled?"

Dylan laughed. "We are like children in Alice's Wonderland breathing in too much fairy dust to think straight."

"Whatever," she retorted. "Feels magical to me."

"Really?" he said, examining the crude stonework and mortar. "This chapel's no more than two hundred years old."

"Can't be."

"Afraid so. A curious mixture of old and new, such as that capitol used to support the east window — and the font by the doorway, which is actually a pillar support, either from St Teilo's Church, or from a much older chapel than this present structure."

"Are you disappointed?"

"Yes and no, because of the location. Though puzzling as to why the line I drew on the map went right through here."

"Yes, but don't you think that might be the chasm and not this chapel?"

"They are associated; there is a reason why this is here."

"Shall I tell you what I think?"

"Please do."

"My first impression is that this chapel and the chasm are physically connected."

"How?"

"By a cave system. You saw that boulder in front of an opening in the chasm, which is roughly fifty feet away from here."

"That's possible, but let's not get too carried away. This structure may not be old, but the inscribed stones are probably sixth-century. Very few buildings survive more than a thousand years in our climate, so what did we expect to see? A chapel of white marble adorned by angels? Let's go outside, drink some tea and go."

They sat on the grass fronting the chapel dedicated to a Shepherd on a lonely rocky tor by the sea, cradled in mystery for two thousand years, as they both wondered if they had truly found what they had been searching for.

Before retracing their footsteps to the village, Dylan—almost as an afterthought, photographed the chapel—unaware that what it would reveal would change everything.

28

Revelation

"Born are warriors straight and true, my earthly life is only two," said Pamela, reminiscing about her childhood during the Blitz, directing its victims towards the light. "Listen to my Song of the Universe:

People of Earth,
Respond to the call,
United we stand,
Divided we fall.
The call comes from afar,
Divine Love prevails,
To bring to an end,
Your earthly travails.

"Do you like it? Came to me in the middle of the night. There was more, but that's all I could remember."

"Beautiful words, Pamela, just what's needed right now."

"We are here to help one another, such as the woman who asked me back last summer, 'Is this all there is? Who are we really? I'm not happy. What is happiness? What is love? Why was I born? Will someone please tell me? I don't go to church, I'm not religious. What are you, what do you call yourself?

A Gnostic? That some weird sect? Oh, it means to know — know what? Through inner experience, like in dreams and stuff? Had some of those, not real are they? Inner knowing, what Jesus said. Wouldn't need a church then, would we? They don't tell us much do they? My husband doesn't love me. He tells me women are the Devil's playthings. He's a Catholic, so I said you should know, you're always playing with them. Why did they do to us all those horrible things, burning and torturing? I am just a little woman, but talking to you, I don't feel worthless any more. My children love me and I love them — isn't that worth something?' Away she would go, her spirit restored with a few words and a lot of love."

Dylan gazed at the garden through the study window, an oasis of calm reflecting nature's innate harmony. More than a week had gone by since his visit to the chapel, which had turned out to be something of an anti-climax, he concluded, observing the branches of a leylandii swaying to and fro in the breeze like the Seven Maidens in the vision.

So long ago, he'd had that glimpse into the Otherworld, the trail from the past to the present, signposts along the way, guiding lights enforcing isolation from the herd. The invisible ones were always there, waiting, watching.

What was he doing now? How far had he come? Had he caught up with his soul yet? Do we ever, or only when the day is done? The trees trembled; even they seemed far from home.

He stood up, agitated, knocking over the camera. It thudded onto the wooden floor. He picked it up — it seemed okay — and plugged it into the laptop to download whatever was there, all those places: Llandaff, St Fagan's Chapel ruin, St George's, Capel Llanilltern, Llanilltud Fawr's roofless ruin, his time there so long ago. Where now? Ogmore? Dunes, castle, Arthur's Stone?

Get it done, it said.

What? he replied.

Just do it — you will know.

I don't need voices, he thought to himself, clicking on the pictures file, meaningless but for the thoughts and feelings of that day. What else was there but the Now of those moments?

Skimming through the pictures of Merthyr Mawr, the stones behind the church, so ancient they smacked of non-existence. *'Pauli Fili M'*, 'Paulinus son of Mauritius', Arthur's brother. A picture of Gail straddling a stile, laughing. *"I'm a good girl, that's why Spirit talks to me. I know things."*

The yew trees, no pictures, just memories of the chasm in the half-light of the deep. Just one, only one, of the chapel — just stone and mortar, no roof, only ivy clinging on, aspiring heavenward. Click off, then on. What was that? Nothing but a trick of the light. What did he see but his thoughts, jumbled with too many images and wonderings, wanting something to happen?

He clicked the cursor a second time. The light, it was bright, it was inside the chapel, inside the gap of the windowless window, bright as the morning sun, big as the moon, no speck of dust enlarged by digital exaggeration, its light diffused into the background stone wall like the feathered edge of frost on a window pane.

He shook. His spine tingled with wonder and awe. It was there and it was real, even to him, a sceptic till proven. What was he to do, or think, or surmise? Miracles happen, the unknown impinges upon our pre-set parameters, if we are lucky, or fortunate, or what...?

"What's the matter?" Pamela asked, as he wandered, dazed, into the kitchen. "You look as though you've just seen a ghost."

"Not a ghost, something else... the chapel."

"What about it?"

Dylan went and got the laptop to show her what he'd seen but could not believe.

"Spirit is talking to you," she said, "telling you that you've found what you've been searching for." Tears came to her eyes as she kissed him on the lips. "I told you that it was a special place, only you wouldn't listen to me, the things I tell you. I always know, you know, whether you believe me or not."

She was right, he rarely heeded her insights. He believed his own visions, though rarely accepted others' without proof. *So much for humility,* he thought, walking into the garden, where frogs croaked in the pond and busy bees fed on pollen-rich flowers whilst the neighbour frantically mowed his lawn before the football match kick-off at three.

He sat on a log beneath a sycamore tree where a Green Man peered through the foliage, the guardian of the forest, overlord of up-thrusting greenwood, a reminder of our origins carved in stone on the tree of Isis, the sycamore, whose seeds would produce a thousand more.

Pamela sat with him and smiled, happy to be involved in his quest, their passions shared, so many things in their lives fulfilled, the love between them constant through time.

"Tell me again the dream of the fish," she asked.

"You mean the angel fish?"

"Yes, that's the one. Please tell it me."

"The fish, yes. We were on a seashore—I don't know where, but it was a sunny day, the sands were golden and the sea was like glass. You are standing on a rock overhanging deep, crystal clear water, and I say to you, 'Hey there's a beautiful big fish just beneath you. Can't you see it? It's huge, look at it—it's a whopper.'

"You peer at the fish, which swims gracefully to the surface, all silver and gold and blue, and leaves the water and holds on to you, becoming part of you in a friendly, loving way, the fish being so good and full of wonderful spiritual significance, clinging to you and touching all your spiritual centres."

"Lovely," she said. "I need that now."

They sat quietly in the silence for several minutes. The lawnmower man had gone indoors to watch football on a big screen.

"Why not give Gail a call to tell her about the chapel?"

"I'll suggest that she meet me at the Ffwrwm tomorrow. Shan't say anything over the phone, better for her to see than for me to describe."

Gail was changing a lightbulb when he called her later that day. "Dylan, is that you?"

"Yes," he said. "Something important's come up. Can you come to the Ffwrwm tomorrow?"

"Of course, but can't you tell me over the phone?"

"Better for you to see for yourself."

The phone went dead, leaving her to wonder what it might be as she replaced the bulb, flicked on the switch and the light came on. *That's it,* she thought. *They are showing us something.*

She couldn't wait for tomorrow. It felt right to share Dylan's dreams in a world where logic crowns truth with the thorns of intellect.

She sat in her garden as the setting sun graced treetops where blackbirds sang a chorus of nature's perpetual choir in celebration of life's mystery. She said a prayer of thanks; blessing everything: the birds, the flowers and all of God's creatures. No longer would she fear the betrayal of her beliefs, feeling an outcast, hopeless and forlorn, the child in her dancing with joy. The spirit within, old with time, travels often to the lands of the past, of many lives gone by, but the child who drinks the dew of heaven is forever young.

Dylan waited for her in the Ffwrwm courtyard the next day. It was already three o'clock and visitors were few, though he'd sold a couple of items, enough to pay the rent for that week. It was difficult for him to sell things; Pamela was much better at it. He did love being there, talking to people, a thousand conversations over the years. He warmed to people, with an intense curiosity. He never saw customers, only stories—where they were from, what brought them there. He was adept at reading their auras; their energy told him much—happy, sad, intelligent, good or bad.

He called Pamela to check she was alright. She said the Social Services had been and gone, and asked him not to be late. Gail arrived just after four, with her lively step and buoyant energy. She had that something, that quality, forthright and quick to respond, always alert.

She sat with Dylan at the stone table on which was a plaque describing the deeds of Arthur and his knights. The laptop was open; he scrolled down the photographs taken that day, of the chasm and the chapel.

She looked closely at the image of intense white light visible through the aperture of the ruinous window opening and she, like him, wondered if the apparition, which was as voluminous as a full moon, was real.

"Holy Mary! Is it real?" She looked at Dylan, who was smiling.

"'And Arthur went into the chapel, and the light descended upon the altar bright as a thousand suns.' A quote from Wolfram Von Eschenbach's *Parzival*, describing the Holy Grail."

She looked again at the image. "You do realise that it is above where the altar would have stood."

Dylan looked closely. "Are you sure?"

"Positive!"

He looked again. "You are right. I didn't notice that."

She sat back suddenly. "Phew! It's a sign."

"I should say so."

"But wait a minute. I also photographed the chapel with my camera, almost the same time as you, but mine turned out blank." She looked again at the image. "What does it mean?"

"I can't say it."

"What?"

"The Chapel of the Grail."

"Have you enlarged it?"

"Many times. The light's diffuse, no clear edge, like it's giving off sunbursts of energy, morphing as if it were alive."

"Dylan, is it the Grail?"

"What else can it be?"

"A portal?"

He thought for a moment. "To the Otherworld, to another dimension?"

She looked at him, tight-lipped. "Make of it what you will, but that's what I think."

"Doesn't matter, whatever it is, it is there. It did not show on your camera, but came up on mine, whatever that means."

"The quest is yours; you were meant to see it. They are showing you that you are right with your thinking."

"About Joseph?"

"Yes," she replied emphatically. "That he is there. What other explanation is there?"

Dylan lapsed into a thoughtful silence, stubbornly refusing to believe that this could happen to him, yet he'd wished for it, longed for it, since the day of the vision of the dancing maidens and the monk who pointed to the treasure less than a mile from the chapel where the River Ogmore flowed around the rocky tor on which it stands.

"What are you thinking?" she asked.

"The vision of the maidens, the monk, the treasure."

|"This is the treasure," she said. "That's it there, right in front of you."

He glanced at her, then at the image of light. "I get what you're saying, but where do we go from here? Unlikely we'll ever be allowed to excavate the chapel."

"There's your evidence," she said, pointing to the light. "What more do you need?"

"Facts," replied Dylan. "Concrete proof that Joseph *is* buried here. We must show this to Iona, and ask her what she and her family know about the chapel."

"No," asserted Gail. "We must keep this to ourselves; tell no one. Who would believe us anyway? They'd say we faked it."

"How? You see it, it's real. How could anyone fake that?"

"Can be done," she asserted. "Any computer bod could."

"Perhaps they could, but we know it's real."

"Yes, just you and I, and that's the way it should stay." She looked at him as he shook his head. "It is a personal message to you, full stop."

"I don't think so. This is just the beginning. We must search through the ancient records for more evidence."

"Of what?"

"Of who else may be there."

"The Prophecy says only Joseph."

"And one hundred and four knights."

"That all?" she said, with a loud laugh. "Why not throw Arthur and his knights into the mix?"

"Let's be serious here," Dylan cut in. "I think Maelgwn knew where Joseph was buried all along, and wrote the prophecy to confuse rather than describe the location. Many have tried to unravel his gobbledegook Latin phraseology, hence there are so many versions, often to suit a certain location—such as Glastonbury which we know to be erroneous."

"So?"

"So take *'Joseph in Mamore'*, which could mean a 'marble tomb' as most believe, or *mamore*, such as a marble-like sea, meaning he is buried near the sea, as the prophecy clearly states. Ynyswitrin being the dunes, derived from *vitrium*, Latin for glass — as in Glastonbury, the glassy isle."

"What of Arthur's cousin, Illtud? Might he not have passed on the secret to his pupil, Maelgwn? He did, after all, live in a cave at Ogmore."

Dylan was wary of forming any definite conclusion, but the image — an image such as described in the Grail Romances — refused to allow objective thought. He'd played on the notion that the stones of the chapel would reveal the source of ancient knowledge in the form of a telling inscription or the discovery of an ancient book, never an actual image of the Holy Grail.

Gail toyed with the image on screen, enlarging it to maximum, revealing an intense white light whose edges splayed outward like a thousand finely frosted needle points in which she sensed a continuous radiating movement.

"But why not an angel?" asked Gail, "A guardian angel, such as you were to Robert Fitzhammon. Tell me again of that dream that you had of him. It is so much more relevant now that this has occurred."

"We were of the same bloodline, which is perhaps how it works when choosing guardian angels."

"All very strange."

"Who'd believe it apart from the experiencer?" Dylan shrugged. "And why Robert Fitzhammon? Because he had inherited the secret passed on through generations."

"Tell me the dream, exactly as you remember it," she insisted.

"All I remember was that I was Fitzhammon's spirit guide, guardian angel if you like, conveying to him that you cannot grasp the meaning until you have grasped God, after which your desire to rule will disappear and you will become the protector of the secret."

"There's your answer: Fitzhammon and you were kin." She pointed to the light. "This has become your responsibility now, so gird on your sword, Lancelot of fame, from whose bloodline Robert Fitzhammon came."

Dylan wondered why him and not someone more qualified to instigate such a discovery, such as a historian or an archaeologist? He didn't want the responsibility; all he wanted to do was to chip away at a block of stone, work on the garden and walk the hills.

"Damn!" he uttered, rising from the throne of Arthur. "I'm not up for this."

"Be careful what you ask for, as the saying goes, because you might bloody well get it."

He walked off into the garden to sit by a marble angel shaded beneath a quince. Arms folded, he gazed up at the blue sky. Beneath his feet lay Isca Silurum, whose story has been told a thousand times, whereas Dylan's lay between the two worlds of past and present, Ariadne's thread his guide into the labyrinth where the minotaur stood guard over Joseph's tomb in the underworld. *"He lies at the bottom of the pit and calls on you to deliver him out of the dark."*

Gail sat smiling on her throne of oak, looking at him standing there tall and brave, yet full of misgivings, his humanity calling him to do this thing like the knights of old who fought for justice and truth.

She joined him in the garden. "Listen to me, Dylan. We can't show the photograph to Iona, not yet."

"Give me one good reason why not?"

"We need to be circumspect. Something of this magnitude must have at least one historical reference concealed within an ancient archive. Can't have gone unrecorded for two thousand years."

"Guardians are good at keeping secrets, going so far as to create a diversionary location at Glastonbury. Fitzhammon had something to do with that, by donating the sapphire altar of Llanilltud Fawr to Glastonbury. De Bloise, the founder of Glastonbury Abbey, knew that Joseph's tomb wasn't there but had no idea where it was. What he had known was that Fitzhammon had direct ancestral links to Melkin, whose forebears brought three books of his to Brittany, the source of the Grail stories emerging at that time. They were the origin of the stories of the troubadours of France, of Chretien de Troyes, who married Marie, the daughter of Eleanor of Aquitaine, who owned a copy of Melkin's book on the Grail."

"Why haven't you told me this before?"

"No reason," he replied, scanning the surrounding walls as if looking for a way of escape. "I'd no idea who Maelgwn was before all this began. I knew of Arthur, but who doesn't? Incredible as it would appear, I just want to drop the whole thing and run."

"Let's be serious for a second," she said, pointing to the image on the laptop. "Do you really think it's what it appears to be? "

"Do angels speak in tongues, or are they devils in disguise and the image is an illusion?"

"You mustn't allow your doubts to cloud your judgement."

"I'm just being cautious."

"Well, I'm not like that. I dive in—that's what I do. I don't care for dancing around the perimeter. All our research, whether from archives, books, or your dreams, will become sand on a beach waiting for the tide to wash it all away. Is that what you want? It is not what I want, so grab the bull by the horns, as you did when that bull stood on the railway track in face of an oncoming train and you grabbed its horns and forced it off the track."

"This is a different kind of bull."

"Not really," she said, watching him sullenly tugging at the ivy growing on the angel. She touched him on his shoulder. "Come on, gallant knight, I know how hard it's been for you."

He took her hand in his. "You are a great help to both of us. Pamela appreciates what you do for her."

"How do you know that?"

"She tells me."

"One of the worst things that has happened to her was me coming along. She's hurt, I know she is—"

"I don't believe that," he interjected. "She thinks the world of you."

"Don't be ridiculous. No woman in her shoes would feel good about another woman coming along and stealing her man."

"But you're not stealing me."

"No, but that's what she thinks."

"No, she doesn't."

"What planet are you on? You live in a dream world most of the time."

"Pamela likes you, I know she does."

"Yes, but she *loves* you, and thinks you're with another woman. Me."

"But I'm not with you."

"That's not the point."

"She knows that what we are doing is important."

"To whom? The future of mankind?"

"Hey now," protested Dylan. "That's not what I'm saying."

"Then what are you saying?"

"That there are situations more important than personal relationships."

"Now you're talking out of your what-not," she said, sitting away from him, the situation fraught with conflicting emotions.

Dylan's intention to do the right thing was hurting the love of his life. What he'd thought would be a romantic quest for the Grail had become one of soul survival.

"If it weren't for Pamela, I'd never have found the chapel."

"I know that," Gail retorted, "but I'm full of misgivings about us. It's only because of your conviction that I'm with you now. Our passion to seek the truth of our history."

Dylan walked off, confused as a bee choosing between two flowers, one whose scent he knew to be good to make honey and the other whose pollen would fruit another generation. The choice he made would change his life or dance like a devil on his dream. Was this the sacrifice demanded?

Raindrops patted the leaves of the tulip tree, and his dreams flitted by like fireflies as the Maidens of the Rose danced along the wall.

Gail came and sat by him. "Just remember, Dylan, I am with you because something brought us together. The quest is our life's work. I know how painful it is for you. I know we cause pain all around, but we don't have a choice. We must go on."

"Yes," he said, half-convinced.

"If you decide not to continue, I shall walk away. I shan't force you or push you."

"I know that you have no ulterior motive, that your passion is the same as my own, which in itself is a marvellous thing. Pamela does know the big picture, and she'd love to be here right now, but she can't, and that hurts me more than you know."

"But I do know, because you can't hide your feelings from me."

"We are all in this together, whether we realise it or not, because in some way Spirit orchestrates our actions from behind the scenes to bring light back into this world."

"I honestly don't know what to say."

"And I don't want the responsibility of it."

"Should we ask permission to investigate the chapel further?"

"Iona indicated that would be difficult with Cadw involved."

"We wouldn't go there with picks and shovels."

"No," said Dylan. "We must back off and not do anything stupid."

"We could ask Iona what she knows of its history."

"We could ask, but she seemed not to know."

"Perhaps her brother?"

"Doubt he'll allow us anywhere near the place."

"Not if we show him the photograph."

Dylan shook his head. "My intuition tells me no, not to pursue that avenue."

He looked again at the image in the chapel. He almost wished it wasn't there, though there was no avoiding its haunting brilliance, ephemeral as the angels who show us the source of our wanderings, who permeate our being with the essence of universal love.

29

The Grail
Conundrum

The anti-climax of the euphoric revelation was a boot up the backside, like waking up from an otherworldly dream.

Pamela's health improved, allowing Dylan more days at the shop, where he hammered on a block of stone and saw to customers, despite feeling as if only half of him were there, the other half being with the love of his life.

This quiet period offered the opportunity to process and evaluate the revelation in the chapel, whilst remaining grounded and circumspect. He'd wander over to the amphitheatre to sit and contemplate the unreality of it all, whilst conjuring up images of Arthur mingling amongst the tourists with their mobiles and cameras as armed knights paraded on horseback in their armoured glory of burnished steel and round shields of blue and bronze, and Sutton Hoo helmets, Celtic in their detailed zoomorphic design.

Were they truly the Knights of the Holy Grail, a religious order of the Holy Mother Church of Jerusalem, hijacked by Arthur? The Order of the Round Table was sometimes called 'The Fellowship of the Ring', which its members wore as an insignia of that order derived from the assembly of knights at the Roman amphitheatre at Caerleon, where Arthur was Supreme King, St David Archbishop, and Maelgwn Gwynedd Chief Elder. Tutor to Talhaiarn the Bard and Merddin Emrys, Maelgwn instituted the Bardic Chair of Caerleon.

Arthur's objective to unite the Celtic Druidic Church of the Culdees with the Church of Jerusalem to stand against the power of the Church of Rome resulted in him being denounced as a heretic and a Pelagian, an attitude of Welshness still prevalent today.

Dylan surveyed the land as though it were a stage on which 'The Matter of Britain' played out. A recurring theme, a recurring dream, over hills and valleys back through time, soaring like an eagle through his mind's eye. Over Cymru's land he flew, to Anglesey and beyond to Skye.

Plagued by visions of the past, white-cloaked men on white horses, white armour, swords and spears strike against the enemy, lightning fast, hit and run, bravest of the brave, no quarter given since the great betrayal, the Night of the Long Knives at the gathering of Cerdic's Saxons on Caer Caradoc.

If the music plays and choirs sing, the people prosper and hope vibrates across the land. If poets recite the deeds of the brave, hope lives in the heart. If a secret is surrendered to placate an enemy, death will follow. Never did the Cymry divulge or teach to the Saxons their beliefs, and so began the march of Rome to subdue the Apostle-taught Christian Celts.

"Hi," Gail said, dropping her canvas shopping bag onto the table. "How are you feeling after the revelation of the chapel?"

"Still shell-shocked, like you, I guess."

"Not really, because I think I know what it is," she said brightly. "It's a portal into the Celtic Otherworld, the light of the Grail visible only to those with clear vision and a pure heart."

"Cuts me out then," joked Dylan.

"Lancelot was allowed to see the Grail but not to touch it."

"Story of my life."

"He was a man of the world, a warrior."

"That's because he was a Druid."

"You still are."

"Damn right I am," he said, gesturing to her to sit. "So then, my number one research associate, what gem hast thou found that you travelled seven leagues from Camelot to the City of the Legions to tell me?"

"You're full of Irish blarney today. Been on the whisky have you?"

"Just coffee."

Gail opened her notebook. "Copied this from the Charter of Patrick, dated 430 AD. He's left France — or wherever he was, as it isn't made clear. Anyway, he returns to Britain and just happens to chance upon the Isle of Ynyswitrin." She looked up at Dylan. "Just like that! Do me a favour, like he hadn't a clue where it was."

"Sure, you and me are good at spotting fabrications. Okay, so go on."

"Quoting his own words now: 'Where I found a place holy and ancient' — "

"Ancient?" cut in Dylan. "St Patrick's concept of ancient could only refer to Neolithic or Iron Age. Just as the twelfth-century Perlesvaus Manuscript states, 'that Joseph's tomb is in a small chapel between the caer and the wild woods beyond, because in front lie the meadows and sand dunes leading to the sea where the pagans lie buried'."

"You mean the caer?"

"Well, yes, what else? Carry on."

"...and there found certain brethren imbued with the rudiments of the Catholic faith, who were successors of St Fagan and Deruvian...."

"Allow me to interrupt you," cut in Dylan, "but there are no churches in the whole of Britain named after either St Fagan (Phaganus) and Deruvian other than those in Glamorgan. And when he says they weren't Catholics, he means they were Pelagians."

"May I continue?"

"Please do," he said with a yawn.

"He goes on to say the guardians were of noble birth of the line of Cunedda Vledig."

"Maelgwn's ancestor."

"Whatever! So Patrick says they showed him writings of St Fagan's and Deruvian, wherein it was contained that twelve disciples of Phillip and James had built the old church in the honour of Mary, and that to those twelve, three pagan kings had granted for their sustenance twelve portions of land."

"Ynyswitrin." Dylan yawned.

"'Now after some time had passed we climbed through dense woods to the summit on the mount which stands forth in that Isle. And when we were come there we saw an ancient oratory, nigh well ruined yet fitting for Christian devotion, and when we entered therein we were filled with so sweet an odour that we believed to be in Paradise...'"

Gail broke as Dylan feigned sleep by snoring loudly.

"Wake up, you!" she yelled. "This might be important."

"Sorry, where am I?"

"About to breathe your last if you do that again."

"I'm familiar with Glastonbury's souped-up version of Patrick stumbling upon the tor by chance, which by itself is highly suspect."

"Then please let me finish."

"I'll try not to doze off."

"Right, so he finds this ruined chapel—"

"Oratory," interjected Dylan. "Different from a chapel."

"So you were awake." Her annoyance was about to boil over. "So, he searched the place diligently and found a volume in which were written the Acts of the Apostles, along with the deeds of Phaganus and Deruvian—"

"Must've been very busy, those two."

"Stop it now, or I won't read any more."

"That a promise?"

"Let me finish," she said, exasperated. "He had a vision of Jesus, who said to him, 'I have chosen this place to the honour of my name.'"

"What, Jesus?" Dylan yawned.

"Of course not, but He was often called what?"

"The Lamb of God?"

"You can be hard work sometimes."

"Obtuse is the word you're looking for."

"Whatever. So stop playing games. Who looks after the sheep?"

"Ah," he said, raising a finger. "A shepherd."

"And what is *buceil*?"

"A shepherd."

"Say no more, I rest my case."

"Which is?"

"That Patrick's story had been stolen from here and placed in Glastonbury."

"How can you prove that?"

"I can't," she said, downcast.

"Yes, you can. Think. The guardians, where were they from?"

"Cunedda Vledig's Kingdom of Gwynedd."

"So what are they doing so far from home in Glastonbury?"

"Good point, whereas here's practically on their doorstep. What else is interesting is that the name of Patrick's Irish companion is Ogmar."

"Ah!" exclaimed Dylan, suddenly alert. "Ogmar as in Ogmore?"

"Read it for yourself," she replied, gathering her notes. "It's in here somewhere."

"I dreamt about the chasm the other night, a dream in which a young woman with short dark hair hovered over the chasm and went away. She did this three times. On a ledge halfway down a man was healing another man using crystals of different colours. So it's not over yet."

"Will it ever be?"

"One day."

"The battle you've been fighting has gone on for a very long time."

"As Chief Sovereign after Arthur, Pendragon of the Isle of Britain, Arthur's Knight of a Hundred Horses, whose son, Rhun, the Shining One, whose mother was Gwallwen, daughter of Avallach. the Galahad who saw the Holy Grail—"

"Yes," she interjected, "but what's it all for?"

"Freedom," replied Dylan.

"I know, but does it ever end?"

"The end is a mystery, as is the beginning. Life on Earth is a testing ground for souls to learn the difference between good and evil, and it is through gnosis we find the middle path where we walk between the two, unattached to worldly things, with a clear vision of the Kingdom within, the Divinity in everything."

"Oh, right," replied Gail. "Never thought of it like that."

"Let me make you a cuppa."

"You know I only drink water."

"Sorry for winding you up just now, just the whole thing's too much with me."

"I understand, but what if Glastonbury is a hoax, and our chapel is the real one?"

"Maybe," he said, only half-listening.

"Good bit of detective work, yeah? Lucius's appeal to Pope Eleutherius for Phaganus and Deruvian to return from Rome to Siluria with Elvanus Avalonius, who'd been living on the site of the chapel, a scholar in possession of books described by Patrick three hundred years later."

"Could well tie in with the chapel," Dylan replied, rising from the Arthur throne to go into the shop to put on lively Greek music on full volume.

Soon, he was dancing on the stone table, much to the amusement of Gail, who thought he'd lost it altogether. Rafi the Goldsmith wondered what was going on and joined them in their wild dancing. Even the Italians who ran the Ffwrwm restaurant 'The Snug' joined in with clapping.

Dylan had had enough of the serious stuff; he'd forgotten how important it was to play. What was the point, if one forgets to enjoy life? All very well questing, to use such hyperbole to describe an old ruin with a light in the window, even though Gail thought it a magical journey, whereas he'd locked himself up somewhere along the way and thrown away the key.

"Bugger it!" he yelled, completely of breath. "Bloody marvellous! Recalled to life, as Manet said when he was let out of prison."

"That's you alright," said Gail. "Welcome back."

30

Interlude

The following weeks ticked by on their own rhythm, staying at home with Pamela, shopping, cooking, everyday doings, no angels with wings flurrying about the kitchen and knocking things over. Dylan laughed at all that now he was back on terra firma.

Pamela couldn't do much to help; she didn't need to—he loved doing things for her, getting certain foods and prescriptions from the chemist, or venturing into the garden if the weather was favourable, where they'd sit for hours without a word passing between them. That's how they were, just being there in the silence of their thoughts.

Her once-blonde hair had taken on a greyish hue, her once-beautiful features had begun to fade, though these outward changes never bothered him as her inner spirit always shone through. Pamela was once beauty queen at the Earls Court Motor Show, so it was hard for her to bear what illness does to our frail biology.

Dylan felt good living a normal existence once again. The Grail escapade had become a faded dream, a schism from the reality of normal living. Gail helped out in the shop several days a week, enabling him to be at home more. Carers came by once a day to help in whichever way they could, making sure Pamela was comfortable and giving her a rudimentary health check, although a cup of tea mingled with lively conversation is the best remedy to lift a person's spirits, better than any medicine.

Grey skies warned of winter's approach as Dylan walked the nearby hills of the Wenallt to ease the emotional pain of seeing the person he loved undergoing discomfort and distress, although Pamela never complained.

Dylan stood on the forlorn, crumpled ruins of Morgraig Castle, situated on a ridge overlooking the City of Cardiff, its megalithic crystalline walls constructed by the Welsh to stop the tide of the Norman invasion.

The ridge sloped gently down into a green and sheep-grazed meadow towards a white farmhouse, the birthplace of Oliver Cromwell in the Commote of Kibor and King Arthur's Caermelin, where Dylan saw him standing on the yellow field as if to say: 'This is my kingdom. Join forces with me once again, for though your kingdom is far from my own here at Kibor, it is ordained that we raise our battle standards together, as one company, to overcome the gathering storm that stands between us and salvation, the final battle before the restoration of the Golden Age. I am always here, always ready.'

31

Vespasian?

Dylan and Gail walked along the winding road that followed the valley which once let in the sea as far as the monastery of Llanilltud, providing safe anchorage for ships bringing supplies to the greatest centre of learning in Europe during the Dark Ages.

Dylan held great respect for the woman with him, who asked for nothing, only to be a part of his quest. Her love was impartial, her thoughts pure as heaven, a child of the Universe. He jokingly called her the Grail Maiden, although it was apparent she'd become that feminine aspect, her passion for the truth clear as daylight.

"Where would you be without me?" she said jokingly.

"Up the creek without a paddle," he replied, laughing.

"Why did Joseph choose here and not Glastonbury?"

"Because England was overrun by the Romans. Lead ingots found a few miles from there stamped with the names of Nero and Vespasian prove it."

"But not if he came here in 37 AD, the last year of Tiberius, as Gildas claims."

"Point taken," he replied. "Who's to know the truth beyond the legend?

"You haven't answered my question; why did he choose to live in South Wales?"

"Kinship between the Silurians and the Hebrews. Druid priests wore a breastplate identical to the Jewish priests. The Silurian Sabbath was also on a Saturday. Taliesin composed verse in Hebrew. The Coelbren alphabet is similar to Hebrew."

"I thought you were a quite serious person when I first saw you," she said, mimicking a down-mouthed grimace. "Very serious."

He laughed. "Now you know I'm an idiot."

"True, you can be wise one minute and totally stupid the next."

"A walking conundrum."

"We have a brief respite here before I go back to Pamela. You know I can't be away for long."

"I know, but it's good to breathe the sea air, which you need more than me. You need to take more care of your health, you know."

"I know," he said absently, listening to the roaring sea in the distance that filled the valley with the timeless sound of water warring against the land, for water, like love, will wear down the hardest of rocks over time.

"What's so special about their philosophy? What spiritual relevance did it contain?"

"Much of what they taught hasn't survived, or was censored by the Church, particularly their veneration of nature and belief in the transmigration of souls."

"Reincarnation?" she interjected.

"The Druids believe we incarnate through many life forms before becoming human."

"I believe we're descended from angels, albeit fallen ones, as the Bible says."

Dylan laughed.

"Don't laugh at me, it hurts."

"Sorry."

"Tell me more of Joseph."

"A merchant in metals, so is said, a Nobilis Decurion, a free citizen of the Empire. Wales has copper, lead, iron, even gold, though he didn't come to buy and sell metal, but for safe refuge. Claudius may have been a closet Christian, yet he'd passed an edict to exterminate all those of the House of David. If it was 58 AD that he came with Eurgain, then it was Nero who was in charge. If it was Vespasian who allowed a prominent member of the House of David to go free, then he had a pragmatic reason for doing so, such as using Joseph as a go-between to arrange a peace agreement with the Silurians, who'd resisted the Roman legions for twenty years. Rome had been humiliated by a small tribal kingdom that made mincemeat of the Roman legions. The poet Juvenal mocked the Emperor Nero when he wrote: 'and is Arviragus still dancing on his chariot pole?'."

"Was there peace?"

"No, the Silurians wanted them gone from Britain, period. This would be around 59 to 61 AD. Vespasian had exterminated the Druids of Brittany and France. The Silurians knew that he'd do the same to them by way of a peace treaty. They would have none of it, and would rather die fighting than surrender their holy men to a monster. Vespasian then took off to Palestine to put down the Jewish uprising before seizing the purple."

"What a story."

"Yet another episode of our debunked history," asserted Dylan. "People may think that because it was so long ago it no longer matters, but it does, which is why the old stories were passed down the generations to let people know that a long line of heroes had given their lives for their freedom."

Gail paused to lean against a wall overlooking the Hodnant brook.

"Twenty-seven arrived here, according to Eusabius, including Phillip, Aristobolus son of Herod Antipas, who became the first Bishop of Britannia. Also Martha, Anna, Mary Cleopas, Mary Salome."

"Would Vespasian have allowed them all to go free?"

"Christianity was already creating havoc with the pagan beliefs that held the Empire together, whether they believed in their gods or not. These were major players deported from Palestine, far from the messianic fever that was sweeping over the Middle East, so why not let them contaminate a principality of no consequence to the Empire, where he could deal with them at a later date? His plan failed, as the new religion evolved through Celtic Druidic beliefs into a unique form of Gnosticism."

Gail scribbled furiously on a notepad, much to Dylan's amusement.

"Isn't holy writ, you know," Dylan smiled.

"Just my way—writing down what people say. You'll write a book about this one day. Then you will thank me."

"But who'd believe it?"

"Doesn't matter," she replied, "because if only one person were to read your book, it would be worth it. We live on a beautiful planet, and our soul's purpose is to love one another and speak our truth. We walk a lonely path in a world where soul talk is ridiculed, but we can't do anything other than speak our truth. Sometimes a voice from Heaven in the guise of a little bird lands on our shoulder and speaks to us."

"In a dream I had long ago," said Dylan, "a man who was Everyman spoke to me, pointing at the sky. 'The stars are just holes in the sky,' he said, and plucked a star. 'You can look at it now that its light has been taken away. Pity their cold lifeless forms haunt space.' I look up to see the Greek Pantheon moving across the sky. 'All the gods are here,' he said. 'Hermes, Perseus, Dionysus. They want an answer: Why are you without money, without home, alone?' To which I answered, 'Because that's the way I choose to go.' 'Then you have their blessing,' he said with a smile."

"Who says the old gods don't talk to us?"

"Archetypes are energy forms that encapsulate our deep longing for wholeness by embodying aspects of our psyche programmed to respond to symbols that resonate within us. Sometimes they are transposed onto natural features of the land to make sense of natural phenomena, the dangers of wild beasts and the powers of Nature, such as earthquakes, volcanoes and storms. We live in a very precarious world, which is why we need a new myth if we are to survive. In other words, man's future myth is man's megalith, which leads me to the second part of the dream."

"There's more?"

"There's always more," he laughed. "I lived like a recluse in those days—reading, writing, meditating, walks in the country, working two, three days a week as a landscape gardener, my life very much one of simplicity."

"How old were you then?"

"Twenty-two, until thirty-five."

"The dream?"

"Yes, so Everyman said, 'The Spirits have returned to Earth once more. Their task is to lighten the burden of salvation of mankind. You won't have to begin, it has begun for you. Here they come, all three of them; they are good and wise and strong. Only follow and the rest will follow.'"

"That's very reassuring, but we still have to do our bit," said Gail, mesmerised by the eddying waters of the brook.

"Of course," responded Dylan. "That's what we're here for."

"What does it mean, 'Only follow and the rest will follow?'"

"To pay heed to the inner voice and guidance from dreams. Belief activates, non-belief smothers the little seed trying to grow towards the light. It's the same battle then as now, the battle for our souls."

"Do you consider yourself blessed to have lived like a monk for all those years?"

"Let's not get romantic about it. The first seven years were tough, the longing to be with friends and family, though I didn't shut myself off completely. Norman came to stay for five years before going on to university and teaching."

"Your brother?"

"Yes," replied Dylan. "A sensitive soul who loves nature. We are like twins in the way we think about life. He's also a damn good poet as well. He married Katriye, who's Turkish. They have three grown up children, and a brother-in-law named Attila."

"Attila?" laughed Gail. "He must be fun to live with."

"Like living with a Gemini who was Maelgwn?" quipped Dylan. "It's fatal to be caught up with past-life memories that prevent us from living fully in the Now, unless something of value needs to be utilised in terms of insight into our origins, of who we are, though not in the ego sense, but in search of truth."

"Yes, I can understand that."

"To think so many believe that they only have one shot to get to Heaven. How cruel a lie is that? Add the belief that you are already born a sinner, and you are crippled with guilt before you can walk."

"Tell me about it," responded Gail. "Mother threatened me with hell and damnation so often I thought it would be a relief to go there if only to get away from her."

Dylan laughed. "Another casualty of religion."

"She couldn't help herself. She was so full of guilt."

"About what?"

"Everything. Doing the wrong thing, being disapproved of by other members of the Salvation Army. Truth is she didn't know how to be happy, crippled with so much guilt. I was only three when I first performed for them on stage. She could not love me; she didn't know how. My father did, but I was only eight when he died. She grieved for years, cried a lot, berating me for the least thing. She was so crippled with guilt, she was afraid to be happy."

She took hold of his arm. "What will happen to us if we find Joseph's tomb? Will they be after us? Will they really want us out of the way... you know?"

"Don't be silly, this isn't *The Da Vinci Code*."

He held her close. She was afraid, not because of her courageous belief, but of the authorities who might prevent their discovery from becoming public knowledge.

"This the same brook that runs through the churchyard?" she said, peering at the flowing water beneath a little bridge.

"The Hodnant, yes."

"The Hodnant, what does it mean?"

"The abundant valley, though William of Malmesebury calls it Rosina Vallis, the Valley of the Rose."

"Such a beautiful name."

"This is the place of the seven maidens and the Rose."

"How significant."

"I've often thought so."

"The Rose and the Lion. What does the Lion represent?"

"Divine Guardianship."

"Oh, never heard the Lion represented that way before."

"Whatever it is, it's a powerful symbol," affirmed Dylan. "'Blessed is the Lion which becomes man when consumed by man; and cursed is the man whom the Lion consumes.' From the Gospel of Thomas, meaning that if a man is overcome by his lower nature, he curses himself."

"Marvellous analogy."

"My favourite is this one: 'When you make the two one, and when you make the inside like the outside, and the outside like the inside, and the above like the below, and when you make the male and the female one and the same, so that the male not be male nor the female female; and when you fashion eyes in place of an eye, and a hand in place of a hand, and a foot in place of a foot, and a likeness in place of a likeness, then you will enter the kingdom.'"

"Whoa!" she exclaimed. "That's deep."

"It's from the Gospel of Thomas also."

"But what does it mean?"

"How to create a spiritual body of light constructed of finer, more subtle matter."

"Which is what the yogis of India do all the time."

"Of course, nothing's new under the sun. Let's get to the beach, it's already late."

"Alright," she said, disgruntled. "We never seem to have enough time."

"We've all the time in the world, if only you knew it."

"What's that supposed to mean?"

"What it says."

They continued at a fast pace towards the beach, the shadows of trees crossing their path as swallows skidded along the valley on their journey to Africa. *An eventful summer,* thought Dylan, *which isn't over yet.*

"What is the meaning of the Rose?" Gail asked

"The mystical union between us and the Creator?"

"And the Lion?" she persisted. "Who or what is the Lion?"

"The Lion *is* the Creator."

Pebbles rattled in chaotic profusion on the beach where Gail sat on a rock as Dylan skimmed a flat stone over the surf. Her serene smile reflected inner peace as Dylan sat by her side.

"Isn't this good?" he commented. "Like the sound of the sea washes all our cares away."

"Always," concurred Gail.

Dylan lapsed into a tangible silence, his head down.

"You alright?" she asked.

"Yes, I'm okay."

"Are you?"

"Yes," responded Dylan. "Just thinking."

"About what?"

"Pamela."

"Oh," she said, suddenly alert.

"Just something I remembered not long after we'd got together."

"Do you want to tell me?" she said in a gentle voice.

"Why not? It was another one of those visions," he said with a wry smile.

"Please tell me. They're always interesting."

"Okay, I'll try to remember it all if I can. It begins with a man who flies over the sea from Palestine at the end of the Second World War, who bounces torpedo-like over the waves to alight upon a tiny island to talk to the two above, which is me and Pam sat on a cloud looking down upon the man standing there."

Gail laughed. "That's so funny."

"This is what he said to us: 'From The Book of Right Thinking. In the beginning was the water, and God parted the water and threw in livestock, and the livestock became people. Then was there war and famine on the land, and the land shook with a thousand hooves, and the sun shone brightly on many and the clouds parted to reveal the truth. The truth spoke of a sentinel who watched and blindly called his name from below, and the rose which was pink and purple became ash. Listen, my brethren, if the clouds part too many times, there will be nowhere for mankind to go, and he'll become numberless and the stars will shake down their dew upon him. Then, my little people, will he know the truth.

"'Amused by his antics they laugh, for they know what he says is true, and they love him for his wisdom, for who can forsake the emblem of the cross and summon Churchillian inspiration to speak for him.

"'God spoke to me, and his words were recorded, and there lying in a tulip field was an emblem of pure gold. It was everything and of indestructible value, and the words flowed forth in a torrent of thanksgiving, and so are the mighty fallen, their death to come. Liberty was at its best then, and stood the test and hammered the message, that all good will prevail, that evil is to no avail. Land and water, heaven and earth, two pastures green, the loved ones serene. These words are simple and so is love when found. The mountains quake and your innards shake when thoughts of love abound.

"'That's enough for now, we don't want to tire ye, do we? Be more to come in another while, lessons to be learned and suchlike, and ye'll do well at it too if I have my say in the matter, so head down now and spill out the words and to hell with all else.'

"He looks up to us and winks.

"'How oft upon my couch I lie, in vacant or in pensive mood,

There sings a little lullaby of heaven and hell, or one such word.

Heaven's hell when there's no love in it, so time and place don't matter.'"

"Excuse me interrupting," said Gail. "He said all that to you and Pam?"

"Long time ago, but very appropriate considering what's happening all over the planet right now."

"That's what I thought. Prophetic, even."

"He finished by saying: 'Well, anyway, the message is: keep your sparky selves up and, laughing inwardly, light a spark of freedom. Blessings to the both of ye. Mark my words, ye are true, ye are, no mistaking that. I loves ye to my bosom, that's a fact as a totem. Bumpy landings.'"

"What a fantastic sense of humour," responded Gail.

"Yes, always makes me smile when I think of the things he said, which are pretty bloody serious, but it's the humour that lightens the load. That's Spirit talking, whereas Armageddonites are full of woe."

"Thank you for sharing that with me."

"Well it doesn't belong to me, I was just the vehicle for it... I seem to recall his name, which was something like Johanne or Johannes Kirsch, lived around 1720, an esoteric philosopher—well into the ancient mysteries and suchlike."

"A real person?"

"Of course."

"That was a gift from Spirit to you and Pam, so I thank you for that."

Dylan glanced at her with a tear in his eye as he stood up and threw another flat stone, which skimmed the water like the messenger.

32

St Samson

Dylan called Gail the following morning to inform her that Pamela had caught a virus and was suffering a fever. The doctor had said she should go into hospital, but Pamela refused, saying that people who go into hospital often die of something other than that which they went in with. Their visit to the chasm would have to wait until a more propitious time.

Pamela wasn't only feeling ill, but often depressed at how unattractive she'd become, having lost weight and her once beautiful hair turning grey. The anguish Dylan felt seeing her like that crucified him, but she never imposed upon him unduly, being such a strong and independent person, though she needed his help to get downstairs or into the garden to see the flowers and the birds flapping about in the birdbath.

The photograph of the apparition had quickly descended into the realms of unexplained phenomena. What did it prove? Very little, though Gail was convinced it was Spirit's way of saying it was the Chapel of the Grail. Dylan wasn't so sure; he'd seen lights before in Brazil, when a star-shaped being appeared close to the healing centre of Joao de Deus, where orbs frequently appeared whenever people gathered to celebrate or to heal, for love was the motivating energy that attracts them.

Glastonbury had made much of its first chapel of wattle and daub, claiming that Patrick had restored it. Dylan thought it far more likely to be the chapel of the apparition, whose present structure was nowhere near two thousand years old.

John of Glastonbury recorded seeing the books of Melkin, as did Leyland and Hardynge. Why would they revere the writings of a sixth-century Welsh bard unless it validated their claim to Joseph's tomb? The answer lay in Melkin's Prophecy, describing the Grail as two silver cruets containing the blood and sweat of the Prophet Jesus. *Duo Fassula* could also mean 'folded twice', referring perhaps to a shroud which was stained with the blood and sweat of Jesus. The Prophecy also stated that he lay buried in or next to a chapel on a rocky tor near the sea, whereas Glastonbury was miles inland.

Frustrated, Dylan looked out of the window at the falling rain, thinking he wouldn't have to water the plants for a while. Grass grows quickly after rain, a bonanza for the blackbirds after worms, which is what he was after — the worm of a relevant word or two to pop out of a book. But which one of the scores lined up on the bookshelves, containing hundreds of names in a who's who of early Christianity?

He'd scanned dozens of book titles until a slim volume with a yellow cover squeezed between tomes on archaeology caught his eye. He flicked it open to a page near the middle to read the words printed there: 'And he caused Amon to come with him, along with the brother of the envious priest, besides the aforementioned Irish brother, four of them altogether, to a very desolate desert, and, having discovered a very delightful caer near the Severn Sea, and in it a spring of very sweet water, he set about making a dwelling for his brothers, while he prayed that the Lord would be pleased to show him some underground cave, and the Lord fulfilled that most faithful prayer. For on a certain day, as he wandered through the forest he found a very spacious and very lonely cave, and its mouth being situated towards the east, he embraced it affectionately as though it had been given by God for a dwelling.'

Leaning back in his chair as if in a trance, he gently placed a bookmark on the relevant page and closed it and smoothed it as if it were a long lost family member. The extract was from the biography of St Samson of Dol, describing the chasm at Merthyr Mawr.

Seven days passed before Pamela had recovered sufficiently for him to go the shop again. He called Gail and asked her to meet him there. It was a quiet day with hardly anyone around. He sat on the throne of Arthur with its telling tale of Lancelot and Gwenhyver, whose liaison caused the unwitting demise of Arthur's dream of the Round Table and a return to a Golden Age, a dream rooted in the psyche of the Celtic people.

A robin hopped close by until a black cat came to scare it away. Birds sing despite danger, people talk freely despite persecution, all living things aspire to overcome fear.

"Hello!" Gail said, startling him out of his reverie. "How are you, and how is Pamela? I assume she's feeling better?"

"She's okay. Things were touch-and-go for a while, but she's a fighter. Though not being able to breathe properly is the killer."

"Yet she still smokes."

"Hardly now, just the occasional puff, as it's the thought more than anything."

"She shouldn't, and you shouldn't encourage her either."

Dylan indicated to Gail to take a seat. "Pamela insisted I come here today, knowing the strain it's having on me. She's independent minded and doesn't want to be a bother to anyone."

Gail saw the tear in his eye before he rubbed it away. "I know that you are brave, doing what you do, and if you think that this is all getting a bit too much, then say. I'll understand. Because compared to Pamela's health, what we are doing is as nothing."

"Quite so, Gail, but you don't understand — she knows how important this is. She wouldn't wish me to abandon it. Besides, apart from the occasional recon here and there, all my research is done at home."

"My God, she's noble! What other woman would do that?"

"Pamela's noble as a queen, her giving and her love go way beyond normal bounds."

"But you just told me that she doesn't want that, that you need this to offset the stress of it all."

"That doesn't let me off the hook of my own conscience."

"Ask yourself what more can you do without going under. I care about your health, so please respect her wishes."

"Home help arrives twice a day now."

"Good, gives you a chance to recover."

"Good to be back at the Ffwrwm. I miss this place."

"Not surprised — it's beautiful here," she replied, sitting on a Hobbit chair of oak. "You said you had something important to tell me?"

"Yes—I came across this information relating to the chapel by chance," said Dylan, before reiterating the passage from Samson's biography.

"What a perfect description of the chasm and the caer. I am impressed."

"It's been bugging me that I'd read somewhere about the place, and just by chance I found the right book."

She thought for a moment, "What of the chapel? Is there any mention of it?"

"On the following page, which I shall read to you now: '...and up to the time when I was in Britain the place, in which the three before-mentioned brothers were, was always reverenced with great devotion, and also an oratory constructed therein, where St Samson was wont to come every Sunday to sing mass and for Christ's communion'."

"Does that mean St Samson constructed the oratory, or that it was already there?"

"Allow me to read the next paragraph. 'A synod having been summoned, when the older men inquired where St Samson lay hid, a certain man came forth and said that he would be found at that cave wherein St Samson was leading a heavenly life.'" Dylan closed the book. "Samson preferred living in a cave like so many hermits and was reluctant to leave there to attend a synod in Paris in 554 AD."

"Merlin and others, didn't they just?"

"Hermits often preferred to live in a cave or to worship in the open like the Druids."

"Why then would he have gone to the trouble of building an oratory if he was happy with the cave?"

"Precisely," replied Dylan. "What is certain is that it had always been regarded as a very holy place by the Britons."

"And now no one knows of its existence — apart from you and I it seems."

"The author, Henoc, was Taliesin's father, after whom Llanhenock is named."

"Isn't that the little village just outside Caerleon?"

"Yes, and the story of Samson's life was related to him by Tigernomalis, Samson's nephew, who attended the college at Llanilltud Fawr. The chapel and the chasm are replete with connections from Joseph through to Arthur. Samson's mother was Anna, Arthur's sister. Illtud was Arthur's cousin. Paul Penychen, or Paul Aurelian, was Arthur's brother. Arthur's stone at Ogmore relates to a monastery there."

"A Piccadilly Circus of comings and goings."

"This is from the *History of Glamorgan*, volume two," said Dylan, retrieving a note from his rucksack. "After reading the paragraph from Samson's biography, it triggered a memory of having read that somewhere else. Then I re-read the section in the Glamorgan History on Merthyr Mawr, and this came up: 'St Samson with several companions settled on a site close to the Severn Sea, which has a chapel within a prehistoric earthwork and a cave with a stream running through it', with the comment that: 'The striking resemblance to the chapel at Merthyr Mawr and its adjacent cave may or may not be a coincidence.'"

They looked at each other and smiled.

"There you have it," affirmed Gail.

"The desert referred to by St Samson being the extensive sand dunes," added Dylan. "The prehistoric earthwork is the caer, and the cave is the chasm. A very accurate description of the chapel and its surroundings, wouldn't you say?"

"Spot on," she said with a happy smile. "Well done for coming across such information."

"Knew I'd read something about a certain saint living in a cave close to the sea. Just couldn't put my finger on it, then all of a sudden there it was, staring at me on a bookshelf: the biography of St Samson."

"Funny how these things happen. You search for something, and up it pops, out of the blue."

"How about we pop to Merthyr Mawr soon to explore the chasm?"

"Especially knowing what we know now."

"I think we should," said Dylan. "Pamela's on the mend, so all being well, we will be able to go there."

"Good," said Gail. "Tomorrow it is then."

33

Oeth and Anoeth

It was a sunny day as they sped along the motorway to Merthyr Mawr. All their energy had been devoted to discovering the missing link between Joseph and the enigma of the Melkin Prophecy, which no one had got close to solving since it was written in the sixth century. Neither had Dylan, during all his visits to Merthyr Mawr over many years, ever considered the possibility of its connection to Joseph of Arimathea.

"I feel excited today, don't you, that we have this opportunity to explore the cave?"

Gail's enthusiasm had little effect on Dylan, who was engrossed in his notes. "Could say."

"You seem miles away. What are you reading?"

"St Samson crossing Cornwall on his way to Brittany, confronts a gathering worshipping an idol of Bacchus, so he persuades them to burn the idol and become Christians."

"At least he didn't burn non-believers alive as did St David."

"One thing's clear from this extract, that there was still a mishmash of pagan beliefs clinging on from Roman times."

"Druids would tolerate what Roman Catholics would not."

"Quite so. Samson's parents went to see a wizard in the mountains to ask for help in conceiving, who said 'bring me two rods of silver and you shall have a child who shall be born wise'. They did as asked and Samson was born."

"The old stories of wizards, goblins and fairies say a lot to our dumbed-down imagination, overloaded with pixels and computer-generated alternative realities when we've yet to suss out this one."

"Nice one, Gail," chuckled Dylan. "Definitely something unusual about Samson; his visions whilst living in the cave of James and John. Scribes often inserted miracles into the stories of saints, but Samson's visions were real, I'm sure. One of his fellow monks was his father, Amon, son of the King of Dyfed. His mother was Anna Ferch Meurig ap Tewdrig, Arthur's sister."

"Were all the monks from royalty?"

"Mostly, a kind of family business," replied Dylan. "Monks were taught to read and write and to know the history of their culture, and the works of the Greek philosophers and Alexandrian Gnosticism, such as Clement, who described the chasm of Anoeth in the second century. Small world."

"People travelled about more than we realise. Samson visited his mother living in Caerwent..."

"Arthur's sister?"

"Living at Caerwent, which is Camelot, which you know very well as you live near there."

"I do," replied Gail. "It's an amazing city with its walls and towers as legend describes the fabled Camelot."

"Pull up just here!" he said quickly.

"What for?"

"Need to check something out."

"What?"

Gail stopped the car, allowing Dylan to scan the run of the Ogmore river to where it had carved a deep pool out of the rock.

"*Pwll y Lech!*" exclaimed Dylan. "The Pool of the Stone mentioned in the Llandaff Charters in 875 AD."

Gail stared into the deep clear water where time had carved its mark two hundred feet below the rocky summit on which stood the Chapel of the Great Martyr.

"The charter is the first to mention Buciel, Greek for shepherd."

"The Chapel of the Shepherd."

"The Great Martyr is the Shepherd."

Dylan studied the rock face where the river had cut in, forming caves, though it was hard to tell how far they penetrated. Gail looked up towards the chapel, invisible amongst the trees.

"The Celtic crosses in the chapel," she asked. "Did you find out what the inscriptions say?"

"The smaller of the two says, 'Conbelinus placed this for his soul and the souls of Glwys, Nertat and his brother'. Same as on Arthur's Stone at Ogmore Castle."

"Who'd ever suspect that tucked away up there, visible only to eagles and buzzards, is the Chapel of the Grail? Anoeth!" exclaimed Gail as her foot hit the pedal.

"What about Anoeth?" queried Dylan.

"He and his knights asleep in a cave, what if..."

"The legend is true?" interjected Dylan. "That he was buried in Anoeth just as the Stanzas of the

Graves say? Wishful thinking we must avoid, and conjecture isn't proof."

"Schliemann conjectured his way to Troy. Howard Carter conjectured the whereabouts of the tomb of Tutankhamen..."

"Just be careful we don't go chasing wild theories," cautioned Dylan. "Wace, author of *Le Roman de Brut*, said regarding the tales of Arthur 'that we have turned fact into fiction, embellished to entertain so that our tales are neither all fable or all true'. Thus ratifying that there was a source book, possibly Melkin's *De Arthurii Mensa Rotunda* — which could have turned up in Brittany via Robert Fitzhammon, which then found its way to the court of Eleanor of Aquitaine whose daughter married Chretien de Troyes who wrote, *Parselvaus*."

"Now who's conjecturing on a book that may or may not have existed?"

"Except we have facts, written evidence, connecting Arthur and several members of his family to the cave. His cousin Illtud knew of it. His nephew Samson, for sure. His brother Paul Penychen, whose name is inscribed on the stone behind Teilo's church."

"Which is where we're heading now," said Gail, as they drove into Merthyr Mawr village with its landscaped vista. A pinnacle of rock amongst trees intrigued Dylan, who made a mental note to explore the anomaly.

They parked outside the churchyard, for the first time since the revelation at the chapel. Dylan paced up and down, looking up at the clouds as if expecting another revelation. He took the photograph of the chapel from his rucksack and stared at the glowing orb above the altar.

"And Arthur saw a flame coming through the window, a hundred times brighter than the sun, descending on the altar."

"Talking to yourself, Dylan?"

"That was a quote from *The Welsh Holy Grail*. And where more fitting than to be buried next to his ancestor Joseph?"

"Now who's getting carried away?"

"We've yet to explore the cave," he said. "Time's moving on, and it will be dark enough down there in the depths of Anoeth."

Again, Dylan noted the fish painted on the gate before knocking on Iona's door, but all seemed quiet, no dog barking or sign of life around the garden or the sawmill.

"What do you suggest we do?" asked Gail.

"She did say we were free to go there anytime."

"But we're going down the chasm this time."

"It is a dilemma, and I don't like doing this, but we have this one opportunity."

The walk towards the chapel woods felt serene. On the distant shore a cacophony of gulls and oyster catchers were feeding off the incoming tide of the Severn Sea, or the sea of the Goddess Sabrina, the original name for the Bristol Channel, venerated by Druids and Celtic Christians alike.

"Why would Samson, a Celtic Christian, choose to live in a cave associated with pagan gods and goddesses unless he were at least part Druid, as was Illtud, who was versed in the Arts of Stipho?"

"Who is Stipho?"

"A Greek of the school of Pythagoras," replied Dylan. "Of gods gone, of Christian ethics maintained. A cross-culture of pagan beliefs, Druidic thought, and Gnostic aspirations. The Silurian Druids recognised the kinship between Christianity and their own beliefs. You only have to read Taliesin's poems to know the truth of that."

They walked the rest of the way in silence, preparing inwardly for what to expect. Dylan carried the ropes over his shoulder, and Gail the torch-lit helmets. It would be risky, but nothing compared to the emotional dilemma of placing an otherworldly apparition into everyday existence, and it was only when they stood on the edge of the chasm, looking into the greyness, that a profound sense of something untouchable overwhelmed them as three rays of sunshine burst through shower clouds in the form of the Awen. Gail and Dylan recognised the portent, tying the rope firmly around a yew tree growing on the upper ridge of the chasm whose dark depths appeared foreboding.

"Pass me the helmet," he asked. "I'm going down."

"What helmet?" she joked. "Health and safety now! Just be careful."

"Aren't I always?" he replied with a wry smile.

"Sure, like the time we climbed that cliff. Only fifty feet to the top, you said, which turned out to be one hundred and fifty feet."

"We survived, didn't we? Anyway, that was up and this is down."

"Then you couldn't see the top, now you can't see the bottom."

"It's there somewhere," he said, sliding down the rope along a muddy slope. "You follow when I reach the cave."

Grasping tree roots, he secured a foothold in a rain-washed gulley, the sheer cliff face opposite disappearing into the darkness below like a grey ghost as loose stones clattered into the blackness to splash into the water at the bottom of the chasm.

Thrusting his fingers into a fissure in the boulder in front of the cave, Dylan wedged his body between it and the rock face. Gail slid towards him, afraid to look down, though her light and nimble body soon joined him, wedging herself between the boulder and the rock face, and giggled like a playful child.

The gap was barely wide enough for them to squeeze behind the boulder, where they discovered a deep-cut ditch big enough to bury a man, though the bones lying there were small, perhaps of a squirrel or a rabbit, the prey of a buzzard. As for evidence of a burial, there was none, as five feet of mud and silt had blocked the cave entrance to its roof, though fissures penetrated deep into the rock towards the chapel fifty feet away.

"Damn!" exclaimed Dylan. "Would you believe it? This mud must be five feet deep. No way we'll be able to shift that."

"Try not to be so pessimistic," Gail said, shining her headlamp into a narrow fissure of crystalline rock. "Bit of Semtex and we're sorted."

Dylan laughed. She always knew when to inject humour into a situation.

"Why does life throw up a major obstacle right on the verge of a major discovery?"

"Did you really believe it would be that easy to find the tomb of Joseph of Arimathea?"

"What do we do now?

"Think," said Gail, pulling her camera out of her beg. "Take a photograph or two and be on our way."

"Neither of us like to trespass, and we shouldn't be here."

"You're right," she replied, as her camera flashed, lighting up the chasm and the stream at the bottom.

"Impetuosity killed the cat, so let's get the hell out of here. This is their domain. The tomb, if there is one, isn't here. We find the chapel, and then the apparition telling us that this is the place..."

"And above is where one prays to the adorable Virgin," interjected Gail. "Isn't that what it says in the Prophecy?"

"'*Super potentum adorandum virginem*'," quoted Dylan. "And if this cave leads to the chapel; '*In Linea bifurcata juxta meridianum angulum oratori*'. Meaning 'He lies on a two-forked line next to an oratory'. And '*cratibus praeparitus*', means 'in a crater already prepared'."

"The chapel being above the cave."

"Therefore his tomb must be below the chapel."

The camera flashed once more into the chasm, its ancient dark rocks lit by digital lightning.

"Our last visit here was euphoric," pondered Dylan, "confirmation of a portal to another world, another dimension? This chasm, where the water flows into a Celtic Hades, Oeth Anoeth, where time stands still and past and present meet."

"This place is full of mystery and will not give up its secrets easily."

"Are you suggesting we go down there today?"

"Of course not," she said. "Besides, the rope's too short, and it'll be dark soon."

They climbed out of the chasm and sat breathless beneath a yew tree, its straight trunk reaching up to the sky whilst its sinewy roots dug deep into terra firma. Other yews grew in a circle around the chapel, thirty-three paces across, creating a hundred-foot arena, the same dimension as the earthwork at St

Llid. South of the chapel, a low-clinging yew spread its branches so wide the ground was touched by its foliage in all directions. Behind that, tall and stately, grew a cedar of Lebanon.

They sat on the grass close to the chapel to quench their thirst and hunger after their escapade. Tranquillity hung in the air like the first day of spring. Dylan glanced through the window where the glowing orb of light had appeared, now just grey limestone walls and the Goblin Stone, whose cross lost an arm centuries ago, giving it the appearance of a grotesque face. The eight-foot-tall cross had once stood in a field a mile away as a boundary marker of the monastery.

Gail was fascinated by the baptismal bath in front of the chapel. Dylan recalled Iona saying to them that a lamb had drowned in the baptismal font at the Chapel of the Shepherd—maybe nature had played a hand there. He stood up suddenly and walked towards the stone-lined bath.

"What's up with you?" she said, intrigued.

He pointed to the bath. "This is it."

"What?"

"Where Joseph is buried."

"What makes you think that?"

"Because it is against Talmudic law to be buried inside a temple or chapel. Now I know the relevance of what I saw in a dream the other night. I saw three crosses and three shrines or ossuaries here, inside this circle bounded by the low wall. One of the ossuaries was right where this baptismal bath is sunk into the ground."

Gail joined him, intrigued. "Do you really think he could be under that?"

Dylan turned to face the chapel. "'On a two-forked line next to the southern corner of an oratory.' It's in exactly the right location according to the Prophecy."

"It is," she said, following his line of sight. "And it's, what, thirty feet from the chapel?"

"About that, but it's the position, and also, I've never come across a man-sized baptismal font before."

"What about the other burials? You said there were six, so who were the other five?"

"Two were ossuaries, which could belong to Jewish disciples who accompanied Joseph. The three others are most likely Celtic Christians."

Dylan examined the mortared white limestone of the bath, filled to the rim though only two feet deep.

Gail put her hands into the clear water to taste. "It must be rainwater," she said. "There's no other source for it to be full like that."

Dylan crouched on the grass. "Why did we not figure this out before now, when it's been staring us in the face all the time?"

"Isn't that the way of it, blinded by other things."

"Phew!" exclaimed Dylan. "That's it, story complete, mystery solved, time to go."

They followed the track through the woods away from the chapel, where remains of the caer's ditches could be seen. Megaliths lay half-buried in the undergrowth but for two, whose craggy shapes looked like beings reaching towards one another though stuck fast in the earth. Leaving the stones, they crossed the meadow with a view of the river majestically winding its way alongside the dunes towards the sea, reminding them that this was the true Avalon of legend.

They returned to the car in silence, deflated but thoughtful, as the Church of St Teilo glowed pink in the evening sun, its pilgrim's cross long gone, along with tales of saints who'd come and gone. They drove slowly past thatched cottages, a child's swing hanging motionless from a tree on a lawn where a peacock displayed its feathers. Tranquillity abounded all around in a holy place of wonders, the legacy of those who'd gone before.

Dylan requested they stop close to the rocky outcrop that had attracted his attention earlier. Twilight was descending as he walked through a half-open gate into a thicket of nettles and Himalayan balsam. It was obvious no one had traversed that way as no telltale signs of disturbance were to be seen.

In front of the rocky outcrop, a small lagoon had formed, home to water-boatmen and other aqueous creatures. Dylan studied with amused interest the craggy rock festooned with ivy and small trees, a rainforest in miniature, an oddity of a sentinel marking some giant's grave.

He looked down at a large flat rock lying at his feet, half in and out of the water, on which was etched the image of a fish, stark white against the natural grey of the limestone, fresh as if inscribed that day. He studied it closely to make sure he wasn't just imagining the shape of a fish, Ictis, the sign used by early Christians. He took out his camera and photographed the finely drawn image, too precise to have been drawn by a child's hand.

When he returned to the car and they drove off, Gail noted that he was unduly quiet, as if in a kind of repose, saying: *do not disturb*. She waited for a signal that he was back on terra firma.

"Well?" she asked, as they'd reached the M4 motorway without a sign of his having returned to the here and now.

"What?" he replied.

"Well what?" she persisted.

"A fish," he declared.

"A living one?"

"No, stone dead, you might say."

"Oh?" she said, intrigued. "Well if it isn't living and it isn't dead, then it must be another riddle."

"A riddle it is," he replied, explaining what he'd just seen, how the stream that ran into the lagoon was the same as ran from the chasm, that there were no footprints or disturbance of any kind to indicate someone had been there in the recent past. And why was a fish also painted on the gate of the Old Forge?

"Who put it there and why?" asked Gail. "Are we being watched?"

"Has someone left a message for us? How would they know I would go there?" queried Dylan. "Unless the Ictis symbol was put there by a devout Christian to confirm Christ's message, that love is the same the world over, that love binds us to the Heavenly Father."

"Where's that come from?" she asked.

"Just thinking about the power of love harnessed to heal. We consider ourselves solid in a world of matter, an elusive interplay of forces beyond our comprehension, that our thoughts have more power to heal than an atomic bomb has to destroy."

"Sri Yukteswar said that there are only two kinds of people in this world: those who are searching for God and those who aren't," said Gail, activating the windscreen wipers. "My thinking is there's only one authenticity, one source to that authentic flow, the inner sun—the Awen, that flow of life—that there has to be structure and order so that it can flow between order and chaos, tapping into that stream of consciousness of a higher nature, the source of joy. Some use the hippy-dippy thing as an excuse for a hedonistic lifestyle. They think it's all love, which it isn't. I see love of Spirit as a tough love; without that love you lose the point, and that's a cop out. Mother is Mother Earth, and without that you have chaos, because there is no true nurturing without discipline."

Dylan scribbled her words onto a notepad whilst keeping an eye on the road, as he knew how easily distracted she could be.

"And if a conviction doesn't challenge to colour every aspect of your life and is just a peace and love 'do what thou wilt' movement of the sixties, it has very little depth. But it's the coming together of a group of people like that, a mass shifting of conscious awareness, that's needed right now. To most it's needful to reinforce, if they have to function in the mainstream world. For others who are fortunate to be out of that, it enhances and encourages our conviction to stay on the path of truth revealed by inner knowing within the framework of still being human. And where there is inner knowing and outward honouring and practising actively the fruits of that, then an authentic life can be lived, true to the Spirit of Creation, the source of all there is, which demands our willingness to live that authentic life of self-checking and not the anything-goes thing.

"Spirit's principle creation wouldn't be perfect without the creation of principles, whether we're up a mountain or wherever, and we dance and whoop it up and laugh with joy, then that is our joy, the reward of living a life authentically with Spirit—not temporal fixes of self-gratification but of eternal bliss. There's a difference; one is temporal and the other is eternal. But none of this can be gained until one knows intimately the moment when Spirit truly reconnects with your soul; not the heart, not the mind—that will naturally follow the first with soul. Otherwise it's like a hollow parody of what we think it is, the mother who opts out of her true responsibility to her child to instil discipline. Then it's not love, and love without discipline is chaos, and without it, not a bird or an animal could survive, and all would become extinct, and life as we know it would be no more."

"Seems I've teamed up with a philosopher," quipped Dylan as the rain blotted out the road ahead.

"Nature is not a singularity," continued Gail, "but an expression of it. We are so used to the notion of Spirit as a singularity, but it is not, it is everywhere and it is everything; it is Nature, and that is why Nature teaches us that you cannot put a label on it. It is us, and we are that, and we are given the gift to see outside that through our intuition, our instructor that sees beyond the illusion of matter into the realms that created Nature out of its own imaginings. So in truth, we worship an illusion that is real and structured; we venerate a straw doll because we made that out of our imaginings, just as nature is real but unreal." She looked at Dylan and laughed. "It's raining!"

"Only for the last five minutes."

"How come I didn't notice?"

"You must've done to have activated the wipers."

"I swear to you, I've no recollection. Where was I?"

"Away with the fairies, or channelling the Pleiadies."

"Oh my, I could've crashed the car."

"What, speeding along a motorway in a thunderstorm whilst delivering philosophical wisdom on the structure of Nature's realm, through torrential rain, visibility almost zero, surreal as an otherworldly celebration?"

"Oh," she said. "So that's what the fourth dimension looks like."

34

The Shepherd

Between waking and sleeping, between mind and imagination where opposites become one, free from the illusion of duality, he plucked a word out of thin air and played with it like a child with a toy. A wondrous thing to play with, a word that rings like a bell, vibrating universal sound all around.

To maps without wings, to rites without passage, many sayings, treatises and words of many labours. Historians miss the point and wonder at the words of God, who wrote the first history of the human soul backwards in time.

Many years ago, a man sat down to write the Gospel of Truth. The truth was prevalent, if obscure to the denizens of lies who lurked around the city of power. Therefore, take a thumbnail and hide it safely away to await the dawn of the Second Coming in the hearts of those who understand the true notion of freedom, moving circular in semi-helical spirals towards the cock of dawn.

'*Nomini Dei Patris et Fili Spiritus Sancti*', 'In the Name of God the Father and of the Son of the Holy Spirit'. Dylan copied these words onto a notepad from an online translation of the inscription on the

Conbelinus Stone at the Chapel of the Shepherd, describing Christ as of the Holy Spirit. The document also mentioned the Houelt Cross at Llanilltud Fawr having an identical inscription, stating that this method of describing the Messiah takes us right back to *The Shepherd of Hermas*, in which Jesus is equated with the Holy Spirit.

He scrolled down the page to read that Bede, author of the *Anglo-Saxon Chronicle*, never deemed the Celtic Church Catholic at all, and refused baptism from them.

Okay, thought Dylan, *that's a plus, being denounced by a recently converted pagan Saxon.* Bede went on to say that 'the Celtic Church omitted the trinity in honour of some Greek'.

Could the Greek be Hermas, author of *The Shepherd*? Dylan had researched archival Church history for years, where the appellation of 'Shepherd' referred to Christ. Depictions of the Shepherd in the Catacombs of Rome were a common motif to those early Followers of the Way. But the chapel was far from Rome, and a connection seemed highly unlikely; on the other hand, he'd never come across a church or chapel named after the Shepherd.

Reading on, he learned that Hermas had been a Greek living in Rome who wrote of his angelic visitations, which he penned into a book entitled *The Shepherd of Hermas*. His first visitation described an encounter with an ancient woman he assumed was the Sybyl of Cumae. "I am not she," he was informed, "but She for whom the world was made." Imbued with feminine symbolism, affirming the role of women in early Christianity.

He called Gail's mobile and waited for a response until the answerphone kicked in. Deciding not to leave a message, he went into the living-room to talk to Pamela about his discovery, but she was sleeping. He wandered into the garden, not hearing the ringing of his mobile.

The recent rain left the grass wet on his bare feet; he enjoyed feeling the earth on his skin. The pond was green with weed, a frog croaked like an old man. His solar plexus energy needed somewhere to go. Could the Shepherd be associated with the chapel whose name had stood for over a thousand years?

His mobile rang for the third time as he re-entered the house. Pamela was awake and asked for a cup of tea, and who kept calling? He told her he'd found out something important and had called Gail to let her know. Pamela had seemed put out until he reassured her, telling her what it was about. Dylan's impetuous and overly enthusiastic ways often led him into deep water.

Pamela suggested he go to the shop tomorrow, as he'd not been there all week because she'd needed him at home. Dylan wondered what Gail knew of the Shepherd, as she'd read the Bible since she was a child. Meanwhile, he scoured his research notes for more evidence of the links between Siluria and Rome.

The Roman amphitheatre at Caerleon no longer sacrificed slaves in mortal combat to celebrate the Emperor's birthday, nor paid witness to a gathering of Celtic Chieftains as in Arthur's day, but the prose of Shakespeare was performed there today. Ten thousand sat there in its heyday, now only two sat on its grassy banks.

"One hundred years before this amphitheatre was built," said Dylan. "Caractacus was a prisoner in

Rome with his daughter, Gladys, renamed Claudia by the Emperor Claudius, who gave her in marriage to Rufus Pudens, a Roman senator. They had four children: Novatus, Timotheus, Pudentiana, and Praxedes. All of whom are mentioned by St Paul, all of whom became martyrs. The Basilica of St Pudentiana was the first church in Rome. Below in the catacombs is a mural of Peter and Paul baptising and preaching to the family, and a wall painting of the Shepherd, also a mural of a woman leading a congregation with arms outstretched in the orans position, not closed and ever-so-humble, but bold and fearless."

"Okay, so tell me of the twist to the tale you wouldn't tell me over the phone? "

Dylan told Gail of the Conbelinus inscription, Bede's remarks, and the comment by a Victorian historian that this way of describing the Saviour goes back to the early years and *The Shepherd of Hermas*.

"So what time-span we talking?" she queried.

"If Caractacus returned to Siluria with Bran in '59, and Claudia married Rufus Pudens before that date..." Dylan broke off suddenly. "Crazy how all the circumstances, beyond imagining, connect the family of Bran with Joseph, Peter, and Paul, at the Palace of the Britons in Rome, also here in this small Celtic Kingdom, whose king was spared by the Emperor Claudius, who adopted his daughter, who marries the half-brother to St Paul, who lived in a house still standing, and whose children are all described as Brethren in the Gospels."

"You still haven't answered my question about the Shepherd."

"It was Pastor Hermas who performed the marriage ceremony for Claudia and Pudens."

"That true?"

"If the martyrologies are anything to go by," replied Dylan with a smug smile. "Fact also: *The Shepherd of Hermas* was the most widely read book outside the Gospels, in whatever form books took then. It was accepted as Scripture, its parables taken as sacred text as if written by Jesus Himself through Hermas's visions of the Shepherd."

"Obviously too close to the true Jesus to become part of the Canonical Gospels."

"That's right—as you and I know there were at least twenty-nine, of which only four were selected."

"And Pudens?"

"Pudens was aide-de-camp to Aulus Plautius, who married Eurgain, Caractacus' sister. He was the military commander of the Romans in Britain."

"Another one to add to the list then?"

"Too much, too many, it's crazy," he said with a gesture of surrender. "Rufus, being a rich man, built a temple in Gloucester dedicated to Claudius, which is how Gloucester got its name. So, Pudens accompanied Caractacus and his family to Rome following his capture. Gladys, which means Princess, went with them, and they fell in love on the journey. I tell you, Gail, the whole story has become stranger than fiction."

"Often ask myself if it's real or an otherworldly hoax being played out on the world stage."

"What more evidence do we need to indicate the importance of the chapel, when all these things occurred practically on its doorstep? Undeniable facts, depending on which books you read, or if your slant is to believe it's all hocum, then you will read whatever confirms that."

"No Hollywood producer would, that's for sure."

"Just to recap: 170 AD, Lucius sends Alvanus to Rome from Siluria. He returns with Faganus and

Deruvian, kinsmen of Lucius through Claudia and Pudens. Hermas was their pastor and performed rituals at their home, the Palatica Brittannicum. The Roman poet, Martial, composed an epigram to Rufus and Claudia: 'Born among the woad-stained Britons, how fully had Claudia Ruffina the intelligence of the Roman people! What beauty is hers! The matrons of Italy might take her for a Roman; those of Attica for an Athenian.' Which means that she spoke Latin and Greek. Just an ignorant barbarian of course."

"The Welsh have always been bright as a button when it comes to things that matter," rebutted Gail.

"Bloody right, it's the Celtic temperament."

Gail laughed. "I'd love what we have found to breathe new life into the people of the Valleys."

"Me too, Gail. It would be great if we can do something to restore the spirit of the Cymry, because the past isn't dead, but lives in us, deep down."

"Go on now, finish what you were saying."

"Faganus and Deruvian arrive in Siluria to do two things: to restore lapsed Christianity, and to rebuild the huts of the Apostles."

"Which Apostles do we know for sure came here?"

"Joseph, of course... and Aristobolus, son of Herod Antipas. Phillip and Martha, some lists include Lazarus and Simon Magus, though we'll never know for sure. The reason I'm bringing this up again is that they would have most certainly brought books with them, including *The Shepherd of Hermas*."

"If it was the number one bestseller with the pre-Constantine Christians, then yes."

"From what I've gleaned from research, Pastor Hermas was a close friend to Claudia and Pudens..."

"In his book, Jesus as the Shepherd spoke in parables, in similar vein as in the Gospels. Hermas became regarded as a holy man, equal to Jesus's Disciples."

"No doubt the reason why his non-canonical Gospel ended up on the bonfire with all the others which didn't suit the Roman agenda of emasculating the sheeple, so they don't think above their station as slaves."

"Most early Christians were slaves," concurred Dylan. "So this is what I conclude: Faganus and Deruvian restored the Chapel of the Apostles and renamed it after the Shepherd, and Hermas being Greek, they called it Buciel in honour of him who wrote the book of the Shepherd, who is Jesus. It also creates a link between the Roman Church of Claudia and Pudens to the Kingdom of Bran the Fisher King."

"Brilliant, Dylan, good to know your brain's still working."

"I do get the odd moment," he joked. "So then Lucius the Great Luminary, in the correct Druidic manner, and with the consent of the people, declares Britain to be Christian, the first country in the world to do so."

"When you say Britain, do you mean the whole of Britain?"

"Lucius was regional king of Wales, called Britannia Secundus by the Romans."

"Just Wales then?"

"Would seem so," he replied. "So much has been taken from this land in blood, sweat, coal and iron, though the irony is the iron in the soul of the Celtic way holds sway to this day."

"Poet now then, are we?"

"A rhyme is not a rhyme if it's written out of time."

"Time to love and time to play, time to sing and time to pray," she said, dancing around him. "When are we going to say what we know? When are we going to act and stop playing around with theories?"

"Theories are all we've got," he said, irritated by her goading. "Truth is, I don't want this journey to end."

"It never will, because it's not meant to. It's a bit like scientists looking for the answer to the Universe."

"I dreamt the words of a passage from *The Shepherd of Hermas*, and came across those same words the following day."

"You dream like poets conjure up words," she said, impressed by this enigmatic man—as many saw him—who'd become a friend, albeit one with flaws like any other.

"The words describe a map to guide the reader into discovering his own country—a kind of spiritual sat-nav as to how empty words and blind faith lead to a dead end, how millions have been fooled following the blind alley of faith."

"Now isn't that the truth? Blind faith is a dried-up well, and they know it."

"Hermas's book is all about restoring the truth of the Gospels, which is why Lucius named the chapel in honour of the Shepherd, who is Christ."

"Faganus and Deruvian named it, you said."

"My dream told me Lucius. Besides, they would have needed his assent."

"Sure does make sense."

"I began this journey as a non-believer in the tenets of Christianity. Now I'm convinced that a great mystery lies hidden within its teachings, that the Grail is simply a metaphor for the Godforce within, knowledge of which has been denied for two thousand years."

"Better get a move on before another two thousand years go by."

"For sure," he replied with a bright smile. "As Grail Maiden, it is your prerogative to lead the way to the Chapel of the Grail. Call it a portal or whatever you like, it's all a matter of perception, as doors open to the open-minded, or close to the uninitiated who believe there's nothing beyond this life."

"The Dark Age of the human soul."

"Which is where we are now," he concurred. "We shall see what comes by rekindling the ancient flame in the chapel, which the camera saw but not our eyes. Why is that? Have we become too civilised?" Dylan stared into the empty bowl of the amphitheatre. "Do you know what I see there?"

"Romans?"

"No. Maidens dancing, celebrating spring, Oestre. New beginnings, new life. They took it all in their stride—the seasons, life and death, it was all one to them, a game of who can ride the wave with courage and fortitude while laughing all the while."

"Mmm," she muttered thoughtfully. "We *are* in a poetically reflective mood today."

"Some years back, I was asked to place a crystal in the centre of this amphitheatre as part of a worldwide grid, from Mount Shasta to Hawaii, Copan to the pyramids of Egypt, some two hundred or more sacred sites. There's a lot going on out there beyond our neck of the woods."

"On the astral as well, by what you've told me."

"That too."

"You've done so much in your life compared to me," she said admiringly.

Dylan laughed. "No big deal. Just being in the right place at the right time with an open heart is all it takes for things to happen."

"That I know," she said wryly. "My life's never been so chaotic since knowing you, like some crazy journey into fairyland."

"And this is just the beginning," he said to wind her up. "So don't worry about it too much. Beats working in an office though, huh?"

"Everything has its compensation," she agreed. "So where do we go from here?"

Dylan peeked at his mobile and realised it was time to go home to Pamela. "I need to get home to Pamela. It's gone six, and I have to buy a few things on the way."

"Then let me take you."

"No need to do that; I'll catch the train."

"You sure?"

"Yes, I like travelling by train."

"Then I'll run you to the station."

"Okay, but I have to pop back to the shop for my rucksack."

"Your rucksack's like the burden you carry, heavy with worry and care."

"That's true, but it's my burden; we all have something to bear."

"Is Pamela still alright about you and me doing our thing?"

"Of course," he quickly replied. "Come on, time to go."

35

Omens

Dylan stood in front of the apple tree, whose withered leaves had been green and healthy three days before. He checked the bark for sings of decay, but there were none, nor had the leaves been infected by a fungus or caterpillars. Puzzled, he returned indoors.

Pamela was sat cosily on the settee reading a book and listening to a choral symphony. He kissed her lightly on her lips. The light in her eyes reflected her spirit, untouched by the outer shell we inhabit in Earth's garden of souls. Nature grooms each, constant as waves washing the sand, impartial as sunlight and falling rain.

"How are you feeling?" he asked.

"How do you think I feel, not being able to breathe properly?" she replied with smiling eyes.

"Your birthday's coming up; I'll write you another poem."

"That would be nice. I love your poems, always have."

"As I love yours. You write very eloquently, mine's a scrawl. Thirty years together — don't know if I can squeeze that many crosses on a card."

"Tell me about Gail. Is she a good person? I've only met her the once."

"What can I say? We've all got issues of some sort or another. She's a great help though, what with her Christian background. An only lonely child, whose mother couldn't find it in her to love anyone."

"That's not good."

"No, but it's made her into a very strong-minded person who won't take nonsense from anybody."

"Sounds like me," replied Pamela with a bright smile.

"Glad you understand how important this Grail thing is to me."

"I know. I wish I could help more. Help me with this cushion, would you?" Dylan propped her up into a more comfortable position. "Do you remember us waking up in the mornings and telling one another our dreams?"

"We did, still do, though not so much now."

"They helped us a lot, on the practical level as well. I know how important your dreams are to you. I know how much you enjoyed going to the Druid camps. It is difficult to put into words how I feel when you go away."

"We're together most of the time; it's just this thing that I have to do."

"You do keep me informed—what you've discovered, the chapel and St Samson, Joseph of Arimathea. Do you think you'll ever be allowed to investigate it properly?"

"Unlikely, being on private land, as you know."

"I know. If it wasn't for me, you'd never have found it."

Dylan smiled. She was warming to his efforts to know the truth of its history, and the meaning behind it all.

"Finish writing the book, that's what they're telling me," she said, looking up at him with her clear blue eyes. "I know things I don't say because I love you and don't wish to hurt you. Just remember me as you used to, for beauty is only skin deep, but what is deeper is the true beauty that never fades."

Dylan disappeared into the study and came back with his latest research notes for her to read. Able to quickly grasp the essentials, she put the notes to one side and closed her eyes for several minutes. With a knowing smile, she looked at the man she'd known and loved more than words can say.

"Do you remember that time when we went to Tinkinswood on Halloween night? Must be twenty years ago now? It was dark when we got there, and as we approached the burial chamber, we saw a light beneath the capstone."

"I remember. We thought it strange, even though it was Halloween."

"When we got there, we peered inside and saw a young couple playing chess by candlelight."

"The weirdest sight we'd seen in a long time. He came outside to shake us by the hand; I recall he had a bit of a beard, his pretty partner had blonde hair."

"That's right, full of enthusiasm. Well, he was young, in his early twenties."

"Introduced himself as an archaeologist and gave me his card."

"Do you still have it?"

"Yes, I believe I do."

"Then why not give him a call?"

Dylan was stunned by her suggestion and quickly fished his wallet from the writing desk drawer. "Got it! It's been in my wallet for twenty years. Why would I keep anyone's card for that long?"

"Because it was meant to be, that's why," confirmed Pamela, enjoying the feeling of being involved with his life once more.

"Well done! He could be the very man we need right now, who can not only verify our findings, but also, all being well with his connections to Cadw, perhaps organise an archaeological dig."

"Let me see it," requested Pamela. Examining the well-worn card, she looked at Dylan with concern. "This may well be out of date, you know, codes have changed since then, and he may not be living at the same address, since this isn't a mobile number."

Dylan frowned. "You could be right. I'll check it out in the morning."

"It is meant to be," repeated Pamela. "You will be in touch with him, soon, they are telling me."

Yet another coincidence, thought Dylan, another affirmation in a long chain of synchronicities drawing them ever onward to the fruition of their goal.

He called the number next day using an updated code, but the line was dead, which he'd half suspected would be the case after so many years. He placed the card into the drawer, chapter closed. What he didn't think of doing was to check online to see if the name came up—Dylan wasn't of the internet generation that did this as a matter of course—but things have a way of connecting when we least expect it.

Three days later en route to the chemist in the high street, he noticed a single book on display in a charity shop window. On its cover, a Roman soldier stood beneath the title, *The Romans in South Wales.*

Its author was Karl Langford James, the same as on the card.

"Here we go again," he said to himself as he paid the two pounds for the book, "yet another synchronicity."

"What the heck is going on?" he said to Pamela on his return. "What are the chances of this happening? It's crazy."

"Marvellous," Pamela said, pleased at his discovery. "I keep telling you how Spirit operates when you put out the thought, so long as it's for a good cause."

"Yes, I know, but even so."

"Call him, then. Arrange to meet, tell him what you know. I feel he will help, though in what way, I don't know. Just be aware that it may not turn out the way you think."

Dylan was puzzled by her remark. "I'm only going to ask if he can be of help in any way."

Pamela became silent so as not to reveal what she knew.

Dylan called the mobile number he'd found in the book and a voice answered. "Hello, Karl Langford James speaking."

Dylan explained his reason for calling, and of their chance meeting at Tinkinswood all those years ago. Karl said that he did remember, and why not come to his talk at Llanilltud Fawr on Thursday? Dylan agreed. He would be there with his friend Gail.

36

Reunion

"Hello! Please come on in," bellowed the interesting-looking man who greeted them with hugs and youthful enthusiasm. "Yes, I do remember that night at Tinkinswood."

Dylan felt quite humbled that he too should recall that night twenty years ago. There was no doubt in his mind that he'd been meant to call Karl. Why else would he have kept his card for all those years than perhaps to investigate the chapel further with professional assistance? The god of circumstance had let loose an arrow of fortunate reunion.

"Please both take a seat. We've not yet started; we've been waiting for you." His cordial greeting and manner put them at ease in an unfamiliar place.

Dylan and Gail sat on hard chairs in the ancient town hall as Karl fiddled with his laptop, adjusting the screen showing images of archaeological excavations, before standing on the rostrum of a small stool.

"On the matter of the archaeology of Britain, we must remember that what is written on the subject of history isn't beyond debate, but that the debate has only just begun. Leslie Alcock's supposed discovery of Camelot at Cadbury Castle was, to put it bluntly,

a media jaunt into the realms of Arthurian fantasy
which led him nowhere. Except that it did prove one
thing: if you set out with a premise in mind, you
will most certainly find something to confirm it. That
is the law of inductive thinking—that if you find a
piece of earthenware pottery, then you have found
what, a fragment of the Grail? Or, as in his case, the
floor of a rectangular building which immediately
became... remember that the world's press were in on
this media event... became nothing other than King
Arthur's banqueting hall, large enough, so he said, to
accommodate all the knights and ladies of the court."

Karl thrust himself forward with arms thrown
back like a bird about to fly. "Excuse me! I am an
actor who knows how to act, but Alcock wasn't even
that. The discovery was immediately flashed around
the world. Come on! We're talking professional
archaeology here, not a no-holds-barred contest
to find King Arthur, but an academic, objective
search for evidence to confirm, not only whether
King Arthur ever existed, but if so, where was his
citadel? Where is Camelot? Does anyone truly know?
Certainly not Alcock with his few shards of pottery
and the supposed banqueting hall no bigger than
your average cowshed."

Dylan and Gail glanced at one another, bemused,
as Karl paced up and down, sometimes touching his
forehead or brushing his hair back with his hands.

"It is ridiculous to assume you've found Arthur
based on such flimsy evidence because of pressure
from financial backers to come up with the goods,
to sell out to appease them and undermine your
reputational integrity as well." He looked directly
at his audience. "I am here for the truth, as those of
you who know me know."

Dylan glanced about the hall, where five men of middle age and four women past their prime sat at tables with notepads, surrounded by a generous distribution of Welsh cakes on paper plates and a Scottish terrier tethered quietly to a bench leg.

Gail was taken with Karl's flamboyant gestures and bold speech, an actor on stage. She wondered what would come next from this obvious renegade archaeologist, who by his own means and conviction was on a path of discovery not dissimilar to their own.

Dylan was also puzzled and a little cautious about Karl's nonconformist ways. He'd expected to meet a serious academic who'd nailed down historical facts in closed-book fashion, instead of an eccentric elucidating a unique interpretation of Alcock's Arthur. Could he be the one holding the key to unlocking the mystery of the chapel?

"Alcock, like so many others," continued Karl, "failed to recognise Arthur as Welsh, assuming as most do that Arthur spent his time roaming around the West Country: Somerset, Glastonbury, the Glassy Isle so wet you need a boat to get about. Tintagel, the archetypal romantic location of Merlin's Cave, sea-washed and dramatic, waves crashing down to drown out Merlin's lament of Arthur's dream of the Round Table because Lancelot betrayed his best friend by shagging his missus. No, that's too crude a description for the underlying beauty of the legend — though in reality that is what occurred. So who are we to judge those who fall short of perfection?

"So if not there, where does that leave us who search for the Once and Future King? Such a hold does Arthur have on our deep yearning for a lost golden age. Was there one? If so, what form did it take? Here at Llantwit Major, which I prefer to call

Llanilltud Fawr, thousands of monks spent a lot of time singing praises to the most high, even though their most high wasn't the same as those who aspire to Catholic doctrine. So what evidence is there for a Welsh Arthur? Do not the dumb stones speak? Does not the inscribed stone across the way declare that St Samson was with King Juthael when Arthur restored the king's throne by defeating the tyrant Conomorus in Brittany? Samson attended the Third Council of Paris in 554AD, which places Arthur in the correct timescale.

"Illtud's bell hangs above us in the belfry," said Karl, pointing to the ceiling. "This was the only college in Britain, if not the whole of Western Europe at that time, where the sons of kings were educated, not indoctrinated, a subtle yet important difference compared to Roman Catholic education meted out to their students of theology.

"No one has yet taken the trouble to lift the turf in the meadow beyond the church boundary here, no one has bothered to investigate what lies beneath the rubble of the villa at Caermead whose mosaics have lain undisturbed for almost two thousand years and which may hold the key to proving Arthur was Welsh. Originally called the Cor of Eurgain, the daughter of Caractacus, who according to legend, returned from Rome following her captivity there with her father, to set up a cor in honour of Christ here, at Llanilltud. Is it possible that she was accompanied by Joseph of Arimathea? How do we know? How will we ever know unless these places are fully excavated? Some say a conspiracy—I say indifference to our own history, as there's overwhelming evidence through many sources of the great importance of Llanilltud Fawr and Caermead.

"I could show you a hundred slides to prove this, but would that make a difference? I could present you with the facts, but that doesn't necessarily make them true, because conjecture plays a great part in proving a fact one way or another. Guesswork is the gambler's way of calculating the odds, but the horse could stumble at the first fence, which is one way of putting it... and oh, let me tell you, gut feeling also plays a role, like when you know when something feels right, which is an unquantifiable no-no as far as archaeology is concerned. Does that make archaeology an empirical science in which intuition plays no part, or is intuition the map that guides, whether we are aware of it or not? Whoever can answer that question wisely may know if they're on right track or not."

Karl gave Dylan a quick but knowing glance before taking a swig of water and turning on a slideshow. "This slide indicates the extent of the monastery in its heyday. Supposition of course, as that's all we have, starved of funds to verify facts. Okay, let's have some fun and suppose Arthur was cousin to Illtud and that Illtud buried him in a cave not far from here at Ogmore. Or that Illtud was an invention of the Welsh monks to provide a link to Arthur. It is possible to construct a myth around a few names as Glastonbury has done — with great success, I may add, judging by the thousands who go there searching for Arthur, and Joseph of course, though no trace of him has ever been found, or is likely to be." Karl glanced at his class, most of whom were scribbling notes. "Questions? Challenge me please, that's what I'm here for."

A woman raised her hand.

"Yes, Maureen?"

"Do you believe he was here?"

"Who—Arthur or Joseph?"

"One or the other."

"Both, though there's no way of knowing until one or both graves are found."

"If they are, what then? If Joseph did come here as claimed."

"I understand your question, but to where and when, we can forever conjecture without sufficient evidence."

"I feel it was to here that he came," replied Maureen. "I mean, that's what I feel."

"Yes, but how much of that is your subjective wish for that to be so?"

Maureen bowed her head in submission, used to Karl's inoffensive, direct way.

"Any more questions to be shot down like pheasants at a shoot?" Karl laughed. "Please don't be intimidated by the cold logic of an archaeologist who wants to be proven wrong. We are logic masters who wear a few sparse facts around our necks like medals, proclaiming unassailable truths. Truth, as history, is as unfathomable as quantum physics."

"What's your take on Joseph?" asked Gail. "Do you believe he came here to Llanilltud with Eurgain, as the ancient stories tell?"

He looked at Gail, her sharp blue eyes intense as a summer storm. "I can't answer you. I don't have enough facts to say yay or nay. Would like to think that he did, I really would, but I dare not stray too far in that direction. There's many think I'm treading the fine line between orthodox investigative archaeology and the crackpot fringe of wild imaginings. I'd soon be out of a job and wandering the clifftops wailing to the wind. I do that anyway," he said with a shriek of laughter. "But that's private, not public. We'll talk later on about why you are here. Dylan came by to seek me out on Samhain Eve, though not even he knew why at the time, because that time was then and this is now."

Dylan felt he knew him, but he was an enigma, a verbal acrobat who could say one thing but mean another, yet was also sincere, as if propounding a truth of any kind could, at the swish of a horse's tail, also become its antithesis.

Karl finished his intriguing lecture and was soon approached by Gail and Dylan.

"I do indeed remember that night twenty years ago," he said to Dylan, quickly putting his gear together. "Actually, it was twenty-one years ago."

"You were playing chess with your partner," replied Dylan. "It was the candlelight that caught our attention."

"Ah, that's when you arrived," he replied with a wicked smile. "We were running around naked when we saw you coming and dashed under the capstone."

Dylan smiled. "What else would you be doing on Samhain?"

"Exactly! Not everything's as it seems," he said unplugging a laptop. "We married, got six kids."

"Are you still together?" inquired Gail.

"No, we split last year, but we're still friends." He looked at her full on and knew she was a live one. He felt in good company, even though their motive for being there puzzled him.

"Is this what you do, lecture on archaeology?" she asked.

"As a self-employed archaeologist, I do whatever I can. I have to earn a living to pay the bills. I do these talks twice a week, here at Llantwit Major and another class at Bridgend. Also online teaching three evenings a week. I'm also an actor."

"An actor?" asked Dylan in surprise.

"Yes, that's what I want to do more of. I see it as my future career. Television's where most of my work comes from. Got a part in *Casualty* next week."

Dylan was becoming quite impressed with Karl, whom he'd last seen as a young man, now full of enthusiasm, an electric energy, focused and swift, as he put equipment into boxes and papers into folders. Gail couldn't work him out, but liked his flamboyant mannerisms, so suited to the acting profession.

Karl, who'd been piling his equipment onto a table, stopped suddenly. "Afraid you'll have to excuse me — will only take a few minutes." He stood still, taking deep breaths with closed eyes as if in meditation, moving clockwise through the four directions.

Dylan looked quizzically at Gail, who smiled knowingly.

"Thank you," said Karl. "Just something I have to do. Do you think you could help put the chairs away? Have to be away in five minutes to catch my train."

"Sure," said Dylan, who began slotting chairs one on top of the other.

"OCD?" asked Gail.

Karl smiled, relieved. "You know? Oh, that's good, means I don't have to explain."

"Takes one to know one," she replied.

"Ah, I knew it, the way you were watching me earlier. Nobody understands us, really. I have to do my little ritual every time I go somewhere. Why? But we don't know why, do we?"

Gail shook her head in agreement. "We do it to keep our life in order."

"Exactly. Though in my case it's something more than just that." He turned away, embarrassed. "It's, well, how can I put it? Magic. That's what I do, perform magic."

Gail listened intently whilst Dylan finished stacking the chairs and putting things straight.

"I know you've come to see me for something other than listening to my talk," continued Karl. "I know you're not here just for that."

Dylan stopped what he was doing and walked up to him. "We don't want to bother you today. You're obviously in a hurry, so we'll talk some other time." He was never one to impose on another if he could help it.

"You said to me over the phone that you had something important to tell me about a certain place, a chapel was it?" Karl asked, his scent for a mystery overriding his due train.

"That's right, but we can talk again," conceded Dylan.

"We believe we've stumbled on something that could change people's view on early Christianity," said Gail, determined not to let the opportunity go by.

"Sorry, guys, haven't the time now — really busy and I need to get home." He looked at them both for several seconds. "Any chance you could give me a lift? I usually catch the train; I don't live far from here."

"Of course we can," affirmed Gail.

"Thanks, guys," replied Karl. "Reckon you can get this lot in?"

Gail gestured at the heap on the table. "How the hell were you going to lug this lot onto a train?"

"A trolley, wonder of technology. Been doing it this way since I lost my licence two years ago," he said with a cheeky smile whilst scratching the top of his head. "What about coming on my ghost walk next Friday?"

"You do ghost walks?"

"Didn't I tell you? Yes, mystery walks on local legends and history, two, sometimes three times a week, if I can get enough people. This Friday we're at Merthyr Mawr."

Dylan's ears pricked up. "Did you say Merthyr Mawr?"

"Seven-thirty, meet outside St Teilo's Church. Only seven pounds. Five if you become a member of Archaeology Cymry."

"Count me in," said Dylan, reaching for his wallet.

"Good man, I'll put you down in my book."

"Not just the ghost walk, I'd like to join your society as well."

"Oh, it gets better. Okay, both, let's sort this lot out first.

Squeezing everything into the car, including themselves, they drove off towards Karl's home in the hills to the north. Dylan was mesmerised; he had hoped to say much more about their findings but knew it would be inappropriate, even though Karl would want to know what he might be getting into. Gail was pleased Karl wasn't the stereotypical archaeologist she'd thought he might be, dry as dust, methodical and precise as a physicist splitting an atom with no room for metaphysics. Crazy as them and delightfully so, this was one of those times in life when chance intervenes to revive a nagging enterprise, a kick up the backside to go that extra mile.

The practicalities of an organised excavation at the chapel and its surrounds would be a major undertaking. Cadw would take a lot of convincing to allow it to happen—there lay the challenge and the opportunity. It was in the lap of the gods, and the gods had found Karl Langford James.

Dylan smiled at the thought. The timing felt right. It is always the timing, whether something turns out good or bad is often a question of the right or wrong time, and if the latter then nothing good will come of it. As the mystery of physics and a surreal journey into an archaeologist's world prove, nothing is what it seems.

37

The Ghost Walk

"Hello!" greeted Karl in a Victorian frock coat and top hat, waving a gold-knobbed walking cane. "So glad you've come, because we've an evening of ghostly surprises in store. You won't be disappointed, I can promise you that. Come and join the others."

"You look like something out of Dickens," said Dylan.

"One must dress for the part. I am an actor, and this is who I am today, Bible black and ready to confront any ghost who comes our way." Karl shook Dylan's hand and gave Gail a hug. "How's my partner in crime? Oh, sorry, I meant OCD," he said with a chuckle as they joined the others wandering about the churchyard.

"You see this tombstone?" said Karl standing over the recumbent stone effigy. "This is where the church used to be, as this chappy would've laid next to the altar because he is its founder, Paul Penychen. His name is on the stone behind the church which was rebuilt in 1857."

"So where are the remains of the church now?" queried Dylan.

Karl spread his arms. "Who knows? But what was it that they didn't want us to know? That is the question."

They continued around the church and over a stile, Karl's wife and son following up the rear. She seemed soft and gentle, awed by his over-the-top antics even though she was used to him by now.

"On we go!" yelled Karl. "For tomorrow we invade Poland!"

He laughed and sang, leading the way like a Pied Piper, waving his stick in the air, with the group walking at fast pace to keep up. Dylan hoped this crazy ghost hunt would reveal aspects of the past of which he was unaware, though it was about ghosts, not history.

"Oh yes! The White Lady of Ogmore Castle, who guards the treasure of ill-gotten gold she'd acquired from an old woman she'd swizzled, whose ghost told her to throw it into the River Ogmore or else she'd haunt her every night till the day she died and then some. Driven mad by the nightly visitations of the old hag, she threw the gold into the river for the sake of her sanity. She'd been told to throw it downstream, but she didn't do that and threw it upstream instead, and the hag continued to plague her until she finally went mad and died 'orribly, and now she's up there watching from the castle turret, keeping out a watchful eye for anyone foolish enough to go looking for the gold."

Karl knew how to captivate an audience, so confident and in control as the walk continued over stiles and meadows close to the chapel.

"Are we going there?" asked Dylan.

"Going? We are going," Karl answered, "but not there, not today, not to the chapel. They don't want people there. I called the owner last week to say about today's ghost walk and to ask permission."

"What was his response?"

"Called me at three forty-five this afternoon to tell me that I'm not to walk over his land." Karl seemed quite perturbed, putting on a performance to entertain, knowing he would be trespassing. "'You must not talk about the history of this land, do you understand? You must not talk about it, do you hear me?'"

"So what was your response?" asked Dylan.

"I told him that it is a public right of way and hung up," replied Karl. "I mean, this isn't the first ghost walk I've done here."

"But why did he say to you not to discuss the history of the land?" queried Dylan.

"He can't tell me what I can or cannot say," continued Karl. "He told me that I would be trespassing if I did this ghost walk, but I'm not giving in to his threats. There are legal rights of way across this land so long as we stay on the paths. Unusual for me to speak that way to anyone, being an actor of eloquent speech and not some East End yobbo."

"What's he afraid of?" asked Dylan. "Why doesn't he want you to talk about this place?"

"Maybe he just doesn't want people walking over his land."

Why didn't the landowner want Karl to talk about its history, unless it was to do with the chapel of Buciel and St Samson, perhaps even Joseph of Arimathea? Whatever the reason, Karl's abusive response wasn't going to help their cause.

Dylan re-joined Gail and the others, who were clambering over a stile to escape a herd of stampeding horses, grappling and shoving one another over mud and manure. The day wasn't going well.

Karl told a story of a man who drove a wagon over the humpback bridge with the river in full flood, who fell in and drowned, and now his ghost is often seen driving his wagon at full gallop towards the bridge over the Ogmore, before relating the tale of the Goblin Stone that once stood in a field close by before it was placed inside the chapel, how the goblin would leap onto passers-by and push their arms though the holes of the Celtic cross. His way with words and poetic licence lent a surreal air to the ghost walk.

"I know what you're thinking," said Gail on their way back to the car. "That it's all over because the landowner doesn't want anyone investigating the chapel."

"Karl's a rebellious eccentric, mad as a rabbit on mescal."

"But a lovely, warm-hearted person who runs his own archaeological outfit and walks his own path as an authentic individual."

"You're right, he doesn't give a toss what people think of him. I like him and his approach to history, a thorn in the backside to conventional historians and archaeologists."

"Reminds me of us," quipped Gail.

Dylan laughed. "Doesn't he just. I feel in my bones he's the only one can do this. Besides, why else would I keep hold of his card for twenty-one years if it wasn't meant to be? I'm a great believer in synchronicity, and we wouldn't have got very far on this quest without it."

"More reason to think carefully as to what to do next."

They walked by several old buildings renovated to accommodate the holidaymakers who flooded to the dunes to re-enact fantastical battles. Running into orcs was a common occurrence as the mountainous dunes transformed into the kingdom of Mordor and the woods and rivers became Elfland.

Karl ran up to them breathless after extricating a dog from a barbed-wire fence, driven there by annoyed bullocks. "Good you both came today, and sorry we've not had time to talk about why you got in touch with me."

"The chapel," interjected Gail.

"You mean the one here?"

"Yes, we were wondering what you knew about it," said Gail. "Especially as you do this ghost walk here."

"I've taken groups there in the past." Karl scratched his head, puzzled by their question. "Is that why you contacted me, to ask about the chapel?"

"Yes, but it's a long story," said Dylan. "One that you'll find interesting."

"Dylan's researched its history for years, and is convinced that someone very important is buried there."

"Who might that be?" asked Karl.

"One of the early Christian saints," lied Dylan.

"What makes you so certain?"

"The Prophecy," said Gail.

"A prophecy!" exclaimed Karl. "Good, I love riddles. Whose? Nostradamus, Merlin?"

"Melkin," declared Gail.

"Oh, that," he said disappointed. "The Glastonbury fraud."

"The Prophecy's neither a fraud, nor a forgery," stated Dylan. "It is real and dates from the sixth century, written by a bard called Melkin or Maelgwn, a contemporary of Arthur, whose brother, Paul Penychen, lies buried here..."

"Okay, hold on here," said Karl, putting his hands up in surrender. "Let's not lose ourselves in fairyland. I am an archaeologist who prefers fact to fiction."

"Tell Schliemann that," Gail threw in.

"Don't hang that one on me. He faked the treasure and lots of other stuff besides."

"He discovered Troy by following descriptions in a twenty-five-centuries-old book called *The Iliad*."

"Okay, got me," Karl laughed. "So what's the connection with this place and the prophecy?"

"Wasn't going to touch on that," said Gail, "only to say Melkin also describes Jesus as a prophet."

"Oh well, out's better than in, especially as you may need my help. I presume that's why you contacted me in the first place?"

"Guess we wanted to see how things panned out before talking about it," confessed Dylan.

"It?" asked Karl, cutting through Dylan's embarrassment.

"The chapel of Buceil."

"I know about the chapel, of course, and the cave system at the bottom of the chasm. So what have you got on that?"

"Definite proof that St Samson worshipped in the chapel that St Patrick had restored one hundred years earlier from the remains of its prior reconstruction by Faganus and Deruvian during the second century, who'd discovered the remains of a dwelling built by Jesus' disciples. Think that about covers it," said Dylan.

"Damn right it does," replied Karl, scratching his head agitatedly. "The chapel does have a lot of history. Something very mysterious about that place. Certain things just don't add up."

"Such as?" asked Dylan.

Karl paused for a few seconds before turning away to look towards his partner waiting patiently by their car. "Great meeting up with you again, Dylan. Come along to my next ghost walk at Monknash—it is a very popular venue, yet another ancient monastery."

"Wouldn't you know?" said Dylan. "Can't walk very far around here without falling over one."

"You're right, it's all there beneath our feet—the reason I became an archaeologist."

"Then perhaps it's about time someone took a good hard look at what's there."

"Got the message," responded Karl, "but don't forget to ask permission from the guardians. A holy sanctuary is holy for reasons we know nothing about, and to violate its protection would be sacrilege."

Karl waved them goodbye and departed, honking his horn and shouting goodness-knows-what like a human jack-in-the-box.

Dylan went behind the Church of St Teilo to look once more at the memorial stone of Paul Penychen standing next to a great wheel cross symbolising the sun god Helios.

38
Full Circle

How versatile is nature, forever changing form, a painting never finished? How strong a tree, how soft an acorn crushed beneath a boot. How small its seed, how slow its growth, millimetre by millimetre; day by day, roots dig deep as branches form. How different are we, who have eternity in which to play out the illusion of time?

Dylan looked at the words written on a scrap of paper, ruffled it into a ball and threw it into the bin. He'd failed to catch the bird of thought that day and hoped tomorrow would be different, which of course it always is.

Early next morning, he opened the kitchen door to take in the sunshine and the scent of the viburnum growing there, but to his dismay all but one of its flower clusters had faded or fallen. The shrub was dying. Pamela had taken one of its sweet-scented clusters with her that day on their coach journey to London with their meditation group, the day their relationship truly flowered for the first time.

Dylan stared at the dying flowers lying strewn on the ground like so many fading memories. The apple tree had died for no apparent reason, now the viburnum, her favourite shrub. His heart knew why, the heart always knows why.

Gail came for him at three o'clock to go to Ogmore. She knew the instant he got into her car that something was wrong. He wasn't his usual self — whatever that meant, being changeable as the weather, bipolar or simply obeying his own inner law, his intuition that defied logic, quirky, with a wicked sense of humour, prone to perceive situations from a distance like a bird up a tree. He said it was a Celtic thing to laugh at the ridiculousness of it all.

"What's with you today?" she asked, knowing his answer would be evasive.

"Nothing!" came his taut reply.

"That the nothing that means nothing, or the nothing that means everything? I know when you have your off-planet head on."

"Can we just get to where we're going?" he said, irritated. "We're limited for time."

"Aren't we always? Rushing here and there."

"You know how difficult my situation is!" he snapped. "Do you expect me to wave a magic wand and it'll all go away?"

"Of course not, but you seem so tense."

"Stop off on the way to get some tobacco, if that's ok?"

"Only if you tell me what's bugging you."

"*Duo fassula.*"

"What?"

"The Prophecy mentions the shroud, '*duo fassula*', folded twice."

"So?"

"So the shroud turned up in Turin in 1345, presented to the cathedral by the granddaughter of a Knight Templar."

"*Duo fassula*, Knights Templar... what are you talking about?"

"Fitzhammon's daughter married Hugh de Payens, founder of the Knights Templar. Do you remember me telling you of the dream where I was Fitzhammon's guardian angel, persuading him to give up his warring ways to becoming the guardian of Joseph's tomb?"

"You think there's a connection between the shroud and the chapel? That Joseph brought the shroud to Britain?"

"Joseph is the only source for the shroud, so yes, it's possible Fitzhammon gave it to Payens or some other high-ranking Templar for safekeeping in view of the Glastonbury clique, who'd already been given Llanilltud's sapphire altar as well as poaching our history."

"Food for thought, Dylan, and we've had plenty of that these past two years."

"Yes we have, and the trick is to eat only what's edible."

"Except that's a bit rich for my taste," said Gail. "I like to keep things simple."

"Life's never simple, no matter how much we'd like it to be," rebutted Dylan. "The shroud portrays evidence of Christ's supernatural resurrection, as the image could only be replicated by a thirty-thousand volt blast of electricity. A similar surge of power transformed Christ into a being of light—which is potentially what we all are, beings of light. That is how those early Christians described the resurrected Jesus."

Gail went into her silent mode, knowing how useless it would be to talk sense into him.

"A moment's revelation," he said, unnerved by her silence, "to find the truth behind the myth, heaven-sent by Joseph, Christianity's precursor who showed the way to the Promised Land."

"Imagination versus common sense—which will win, I wonder?"

On arriving at Ogmore, Dylan told her he was going to try to locate the lost Roman city of Bomio by following the fragmentary Roman road by Ogmore Castle, which he'd seen on an old map and might indicate where the city lay in relation to the chapel.

Dylan set off, leaving Gail perched on the castle wall close to several teepees, reminding him of the Native Americans who venerated Nature in all its forms, whose wisdom mirrored the Celtic veneration of the Great Spirit.

He waved to Gail, who feebly waved back, feeling ashamed for allowing his black-dog mood to affect her. He threw cupped handfuls of river water over his face and neck, as every day felt like a baptism of some sort. Looking towards Chapel Hill half a mile to the north, he thought of the light in the chapel. They were no closer to a final resolution than before. Had they been shown the light in the chapel to keep them going when they still had far to walk? Would they have persevered without it? Dylan thought not. His life situation had become so demanding he doubted that they would have continued to this point without it, but this point was the end. Great changes lay ahead.

"Well, Mister Schliemann, did you find your Troy?" she asked, as Dylan bounded over the stepping stones.

"Very funny," he replied. "Truth is it's me that's lost."

"Wouldn't be if you let me be your compass," she said, throwing a rock into the river, which splashed all over him.

"What's that for?" he yelled.

"What do you think it's for, you miserable sonofabitch!"

Realising he'd gone too far, Dylan slunk off to sit on the castle wall to roll a cigarette. The tobacco was wet. He fished into his rucksack for the flask of tea and offered it to Gail, but she refused.

"Will you please tell me what's wrong?"

"There's nothing more we can do. The landowner hasn't responded to my request to investigate the chapel. Karl, who's a first-rate archaeologist, insulted the landowner whose cooperation is desperately needed if we are to resolve the mystery of the Chapel of the Shepherd."

"Doesn't sound too promising I admit, but—"

"But nothing!" he interjected. "We're scuppered. Winter's fast approaching and Pamela's very ill. I'm only here today because her sister, Carol, is over from Germany. I'm exhausted, and our dream of finding Joseph has evaporated. It's over and I'm like a split pea; one half in a pot of boiling water, and the other chewed between the teeth of circumstance."

"I can understand your misgivings, despite what we know of the early church and the relations between Pastor Hermas and the house of Claudia, the first Church of Rome."

Dylan turned around to face her. "I dream a lot, as you know. I read signs and often know in advance when something bad's about to occur. I knew what would happen to Max before he died, because I dreamt I saw him fall outside the gates of a cemetery. Two weeks later, he fell over and broke his pelvis, and he died a month later. I knew my brother was going to die when I dreamt I couldn't find his name in the telephone directory when all my other brothers and sisters were listed there."

"What are you saying, Dylan?" Gail placed a comforting hand on his shoulder. "That something's going to happen to Pamela?"

Dylan was reluctant to confess the reasons for his fears about Pamela.

"Tell me," Gail urged. "I know you know these things."

"Isn't something I wish to acknowledge, that Pamela might not be here for much longer," he confessed, torn between his sensitivity and fear, hoping by some miracle that all the bad things would right themselves, that Pamela would suddenly be healed and whole once more. "The apple tree died for no apparent reason."

"Yes, I remember you telling me about it. But it's just a tree, and trees often die without cause."

"Pamela loved that apple tree."

"You're not going loopy on me now, are you?"

"Today the viburnum died. Her favourite shrub, with its beautiful white flowers and exquisite scent." He paused and stared at the river. "I'm not going crazy, these things happen. Max told me that Pamela and me would be together for thirty years, and this year is the thirtieth."

Dylan lapsed into silence, unable to voice the unbearable implication of his thoughts. Gail felt for him, but smothered the urge to touch and comfort him.

"Have you had any other premonitions?" she asked.

"No, but I know she doesn't wish to go on living breathing through a tube. She told me many times

over the years that she would never be a cabbage,
whether at home or in a hospital, if she had any
say in the matter. 'Life's about quality not quantity,'
she'd often say. 'Life lived true to Spirit is the only
thing that matters.'"

"A lot of truth in what you say, but aren't you
putting her on a pedestal, just a little?"

"No!" Dylan retaliated. "You've only known
Pamela since her illness, but she has an inborn
understanding of how Spirit moves in all things."

Gail turned away, knowing how deep his love
was for Pamela, that they were deeply connected on
a level she could only hope to understand despite her
feelings of affection for Dylan, knowing he loved her
as much as he was able to.

They walked in silence alongside the flowing
river, where graceful swans floated upstream with
the incoming tide, nature's synchronised movements
of the dance of life between heaven and earth like
twin-souls on their journey toward perfection, just
as Gail and Dylan tip-toed over the stepping stones
towards her flower-painted car to journey towards
whatever fate lay ahead.

Three weeks later, Pamela was rushed to hospital
suffering from pneumonia. Her brother Derek arrived
from Washington DC with his wife, Betty. Pamela
hated for them to see her in her present state, even
though good people see only the inner spirit.

After all was done to save her, Pamela passed
away quietly, her eyes fixed on who was in the
room beyond the physical spectrum, and Dylan knew
all was well when they came to take her home,
reminding him of the Native American who'd looked

into her eyes and said: 'By Guni! Heaven sent her, I haven't seen that before.'

Death's truly a great leveller, and we only see what we want to see when we walk between two worlds and put on the iron-clad armour of protection, shielding us from our emotions and making us into a functioning robot arranging funeral details.

The day came he hoped would never arrive. Friends he'd not seen in years came to honour the love Pamela had given freely over the years. Richard was solemn, but with a knowing look in his eyes. Platitudes fell like peelings on the floor to reveal the fruit inside. Dylan's opera singer nephew sang *Una Fatima Lagrima*. Gilbert Biberan, world-famed master of the classical guitar, paid tribute in humourful words, denying death of its mournful overtones: "I have performed at Carnegie Hall and the Royal Albert Hall, but the place where I love to play most is at the Ffwrwm with my friends Rafi and Pamela, whose love is tangible as the sound of my guitar. God bless her beautiful soul."

A window opens and shuts like a thin veil of matter, invisible to our eyes. We are the same on both sides, as we cannot be otherwise in accord with the Law, which is the Law of Immortal Life.

Dylan was not tinkering with words to find their true meaning, or to avoid the pain of acknowledging that his love had gone to another place, far from here it seemed.

We know that this is what we conclude: that we do not know the true reality, locked inside a tin can of narrow vision, but that will disappear when the day of change arrives to open the window into the realm beyond.

≈≈≈

The sandy soil felt soft and cool between his fingers as he dug between the roots of a Scots pine. He didn't see the buzzard watching him from the branch above as he focused his thoughts and energy digging a hole in the sandy hollow in the place Pamela had loved most, the tranquil surroundings of the dunes at Merthyr Mawr. Happy times lying in the sun, listening to the birds, delighting in the violas and evening primrose, enjoying the peace of one another's company in the healing sanctuary of nature's garden.

He burrowed until he could go no deeper and, looking around to make sure no one was watching, he pulled the ring off his finger and tied it to hers, rings they'd purchased the same day at an antiques market, gold with sapphires. Dylan carefully placed them in the ceramic vase containing her ashes, sealed the lid and slid it into the sandy cavity.

Then came the tears, shaking and trembling with the emotion. Pain could not retrieve one moment of the physical presence of the person he loved. Why couldn't he just sit with her one more time, to prepare him for that deep dark plunge into unfettered grief? Even though he knew with certainty that she'd returned to the world of Spirit, whose loving vibration he could only sense through love that is true.

"You have your freedom now," she'd told him in a dream three days after she'd gone. *"Use it wisely."*

She knew the true purpose of earthly life as she watched him place the flat stone on which he'd carved her name, with the words 'Love is all' and symbols known only to initiates into the mysteries. Carefully placing her memorial stone with her ashes, he concealed them and brushed leaves over the surface.

Peace descended on him like a dove as he conjured up memories fragile as rose petals, memories of yesterday fading into the ether, imprinted onto nature's tapestry to be enshrined into the fabric of our existence. He smiled and gave thanks for the privilege of knowing her, and plucked three oak leaves from a nearby tree, which he would press into a book as a reminder of this place beneath the tall pine.

It was sunny and warm for March, and life-affirming activity was all around as green shoots pushed through the soil. The more you love the more you hurt; nature's life and death is all around, change and renewal of eternal cycles teach us to let go, to know that we have this allotted time to explore the imagination of our existence.

Gail was waiting in her car. She would stand by Dylan's side to help him through the ordeal of grief with forbearance, respecting his needs without presumption.

"Where would you like to go?" she asked, observing his red eyes and remnants of tears.

"The spring in the dunes where the Neolithic people buried their dead. They knew the true meaning of life, that when we die we go to the Otherworld."

"I'm so glad you refused to wear black at her funeral," she said as they walked towards the dunes reflecting the gold of the sun.

"Black is for those who see only gloom in death. Pamela wasn't like that. Life and death are the same with different coats, neither of which is black. Years ago, before we met Karl even, we went to Tinkinswood. It was a warm summer's evening—you know, one of those days of calm—and as we approached, she stopped. I said, 'Why have you stopped?' She said, 'Because I am seeing something.'

A Neolithic celebration. Someone has died and all the people are wearing colourful clothes and playing music and dancing, and the children are running about with posies, laughing, because the person who'd died was going home.'"

They walked the half-mile to where a spring gushed between two rocks in the depths of the dunes, forming a deep pool of crystal clear water. Dylan drank deeply and poured it over his head as a baptism into a future of new beginnings. Gail drank in the hope of dispersing the clouds of anguish hovering above them, asking Spirit to help see this through to the end, though what end that was, she'd no idea.

Dylan stared out to sea to the land on the other side, at how inviting it seemed, that faraway country of yesterday. He'd no wish to impose his cares onto her shoulders, strong and supportive as she was, and he thanked her for that. Personal memories demand solitude to relive moments shared with someone who has gone away, because thoughts cemented by love deserve attention, else they gather dust in our minds to become inconsequential snapshots of a holiday of long ago, to be put away and forgotten.

They sat on top of a Neolithic tumulus close to the spring as a heron flew overhead on its journey towards the setting sun.

39
Zorba's Dance

Gail sat at her piano playing Chopin's *Moonlight Sonata*, her fingers trembling on the keys. Dylan had vanished; he'd not been seen at the shop for days. Richard had contacted her to say he'd seen him half-drunk in the Hanbury Arms, that he had a message for him from Spirit to say that it was important he finish the story, that its ending would not be as he hoped. Richard told her that Maelgwn had been told of Joseph's tomb by Arthur. He also said that Maelgwn constructed the prophecy to conceal in coded language a riddle so that only someone guided by inner vision would know the truth hidden there, and that person would be Maelgwn in a future time.

Aware of Dylan's predilection to being near water, Gail searched around Ogmore and the dunes to no avail. Had he gone to Caer Caradoc and the Dancing Stones, or the Lake of the Maiden where he'd encountered the Goddess of the Waters, or the Cor of St Llid, where he'd spent time with Pamela?

Her footsteps resounded on the stone floor of the West Chapel of St Illtud's Church, where the Arthmael stone stood upright and unmoving, sure of its destiny. She stepped outside to examine the tile of the Rose and Lion set in a corbel above, reminding her of Dylan's vision of the seven maidens that correlated with the Seven Maidens of Hermas' vision, Guardians of the White Tower, representing Faith, Continence, Simplicity, Knowledge, Innocence, Reverence and Love.

They had knocked on the door of the Grail Castle, but no one answered. Why does daylight dance through the trees as if to say, 'We know the great secret; it is all around. Can you see it? It is in the air, in the waters, in the sky. When you walk, do you feel the earth touch your feet? Do you see the white clouds? Do you know what they say? The bird that sings knows the secret. Will you follow the rainbow? The rainbow's end is everywhere. Do you know where you are? Do you know where you have been? Do you know where you are going? Do you know the secret of the Awen? The Awen is the God inside you. When you go to the Circle of Prophecy, what will you find there? What is there that's unseen? Who stands by the big stone? Do you know his name?'

The road to the sea wound through the valley, once a natural harbour of the monastery of Llanilltud. Her feet padded at a rapid pace as her solar plexus radiated anticipation. Would he be there, walking on the pebble beach, listening to the waves of his thoughts drenched in melancholy? Or would he be the Dylan she knew, the dreamer?

The seascape opened up before her; grey-blue against white crashing waves. Dog-walkers were silhouetted on the horizon. There was no sign of him. Her hopes sank and she hugged herself tightly, when she felt a tap on her shoulder. She spun around to see him smiling at her.

"Dylan!" she yelled. "Where in God's name have you been? I thought you were dead."

"Not yet."

"What then?"

"Just needed time out."

"Can say that again," she said. "Where were you?"

"Behind the gorse bush over there," he replied. "I saw you coming, so I hid."

"No—I mean where have you been until now?" she asked, observing his week-old stubble and unkempt hair. "You look like you've been sleeping under a bush."

"No," he laughed. "Just here and there."

"Where have you been staying?"

"Like I said, just here and there," he replied, seeing how upset she was, wishing not to hurt her, but he had. "Must think me very ungrateful, after all you've done to help."

"Not even a phone call or a text?"

"Sorry, all of it hit me after the funeral, holding everything in, no time to grieve. I fell apart and knew that I had to do this alone."

"I understand, but I was concerned, naturally."

He looked her in the eye. "None of us know how we'll be when these things happen."

"Of course not."

She'd never imposed herself on his life with Pamela, and his respect for her had grown during the time they'd known one another.

"How about we walk along the beach? Pebbles everywhere, and I know how much you love pebbles," he suggested with an encouraging smile.

"Yes." She returned his smile. "I'd like that."

They walked in silence, contemplating the waves and seabirds pecking titbits in the sandy cove as the mesmeric effect of the breaking surf eased the tension between them, though she knew that what she had to say would not go down well.

"You do know we've reached the end, don't you?"

"The end?" he queried. "End of what?"

"We've knocked on the door of the Grail Castle, but no one answered our call."

"Perhaps we should knock harder."

"No, Dylan, you're not getting what I am trying to tell you."

"What are you trying to tell me?"

"That it's over."

"The search for Joseph's tomb?"

"Think about it. What more is there to achieve? We have seen the Grail, what else is there?"

"Joseph's tomb." Dylan looked at her in dismay. "We've come so far, we cannot quit now."

"Yes, we can," she replied. "Why disturb him? Why not let him rest in peace?"

"We're right at the point of a great discovery, and you're telling me to quit? That there's no need to continue?"

"Think about it," she said, sitting on a rock. "It's pointless to continue in a struggle we cannot hope to win."

"The Grail means steps to enlightenment, and those steps are fraught with difficulty, but you don't give up—that's the coward's way. I'll fight all the way if I have to."

"Who or what will you fight?"

"I'll fight to resurrect the truth of our history."

"Do you think Joseph will give that to you, that he will take the journey for you?"

Dylan suddenly awoke from his delusion. "Of course not..." He broke off to look away. "It's just that we're so close."

"Yes, we are," she said, responding to his sense of failure. "But this has nothing to do with us, our sense of achievement, our egos."

"It's not my ego that's involved here, but the bringing to light of the truth of the beginnings of Christianity in Britain."

"You know the story of Sri Yukteswar, who appeared before Yogananda ten days after his death in full physical form, and spoke to him of the divine dimensions and the many plains of existence. Yogananda touched him, saying, 'But you are real, how is this possible?' Yukteswar explained that those who overcome all desire and karma of their past lives, who live in accord with the Creator of the Universe, are able to recreate their physical form with lifetrons, a form of matter infinitely more subtle than the gross material bodies we inhabit. Many avatars and Christ figures have lived in India. We in the West have been blessed with just one, Jesus, and He they hold aloft like a flaming torch, unreachable as the stars.

"How often have you been guided by otherworldly forces, Dylan? Perhaps you should listen to what they're saying instead of convincing yourself it's right to go steaming ahead in face of so many obstacles. Maybe they'd say to you, 'Job done, time for you to return to the here and now.'"

Dylan bowed his head as she stood above him on a rock, her poise firm and determined.

"Unless we're shown a way forward, we shall have to abandon the quest, which may not be a bad thing if you think about it. We would have to go on the run to hide from the ramifications, and our lives would never be the same again. You do realise that, don't you? Our lives would be hell; whether praised or vilified, it will never be the same."

"A mite dramatic, but I get the message," he said, climbing onto a rock jutting over the sea and standing facing the crashing waves. "Would you mind passing my rucksack to me? Something I must do — the reason why I came here today."

She handed him the rucksack, from which he took out a sealed plastic bag. He sat cross-legged as pounding waves sprayed him with salt water.

"Come and join me," he said, his composure somewhat restored.

She climbed onto the rock and stood by his side. "What are you about to do, Dylan?"

"Pamela's ashes, I want to throw what's left into the sea."

Gail choked as he opened the bag and uttered a prayer she couldn't hear because of the wind and the sound of the waves as Pamela's ashes flew into the air like a white mist.

They sat to ponder the ceremony he'd just performed. Nothing seems real when the person you love has gone from your life, neither platitudes nor all the love in the world can disperse that. It is only when you know that life is eternal that a certain perspective changes grief to the joy of knowing they've only gone next door for a chat and a cuppa.

Gail praised him for putting the remainder of Pamela's ashes into the sea. "You've been living this quest for so many years. Not an obsession exactly, but a great part of who you are. I can only ask that you see your situation from a different angle. You're always telling me there's a right time and a wrong time for something to happen, so maybe now isn't the right time. Spirit has guided us, measured the pace of our search, also the synchronicity of meeting people at the right time. I only know what is meant to be will be. We are their instruments, and for that to happen, we have to get ourselves out of the way."

"You're right, but I'm just a human being with an objective," confessed Dylan.

"As long as it doesn't become objectionable," she teased, to lighten the tension.

"If we walk away, I shall write the story, see what comes of it, though it still feels to me like a cop out."

Dylan skirted the surf, scanning for driftwood or fishing nets and ropes he could turn into something, wishing life were that simple. He had to decide now before going any further whether his life was worth the challenge of taking on the authorities. Though he'd sworn to himself to see it through to the end, maybe life had other plans and this wasn't the right time. But if he were to get a book out there, it might inspire others to continue the search. Accolade was the last thing he wanted. He'd done his best, and that's what mattered.

"Shall we go on now?" he said, throwing a pebble into the foaming surf.

She laughed, knowing his hurt was beginning to mend. "When I think it all started with a simple conjecture."

"Conjecture frees up the imagination." He threw another pebble into the sea. "Conjecture's the hound that pursues the quarry with a mere whiff of its scent."

"Conjecture plus intuition," added Gail.

"Well, here's my conjecture on the Chapel of the Shepherd, conclusions I've formulated these past few days, wandering about half out of my head."

"Go on, I'm listening."

"The chapel is built on a telluric hot spot. The chasm and the water running through it, the picture of the orbs coming up out of there, the stone circle, point to it as a place of initiation. The Sybil of Cumae, the Oracle of Delphi, Stonehenge, Newgrange in Ireland all have this in common—that wherever telluric energy is concentrated, a gap between worlds is created."

"You mean like a fissure, a crack in the rock?"

"Look at it on a different scale. It is a known fact that an atomic blast tears the space-time fabric between dimensions. On a much smaller scale, this is what occurs at Merthyr Mawr, why Illtud and Samson and others were drawn there. Being sensitive souls, they knew how to harness the vibrations. Samson experienced visions there, and was very reluctant to leave the chapel. The author of his biography commented that the place had always been regarded as very special."

"Convincing explanation of the orb of light in the chapel." Gail frowned, deflated but not disappointed. "But it could also be otherworldly."

"A gateway to the Celtic Otherworld," affirmed Dylan. "In common parlance, an interdimensional wormhole through which communication with the ancestors is possible."

"Seems we lack that sensitivity to know these places through feeling alone."

Dylan smiled. "Truth is, Gail, it has always been that way. Tribal shamans are rare, as are initiates like Taliesin, who wrote of his multidimensional experiences. So there you have it, and we were fortunate to witness this phenomenon."

"Where does that leave Joseph?"

"Where he is, lying beneath the font to the south of the chapel, exactly as described in the prophecy. His Jewish beliefs forbade burial inside a church."

"That dream you had of three shrines and three Christian burials there makes sense in view of that, as all were outside the chapel."

"Yet another confirmation. But we'll leave it be, because what would the discovery of his tomb prove, other than he lived in Wales for a time?"

"Who knows if it won't spark a revival of Celtic Christianity?"

"That's happening already," confirmed Dylan. "Many are asking the same questions as you and me; all things are coming to the surface from the past, hidden secrets. All must be known to make way for the new."

"But why did the light appear above the altar?"

"Because the altar was placed above a hot spot, and what you see depends on your perception, so it would be a sign from God if you were a Christian, or a quite natural phenomenon to twenty-first-century understanding of earth energies."

"Oh, that's so disappointing," said Gail.

"Not really, as it's a valid confirmation of the fragility between overlapping dimensions. Sensitive people are those who value spirituality, the Godforce, if you like. And the more awakened you are, the more you see, which is why the Grail appeared to some but not to others; the more the world is with you, the less you see. It all comes down to heightened perception."

"But why did the camera pick it up and not us?"

Dylan paused for thought. "Maybe our perception isn't tuned sufficiently to see it."

"A camera isn't human, it's just a thing that records pixels of light."

"Don't know the answer to that, Gail. My knowledge of a digital camera is limited to pressing the button. The conundrum of the chapel," said Dylan, looking out over the sea. "One mystery pervades another and so on, just as the mystery of physics remains out of reach, allowing the adventures into the unknown to continue, drawing us ever on towards the truly Divine."

"I love it!" shouted Gail.

Dylan laughed. "Me too! The Creator of Heaven and Earth entices us forward, questing, searching for the elusive phantom within our soul, forever reaching for the ultimate conclusion, the answer to who we are, why we are here, where are we going?" He began a slow dance in the surf. "The party isn't over. From one beginning to another, the circle of beginnings and endings which begin at the beginning all over again. Wouldn't wish it any other way, would you?"

"No," she laughed.

"We are like children playing in a garden of wonders." Dylan clapped his hands. "Yes, Gail, the truth of freedom to explore freely the magic of creation. We are truly the playmates of the One Creator. Remember Zorba — the worse things got the more he danced."

Dylan snapped his fingers and jerked about on the sand, lifting one leg then the other, the Greek way. Gail laughed, appreciating his sudden lightness of spirit. She joined him in the dance, clapping her hands and moving her hips in a delightfully rhythmic and sinuous way as sand flew in all directions. The sound of the surf was nature's orchestra and the squawking seagulls the audience. Dylan leapt and jumped, shouted and clapped in an uncoordinated rhythm of wild emotion. Gail danced with grace, her lithe femininity in contrast to his jerky movements. They were complimentary opposites, a juxtaposition indicative of the challenges to come.

Their crazy lives dancing between two worlds had been the antithesis of normality — a Greek word. The catharsis of surviving inner turmoil — yet another Greek word. They knew a thing or two about existing on the flipside, which is why Greeks dance with such crazy abandon.

"Oh, so we have potential," she said laughing.

"For dancing?"

"Yes," she replied. "Not bad for a big guy who dances like a demented leprechaun."

"I'm only half Irish."

"Only half mad then."

"And the Welsh bit can't sing."

"You do talk a lot of blarney."

They danced on, laughing, letting go of preconceptions and everything else that weighed on them. The Grail had become both a goal and a gaol. Hubris, yet another Greek word; don't fly higher than the wings on your feet can safely take you. The game was over, there was no reason to find what was gone.

They danced like dervishes on the sand by the sea, beneath the light of the sun, the waves synchronising their movements to the timeless ebb and flow of creation as they sang and shouted in elation above the sound of the surf, the pulse quickening in joyful celebration as the image from the chapel joined them, an unseen companion that whirled about their bodies until the love of its presence healed the pain and lifted their spirits to gnosis, yet another Greek word, rekindling the flame of love within the Grail of All.

Author Profile

The author is a sculptor and writer living in South Wales.

He has a passion for history and is a keen amateur archaeologist. He is a great believer in how we can truly connect with the natural landscape to reveal its secrets. Shamans do this whenever a cure is needed, and Carlos Castaneda was well known for using this method of communing with the plant world.

He also has a love and talent for creating gardens that reveal a spiritual connection to nature using rock, water and varied plant life to reflect the Welsh landscape.

Dreams have always played an important part in his life, not only in helping to reveal our true selves but also in connecting us with the divine aspect of the inner spirit. *"The answer to our problems is already inside us in our dreams. Dreams are free downloads, often from other dimensions. So who needs AI when we are already light years ahead?"*

Alec recommends we return to the natural world and our ancestral roots and listen our inner voice. He believes that we should sing and dance more, to celebrate life as nature intended.

Publisher Information

Rowanvale
Books

Rowanvale Books provides publishing services to independent authors, writers and poets all over the globe. We deliver a personal, honest and efficient service that allows authors to see their work published, while remaining in control of the process and retaining their creativity. By making publishing services available to authors in a cost-effective and ethical way, we at Rowanvale Books hope to ensure that the local, national and international community benefits from a steady stream of good quality literature.

For more information about us, our authors or our publications, please get in touch.

www.rowanvalebooks.com
info@rowanvalebooks.com